THE REREDOS OF
ALL SOULS COLLEGE
OXFORD

THE REREDOS OF ALL SOULS COLLEGE OXFORD

Peregrine Horden, Editor

AD ILISSVM

CONTENTS

ACKNOWLEDGEMENTS

The editor's warmest thanks go to the Warden and Fellows of
All Souls College for their encouragement of this project, their
funding of the scientific investigation of stonework and polychromy
and of the symposium in which this volume originates, and their
subvention towards the costs of its publication; to Paul Holberton
for agreeing to publish; to Laura Parker, the book's designer;
to John Drury, chaplain of All Souls and 'onlie begetter'; to Robert
Franklin; to all who took part in the symposium whether as speakers
or audience, and especially the speakers for their willingness to write
up and rewrite their papers and for meeting the costs of securing images
and permissions for material not already in the College's collection;
and to Gaye Morgan, Librarian in Charge, the Library, All Souls, and the
late Bronac Holden, for indispensable help with the College archives.

CONTRIBUTORS

Robin Darwall-Smith	All Souls, University and Jesus Colleges, Oxford
John Drury	All Souls College, Oxford
Eamon Duffy	Magdalene College, Cambridge
S. J. D. Green	University of Leeds and All Souls College
Michael Hall	*The Burlington Magazine*
Emily Howe	independent wall painting conservator
Peregrine Horden	All Souls College
Richard Johns	University of York
Michael Liversidge	University of Bristol
Diarmaid MacCulloch	St Cross College, Oxford
Tim Palmer	Aberystwyth University
Ruth Shaffrey	Oxford Archaeology
Christopher Wilson	University College London

ABBREVIATIONS

ASC	All Souls College
BL	British Library
Building Accounts	S. Walker with J. Munby (ed.), *Building Accounts of All Souls College Oxford 1438 – 1443*, Oxford Historical Society new series vol. 42 (Oxford, 2010)
Colvin and Simmons	H. Colvin and J. S. G. Simmons, *All Souls: An Oxford College and its Buildings* (Oxford, 1989)
CTM	C. Trice Martin, *Catalogue of the Archives in the Muniment Room of All Souls' [sic] College* ([Oxford], 1877)
HUO	History of the University of Oxford
ODNB	*Oxford Dictionary of National Biography*
RCHM	Royal Commission on Historical Monuments (England)
TNA	The National Archives (Kew)
Unarmed Soldiery	J. Catto, R. Evans, J. McConica, S. Walker and A. Watson, *Unarmed Soldiery: Studies in the Early History of All Souls College* (Oxford, 1996)
VCH	*Victoria County History*

PREFACE

JOHN
DRURY

The reredos in All Souls College Chapel is a wonder – 'marvellous',
wrote Pevsner – not widely known or thoroughly understood. This
was made very clear when Anna Eavis of English Heritage was brought
to see it by Rosemary Hill a few years back. Wonder led to amazement
that our knowledge about it, historical or material, was so sparse.
Caroline Elam suggested a symposium to remedy this. The College's
historians, Keith Thomas, Peregrine Horden and Simon Green planned
one with me. It would approach the reredos in narrative mode from
its making; through its breaking by Reformation iconoclasm; its
covering to support a classical or baroque ensemble; and its brilliantly
tactful restoration by Sir Gilbert Scott in the 1870s. Each phase showed
the persuasions and passions of its time: changes in religious beliefs
and practices, in styles of architecture and the visual arts, as well as in
national and College politics. All this would rest on a basis of material
analysis (pigment and stone) along with recording and imaging, guided
by Andrew Wilson.[1] Here is the result.

    The east ends of English churches and chapels are historically restless
places, altered again and again under the pressures of devotion and
denial, notions and rituals. All Souls Chapel began by manifesting a
lavishly visual religion, superseded in a century by an austere religion of
the word, then an assertive celebration of established order (the screen
between the outer and inner chapels, a superb interruption, witnesses
to this) and finally a reclaiming of original splendour, though beset by
acrimonious College debate, so beautifully carried out by Scott and his
Victorian masons. It should be sadly recorded that Gavin Stamp, who
knew all about Scott and was to speak about this last phase, died before
the symposium met. Michael Hall, generously and expertly, stepped in.

    The sheer beauty and splendour of the reredos, which stopped
Pevsner in his tracks and delights so many people, is the prime mover

---

1   Professor of the Archaeology of the Roman Empire, All Souls College.

of the symposium and this book. It dominates the chapel. But it is not oppressive – rather, uplifting in a very precise sense. The scheme of regular niches and canopies, and of the variously inclining figures within them, is significantly graded. It is not (as at New College) a stack of shelves as in a bookcase. Rather, of the thirteen vertical bays, the central five support figures higher than the four flanking them on either side. They make up a tableau of Christ's crucifixion, the redeeming sacrifice on which the world turns, flanked by the college's two founders: Archbishop Chichele and King Henry VI. This surmounts the altar. Next, within that five, three figures arise, the risen Christ at the centre. Then, the archangel Michael with the scales of justice rises higher still. Above him Christ sits in judgment on the rainbow with naked and risen souls approaching him from either side. Above him the command is inscribed *surgite mortui venite ad iudicium* (Arise, ye dead, and come to judgment).

This is laboriously put but the effect, by contrast, is of uplift: the eye is drawn upwards from the lower terrestrial level to the throne of heaven and to the one Christ, sacrificed below, now supreme. This formalised sense of ascent is confirmed by the diminishing sizes of the figures. Perspective is understood.

There is another way in which the excellent design counteracts heaviness. This is only discernible from close up, but it tells from further off. The ornamental carved panelling behind the figures is not solid or 'blind', but pierced. This way too, the eye is not balked but led on.

Such dedicated and intelligent creativity gives this complex survivor of some six turbulent centuries a serene and direct appeal to the present – and makes the study of it so rewarding. All thanks to the participants.

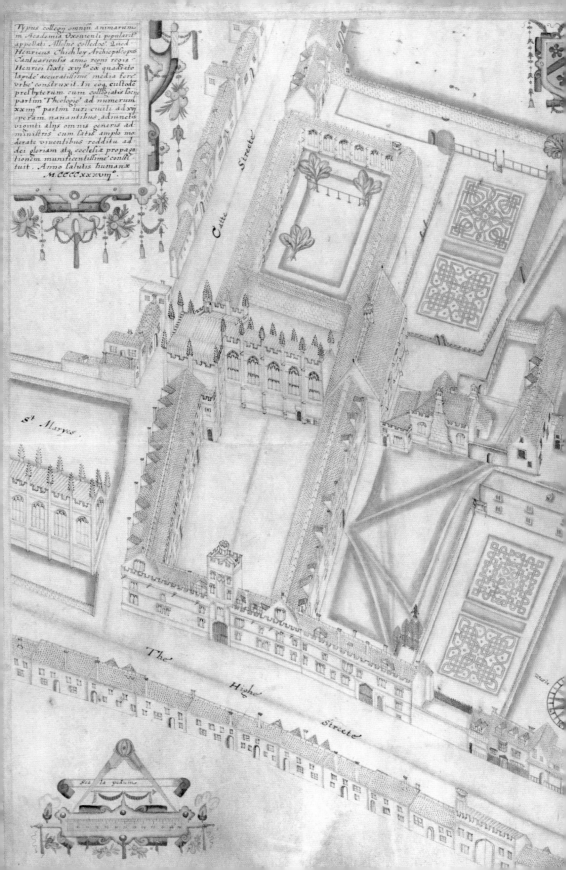

Typus collegij omniu animarum
in Academia Oxonienfi populariť
appellati Allefne colledoc. Quod
Henricus Chichley Archiepiscopus
Cantuariensis anno regni regis
Henrici sexti xvjᵗᵒ ex quadrato
lapide accuratisfimè media ferè
vrbe construxit. In eoq; custode
presbyterum cum collegiatis focijs
partim Theologie ad numerum
xxmͫ partim iuris ciuili ad xvj
operam nauantibus adiunctis
viginti alijs omnis generis ad
ministris cum fatis amplo mo
derate viuentibus redditu ad
dei gloriam atq; ecclefie propaga
tionem munificentisfimè conſti
tuit. Anno falutis humanæ
M.CCCCXXXVIIᵒ

Castle Streete

St. Maryes

The

Highe

Streete

Scala pedum.

INTRODUCTION
THE BUILDING OF THE CHAPEL; THE EVOLUTION OF ITS EAST END

PEREGRINE
HORDEN

Foundation

All Souls College, Oxford, was founded by Henry Chichele, the elderly archbishop of Canterbury, with the teenaged King Henry VI as his nominal co-founder. The king granted the foundation charter on 20 May 1438, but the business of designing, endowing, building and populating the College with its warden and 40 fellows (enlarged from an original 20) was inevitably protracted. Chichele had been planning the College for some years. Its first fellows were already being selected, and land purchased for it, in 1437. Building work began in February 1438. The chapel was licensed by papal bull in June 1439 but Chichele did not consecrate it and say the first mass there until June 1442. Finally, at Lambeth in early April 1443, the ailing archbishop handed his first warden the approved copy of the College statutes. Ten days later he was dead.[1]

His vision of the college and its purposes had remained constant. It is there in the royal letter patent of 1438 and in the statutes of 1443.[2] It was two-fold. All colleges in the medieval English universities had a chantry function, supporting priests to pray for the founder's soul. Thus All Souls was first and foremost a chantry, and specifically a Lancastrian military chantry, in which prayers would be said for Henry VI and Chichele while alive and their souls after death, and the repose of the souls of Henry V, his brother the Duke of Clarence, others 'who had drunk the cup of bitter death' in the Hundred Years War — and the souls

---

0.10 The 'Typus collegii', bird's-eye view (axonometric drawing) by Thomas Langdon, c. 1600 (ASC archives, Hovenden Maps I, 1)

1   What follows, related to my forthcoming history of All Souls from its foundation to the end of the seventeenth century, is based on College archives. It is also of course indebted to its predecessors in the field: *Unarmed Soldiery* (especially the contribution of the late Jeremy Catto); Colvin and Simmons (see Abbreviations); the contributions of E. F. Jacob and A. H. M. Jones to the entry on All Souls in VCH *Oxfordshire*, iii; E. F. Jacob, 'The Building of All Souls College, 1438–1443', in J. G. Edwards, V. C. Galbraith and E. F. Jacob (eds), *Historical Essays in Honour of James Tait* (Manchester, 1933), 121–33; the edition of the *Building Accounts*; also J. Harvey, *English Mediaeval Architects: A Biographical Dictionary down to 1550*, revised edn (Gloucester, 1984).

2   *Statutes of the Colleges of Oxford*, 3 vols (London, 1853), i (section 7), 'All Souls'' [sic], separately paginated, cited below by statute number.

of all the faithful departed. For which reason the college would be called 'All Soulen College'.

The second purpose of All Souls was military in a different sense. It was to provide a remedy for the decay in quality and number of the 'unarmed clerical militia', the priesthood. It would do this by taking from other colleges – not straight from school – those who had graduated or were just about to graduate. It would provide this select number of advanced students with the fellowships that would enable them to study for higher degrees, proceed to holy orders, and serve church and government as leaders, administrators, or advocates, their thoughts and deeds underpinned by the rationality instilled in higher education, not least the rationality of legal training. In a nutshell: 'prayer helped the dead as law helped the living'.[3] Chichele's own career had been as scholar (at New College), civil lawyer, diplomat, grand strategist (in the invasion of France), bishop, scourge of heretics, and archbishop. It not coincidentally exemplifies the ideal of rational learning and sound religion placed in the service of church and crown that he hoped the fellows of his college – twenty-four in arts and theology, sixteen in canon and civil law – would uphold.

To the corporate life of this fellowship, worship was central. The statutes give some attention to the reading of the Bible during meals which were otherwise to be silent (ch. 12) and to the private prayers to be said by fellows in their chambers (23). But far more space is devoted to the round of services from vespers to compline that were to be sung, following the 'Sarum rite', by the whole College on Sundays and feast days, and to the services in commemoration of the dead that were to be said weekly (chs 22, 23). The main liturgical round has been estimated at over 1,000 services a year spread across 200 days.[4] In his statutes Chichele did not specify a choral foundation as had William of Wykeham at New College in 1379, even though Chichele had been a graduate and fellow of New College and its statutes were in many respects his model for those of All Souls. But it is clear from occasional mentions in the All Souls statutes and other evidence that the College supported chaplains, clerks, choristers and organists, was well equipped with books of polyphony, and had an organ probably donated by the founder himself.[5] The fellows were expected to be competent in plainsong and to participate fully in the liturgy.

---

3 Margaret Bent, sermon preached in All Souls chapel, 2 Nov. 1997.
4 Estimated by John Harper, at the original symposium on the reredos.
5 B. A. Lee-di Amici, 'Cum nota solenniter celebret: Music in the Chapel of All Souls College, Oxford, 1445–1550', Renaissance Studies, 18 (2004), 171–207.

Building

We learn about some of the chapel personnel from the early archives. The archives also contain a unique survival as far as medieval Oxford is concerned, a fair or presentation copy of the building accounts of All Souls. These accounts supply plentiful details of most basic aspects of the construction of the College, such as the labour force, the materials and the costs – but are unhelpful on chronology. They are also for the most part about the College in general rather than the chapel in particular. Walls are referred to for the first time in September 1438; carpenters appear in January 1439.[6] By August 1439 the walls had reached first-floor level, for carpenters were paid to work on the supports of the floors of two upper chambers. The residential ranges were apparently begun first. But as these inched towards completion in the course of 1440, work on the chapel was also well advanced. By late 1441 a glazier was occupied in the choir of the chapel filling eight windows and the roof was being decorated with angels. We know that the vestry was paved and that the roof was being worked on during 1442. The chapel was consecrated by the archbishop in June 1442. Mass was followed by a celebratory breakfast, presumably in the antechapel. This was Chichele's only visit to the College.

Still, the list of dramatis personae involved in the appearance of chapel and College generally must start with Chichele. He would, from Lambeth or his palace at Croydon or wherever else he happened to be, have taken an active interest in the design and development of his foundation and was visited several times by his supervisors, sometimes in the company of the master mason.[7] Chichele had previously worked with Thomas Mapilton, the royal master mason since 1421, on the south-west tower of Canterbury Cathedral and the Lollards' Tower of Lambeth Palace and Mapilton might have drawn up some initial plans, but he died in 1438. The 'supervisor of the work of the new college'[8] was a clerk named John Druell, future fellow, one of Chichele's men whose family had connections with the archbishop's birthplace, Higham Ferrers. Druell collated the building accounts for annual audit from February 1438 onwards. He was succeeded in September 1441 by Roger Keys, soon to be warden of the College, who accounted up to at least November 1443, when the surviving manuscript breaks off abruptly. The main concern of these men was the purchase and transport of raw

---

6   Building Accounts, 26, 39, and, for what follows, 70, 224, 230, 239, 257, 293.

7   For what follows see Colvin and Simmons, 4ff.; Building Accounts, xix.

8   Building Accounts, 1.

materials. In charge of the work force, the 'clerk of works' was first, appropriately, John Clerk and then, from April 1440, John Medehill, later to be clerk of works at another royal foundation, Eton College. The master mason was Richard Chevynton, a now obscure figure who may have recommended himself to All Souls through working at Abingdon Abbey. He supervised the cutting of the stone in the quarry. The second or deputy master mason was Robert Janyns, who would have been in charge on site. He went on to supervise the building of the bell tower of Merton College and, concurrently, also to work at Eton. The chief carpenter was John Branche, again perhaps from Abingdon. These were worthy men, of considerable experience and skill; but the one figure of national renown, most closely involved with the reredos, was the sculptor John Massyngham. Together with his son, also John, and his assistant Thomas Whitlock, he was responsible for the figures of King and Archbishop above the entrance to the College and a coloured 'image of the Trinity' among other sculptures above the high altar.[9] Massyngham was paid 4s. 8d. a week, significantly more than Chevynton or Branche.[10]

We cannot tell how much the chapel cost. We know only that the total expenditure on building work, between 1438 and 1446, was in the region of £4,500.[11] In the early years annual expenditure on construction was just over £500 a year, but as the College neared completion that figure doubled. Chichele was an old man in a hurry. At the time of his death in 1443, he was pouring into his final great project moneys equivalent to around one third of his annual income from the lordship of Canterbury. The building project was not only well funded, it was well managed. Thus it was completed with relative speed. Compare the £17–18,000 that Henry VI spent on Eton over a longer period, from 1442 until his deposition in 1461, a period that included the demolition of the partially constructed first chapel in 1448 to make way for a grander conception.[12]

We know, then, from the building accounts, who provided the funds. We know who managed the works and had some responsibility for the design. We also know where the materials came from.

---

9 Building Accounts, 167, 264. See further Wilson, this volume, 97.

10 Colvin and Simmons, 5.

11 Building Accounts, xxviii; Colvin and Simmons, 8.

12 R. Allen Brown, H. M. Colvin and A. J. Taylor, The History of the King's Works, Volume I: The Middle Ages (London, 1963), 292.

The primary consideration naturally had to be the supply of stone and timber.[13] The ragstone for foundations and walls was brought from Headington, where the College purchased rights to a quarry of its own.[14] Taynton, northwest of Burford, and about 20 miles from Oxford, was used for the better quality and more readily carvable freestone and thus for some mouldings and tracery. The College again leased its own quarry. Visual inspection suggests, however, that Taynton stone was not used in the medieval reredos, which is predominantly of oolitic freestone from other quarries in the region of Burford such as Sherborne.[15] For the finest work, such as the statuary, stone was brought from 'Rysborgh', presumably Prince's Risborough, as well as Taynton.

The timber for roofs and fittings was nearly all oak, from nearby woodland at Shotover, Stow Wood, Eynsham, Cumnor, Beckley, Minster Lovell and Horeham (presumably Horeham wood near Marlow). Iron came mostly from London, lead from Derbyshire, slate from Oxford.[16]

We have all this tantalizing detail. Yet we could not tell from reading the building accounts, or indeed from any of the other college muniments of the time, how the chapel building looked, inside or outside. Apart from the angels under the roof, we know there were *imagines* above or on top of the high altar, including one of the Trinity that was gilded, and that is about all.[17]

Other, later material in the archive will of course help here and there, but we have to judge the original outcome of Chichele's expenditure mainly by what survives today: that is, by the front quadrangle of the College. As a preliminary to focusing on the chapel and on its reredos in particular, we should appreciate the place of the chapel within the overall site.

Site

In that sense the history of the All Souls College chapel begins in 1437 with a modest property transaction.[18] The property was Berford Hall, located at the corner of Catte Street and the High. It was one of the many domestic establishments in which the majority of Oxford's 1500 or so undergraduates still lodged in the fifteenth century before the

13 Jacob, 'Building', 125–7.

14 CTM, 162, no. 173.

15 For all this see further Palmer and Sheffrey, this volume.

16 *Building Accounts*, xx-xxi, 162; Colvin and Simmons, 6.

17 *Building Accounts*, 167, 264; Wilson, this volume.

18 Ibid., xvi–xvii.

colleges came to dominate the landscape. Berford Hall used to be known as Charlton's Inn and was a substantial tenement with a High Street frontage of perhaps 70 feet, and, apart from the accommodation, several shops on its ground floor. It had once belonged to a royal mistress but was now, in 1437, in the hands of a gentry family of MPs, the Bromes of Warwick. On 14 December John Brome senior and John Brome junior, presumably his son, sold the plot to Chichele's feoffees. These men, including the archbishop's brother, Thomas, became joint tenants who would next surrender it to Henry VI. The king would then, as co-founder, grant it to the college. This is the process by which other sites were acquired and then conveyed to the nascent college in both legal and practical terms. A variety of individual and institutional landlords had to be reckoned with, but the times were propitious. Oxford, even near its centre, was a buyer's market thanks to a slump in rents. In addition, ecclesiastical landlords with properties in the right place, such as St Frideswide's Priory, Osney Abbey and the University Church of St Mary the Virgin, might have been glad simultaneously to abandon unprofitable rents and ingratiate themselves with the primate. Even so the technicalities could take time. In several cases some informal agreement or interim lease must have preceded the legal arrangements because building had begun before the properties had been conveyed. The antiquary John Rouse would record that *six* academic halls had to be destroyed to make space for All Souls, but this may both obscure the extent to which some of them were already in decay, and yet also create the impression that Chichele could 'bulldoze' freely. In fact the College was planned, at least according to the letter of Henry VI dated 20 May 1438, as being only 160 feet wide (and 172 feet long), and its main building seems to have occupied the sites of at most *four* former tenements.[19]

This smaller number is important because it means that the College quadrangle was deeper north-south than it was broad, and from the front has a slightly constricted air. The east-west constriction is marked, especially if we remember that the façade, running east from Catte Street, stopped (until the mid-sixteenth century) at the point where the High Street changes direction a few degrees to the south; and it may explain the fact that the original dining hall projected north from the north-east corner of the quadrangle.[20] The chapel of course had to be

---

19 Jacob, 'Building', 124.
20 *Building Accounts*, xix. H. Colvin, 'The Building of St Bernard's College', *Oxoniensia*, 24 (1960), 37–48, points out that a north projecting hall was also a feature of Cistercian houses, and St Bernard's (the future St John's) was Chichele's previous collegiate foundation.

aligned east-west. It therefore occupies the shorter side of the College (although its north wall is further from the frontage than the 172 feet longitudinally allowed for by King Henry, and St Thomas Hall, lying to the north of Charlton's Inn, had had to be purchased to accommodate it). That in turn had consequences for the chapel's position within the College's overall layout. Chichele had, through his agents, secured a prime site for his foundation, on the High, next to the heart of the University, St Mary's, which included the convocation house where the 'regent Masters' met, and not far from the Divinity School, still under construction at the time. (It was also as it happens opposite the city's red-light district on what is now blandly called Magpie Lane.[21]) Chichele and his master mason (the equivalent of architect) surely would not have considered placing the main entrance on cramped Catte Street: it had to be on the High. If they had wanted to see the effect of facing on to Catte Street they could compare Lincoln College, largely built from 1427 to 1437, with its front on the narrow Turl Street (as it is now called).

The north-south orientation of All Souls towards the High entailed a departure from the layout of William of Wykeham's foundation, New College, which in so many respects, not just its statutes, was Chichele's inspiration. Wykeham's college was large and imposing, much larger than All Souls in every respect. But it had been aligned east-west, under the city walls to the north, and with its chapel and hall together forming the northern range of the quadrangle. Similarly, Chichele's plan for St Bernard's College for Cistercians, on the Northgate Street, now St Giles, also has the hall, kitchen and chapel on the left of the small quadrangle, for St Bernard's orientation was also east-west.[22] Chichele clearly liked his Oxford foundations to stand four-square on one of the city's arteries.

The layout of All Souls was thus determined by the fact that its main frontage stood on the High Street. Other aspects of the overall design were more straightforward. In Oxford, the quadrangle had first evolved, haphazardly, at Merton. New College then established it as the default shape of planned collegiate building in Oxford. It was monastic in essence (though the quadrangles of the monastic Gloucester and Canterbury Colleges postdate Merton's), but also with more than a hint of the college of priests and, more specifically, of the rectangular former cloister housing canons in the lower ward of Windsor Castle and the

---

21 H. Kavanagh, 'The Secrets of Magpie Lane: Prostitution in Medieval Oxford', *The Local Historian*, 45 (2015), 40 – 54.

22 Colvin, 'St Bernard's', 39 – 41.

extremely regular upper ward, with hall and chapel set end to end.[23]
Access to the Oxford quadrangle led through a gatehouse in the form
of a plain tower. (If Oxford colleges, with mainly royal and episcopal
founders, are like religious houses in this period, their Cambridge
counterparts, with a preponderance of lay founders, more closely
resemble manor houses and boast correspondingly more impressive
gate towers.[24]) In the tower, the head of the college would reside
like an abbot or a prior − in a quasi-panopticon with views over the
quadrangle as well as the outside world.

Chichele's College thus took the form of a south-facing frontage and
gate house on a main street with a quadrangle behind, the northern arm
of which was constituted by the chapel. The chapel was at the heart of
the College's existence, as a place of worship and also of secular events.
One could cross the quad to reach it by the shortest route since in 1442
the quad was paved, an unusual feature (figs. 0.2, 3).[25]

The two-story gate tower might be said to have a military as well as
a monastic aspect.[26] As at Lincoln College, recently completed (1437), it
is a simple upward prolongation of the walls with no projecting features
and no interruption to the main string course.[27] Deliberately or not,
its crenellation echoes that added to the tower of Merton College. But
the All Souls gate tower also conveyed a religious message: between its
statues of Henry VI and Chichele, the College's co-founders (fig. 0.11),
within a central niche stood a figure of Christ atop a relief showing
souls rising from the tomb. You entered the College passing under these
figures and there at once, straight ahead, the windows of the chapel
'hit' you. The library, home of learning, the other pillar of the College's
existence, lay to the right of the person entering, as at New College;
the hall on the other hand was concealed beyond the north-east corner.
The symbolism of the layout cannot have been unintentional.

23 J. Harvey, 'Architecture in Oxford 1350−1500', in J. I. Catto and R. Evans (eds), HUO, Vol. II: Late
Medieval Oxford (Oxford, 1993), 755−6; C. Wilson, '"Excellent, New and Uniforme": Perpendicular
Architecture c. 1400−1547', in R. Marks and P. Williamson (eds), Gothic: Art for England 1400−1547
(London, 2003), 105.

24 Colvin and Simmons, 12.

25 Jacob, 'Building', 131; Colvin and Simmons, 6.

26 J. Harvey, The Perpendicular Style 1330−1485 (London, 1978), 139−42.

27 Harvey, 'Architecture', 754; Colvin and Simmons, 11−12.

Style

The style in which the College and its chapel was built is usually described as Perpendicular Gothic. Like other phases of English medieval architecture, the term was invented by the architect-antiquary and Gothic revivalist Thomas Rickman in 1817. It has been flavoured from his time to that of John Harvey (d. 1997) with English nationalism and wrongly seen as largely immune to Continental influence.[28] But the term, though anachronistic, does capture the unity, based on repetition of forms, the essential clarity and simplicity of overall conception, the subordination of individual features to the effect of the whole, and the rectangularity that characterize so much architecture right across the country in the late fourteenth and fifteenth centuries.[29] In Oxford the Benedictine Canterbury College of c. 1364–97 had had Perpendicular tracery. The 'spirit' of Perpendicular, as far as the 1430s in Oxford was concerned, is captured in the instructions given to the new master mason brought in to work on the Divinity School – to avoid superfluous and irrelevant 'curiosity'.[30] It cost too much and slowed work down, and more importantly perhaps did not befit the University.

The applicability of the term Perpendicular is less obvious when one looks at the All Souls High Street front, despite its austerity (the chimneys and oriel windows visible today reflect exuberant re-Gothicizing in the 1820s). But once we are inside the College, the chapel's five bays with their buttresses and parapets with pinnacles, and the windows' transoms and strongly vertical 'gridiron' tracery that runs from sill to soffit beneath four-centred arches, are all unmistakeably Perpendicular.[31]

The chapel rises on the line of the inner front of the eastern range of the quadrangle, up against the fan-vaulted vestibule of the north-south-orientated hall. The hall was served by a buttery the cellars of which extended under the chapel, meeting up with its crypt, so that the beer was stored beneath the high altar, a nice and unusual alignment of two

28 For Harvey's extreme politics see G. Macklin, 'The Two Lives of John Hooper Harvey', *Patterns of Prejudice*, 42 (2008), 167–90.

29 Harvey, *Perpendicular*, 215–16; Wilson, '"Excellent"'; Wilson, this volume.

30 R. H. C. Davis, "The Chronology of Perpendicular Architecture in Oxford', *Oxoniensia*, 11–12 (1946–7), 75–89 at 79; Harvey, 'Architecture', 750, 763; Wilson, '"Excellent"', 117, with Wilson, this volume, 178 n. 92. In his chapter Wilson (e.g. at 153–4) registers departures from the Perpendicular ethos in the canopies of some reredos niches.

31 Davis, 'Chronology', 79; RCHM, *City of Oxford* (London, 1939), 17, which has been my guide for technical architectural description.

of the poles of the College's daily existence.[32] Thus fortified, the chapel proceeds westward for five bays. Its chancel and choir are together almost 74 feet long inside.[33]

The two bays of the antechapel thrust south into the quadrangle, meeting the western residential range in a vestibule with a room for fellows above. The bays have similar parapet and buttresses to those of the chapel and there are two similar but smaller windows on the east wall. The north arm of the antechapel also has two bays. There is a window in its north wall and another on its west wall. The main walls of the chapel each continue virtually across the antechapel as a pair of tall arches, with two-centred arches springing from slender piers. Mouldings run up the whole height of the antechapel wall, in an extreme refinement of the Perpendicular ethos.[34] The west front has a seven-light main window and two three-light ones either side, transomed like the others (figs. 0.5, 6).

The T-shaped plan, according to which all that we have are sanctuary, choir and transepts, without the nave one would expect in a larger church, has an Oxford history of its own. At Merton there might have been plans for a nave, but it was never built.[35] At New College, Wykeham's chapel might have been intended also to include a nave but ended up with a cloister instead. In the limited space of the town centre, Chichele's chapel was literally brought up short by the ancient north-south thoroughfare of Catte Street. This was immovable, and the College, smaller than Wykeham's (40 fellows to 70), did not need a larger chapel. Hence antechapel rather than transepts. The sovereignty of the street is declared in the antechapel's west wall, which follows the street's contours and thus makes the antechapel wider at south than at north end.

Interior

Within the chapel, the most striking feature is the original roof, because of the way in which (as Wilson shows below) it fits in with the programme of the topmost part of the reredos, the tympanum (fig. 0.8). As at New College, the roof is shallow-pitched and hammer-beamed in seven bays with moulded main timbers. There are carved angels at the ends of the hammer-beams and foliage bosses in the middle of the

---

32 Colvin and Simmons, 9.
33 I am indebted to Paul Gardner, Manciple of All Souls, for estimates based on electronic plans.
34 Davis, 'Chronology', 80; RCHM, 17.
35 Harvey, 'Architecture', 759.

collars. The roof rests on stone corbels carved with the heads of kings, bishops and, in one case, a queen. The roof of the antechapel is similar but in two bays, with tie-beams and curved braces forming four-centred arches.

The medieval glass was the work of John Glasier in the chapel itself and of John Prudde, the king's glazier, in the antechapel. Its general quality has to be inferred from what survives (restored 1870−71) in the east windows of the antechapel.[36] The original programme is described by the soldier-antiquary Richard Symonds, who made notes on it 'between December 1643 and April 1644, when the Royalist army was in the City'. He records in the lower register of the south windows a sequence of the fifteen kings from William the Conqueror to Henry VI (one per light therefore), Church fathers and saints above them (which must have included the 'Four Doctors of the [western Latin] Church' to whom the chapel was dedicated − Ambrose, Augustine, Gregory, Ambrose); and on the north side, above, some Greek fathers including the eastern 'doctor' Basil, and, incongruously in that company, the venerable Bede, with some of the twelve apostles, St Paul and John the Baptist below.

In the lights of the antechapel east wall we still see the full twelve apostles and below them a striking array of holy women from Anna to the Exeter saint Sidwell or Sativola, who also appears in the wall paintings of Eton College chapel.[37]

A full description of the All Souls chapel would give some space to the sedilia, of which part is original;[38] to the floor tiles, a few of which survive in the choir; to the stalls (more than enough for all the fellows, although at New College there were only 62 stalls for 70 fellows), almost all original, and with an attractive set of misericords;[39] to the monuments and their inscriptions;[40] to the sequence of screens;[41] to the entrance to the vestibule from Catte Street, blocked in 1784 (fig. 0.4); to the vestry

36 F. E. Hutchinson, *Medieval Glass at All Souls College* (London, 1949); 'Corpus Vitrearum Medii Aevi', All Souls College, Chapel, http://www.cvma.ac.uk/jsp/location.do?locationKey=870&mode=LOCATION (accessed 20 Aug. 2020).

37 E. Howe et al., *Wall Paintings of Eton* (London, 2012), 140−41.

38 See further Wilson, this volume, 130, 154.

39 Colvin and Simmons, 9; http://www.misericords.co.uk/all_soluls_oxford.html#miseri (accessed 20 Aug. 1990).

40 F. E. Hutchinson, *Monumental Inscriptions in All Souls College*, revised edn by M. A. Screech (Oxford, 1997).

41 There is no record of the appearance of those funded by Chichele and by Bishop Goldwell in the 1490s (Wilson, this volume, 115). Sketches for screens by Christopher Wren (All Souls College, Wren II: 67; IV: 117, 157) make up the next chapter in the screen's history. The current screen, paid for by Sir William Portman in the 1660s, was remodelled by Thornhill (Colvin and Simmons, 58; Johns, this volume, 230) in the early eighteenth century and regilded in the late twentieth (fig 0.7).

and the cloister, both on the north side, the cloister slowly built during the second half of the fifteenth century and both demolished in the eighteenth; and to the sundial, reasonably attributed to Christopher Wren, dateable to 1659, and removed from the central bay of the chapel's south wall to the equivalent on the Codrington Library in 1877.[42]

But these are Hamlet without the prince – the reredos, our focus here. Why is there a reredos? In part, because as at New College, and wherever chapel and hall share a party wall, there can be no east window. Yet there were various ways of filling the necessarily windowless space. The original ranks of *imagines*, including a Trinity, rising to the inscription under the roof – 'rise up you dead and come to judgement' – was obviously fitting in a college of all souls in which prayer for the dead was a regular obligation. Yet the reredos may not originally have looked quite as we fancy it did.

What survives in the reredos, is, to put it in dynastic terms, Lancastrian or early Tudor painted niches, populated by high Victorian unpainted statues. The purpose of this book is to explore and explain both initial and current state, to recreate the various phases of destruction and covering-up that came between the Tudors and the Victorians, and to convey the tides of taste that those phases reflected.

Conspectus

We begin with the appliance of science to the materials of niches and figures. Tim Palmer and Ruth Shaffrey provide what is in effect a detailed commentary on and amplification of the evidence of the building accounts. They show us what stone was used where and which quarries it came from – and find no great changes or discrepancies that would mark out one phase of initial construction from another. They also show the care of George Gilbert Scott's Victorian restoration.

From stone to its coloration. Emily Howe records, for the first time, the extent and condition of its surviving medieval polychromy. The range of pigments employed was, she shows, extensive and extravagant. Furthermore, her examination has brought to light an unprecedented array of embellishment, ranging from silver leaf to sumptuous gilded tin relief fashioned to emulate luxurious brocade textiles. It must originally have been a wonderful sight. Technical sophistication was

---

42 Colvin and Simmons, 15–16; Green, this volume, 269. The sundial has been photoshopped back into its original position by Deborah Oxley: https://talbot.bodleian.ox.ac.uk/2018/07/20/summer-pleasures-sundial-symmetry-and-simmons/ (accessed 20 Aug. 2020).

0.12 (2.6) Niches S1.II-IV on the south side of the bottom register, with residual iron oxide decoration

not, however, matched by coherence of design. The craftsmen seem to have been left to their own individual devices and to have learned how to systematise their colour schemes as they proceeded upwards, from base to Judgement scene, in a sequence of campaigns, possibly undertaken by different groups of craftsmen. Moreover, they were painting the niches working around statues that had already been installed (see fig. 0.12).

Those details are important for the historical chapters that follow the scientific ones. After a panorama of the cultic and devotional practices of Chichele's world by Eamon Duffy, Christopher Wilson provides a detailed and radically new interpretation of the 'medieval' reredos. It had always been known that some work was still being done on the reredos in the years around 1500. But that work had been interpreted as the completion of a sculptural scheme that might have been left incomplete in the 1440s. Through a rereading of the archives, and an eye for the inconsistencies of the surviving early niches with their surroundings (especially where they meet the Judgement scene on the tympanum), Wilson separates out a Chichleian reredos which occupied only the central part of the wall (Reredos I) from an early Tudor reworking of the entire wall with the exception of the tympanum (Reredos II); and he places the newer work in its contemporary, often Netherlandish, stylistic context. It is important to note that the

0.13 (4.5) All Souls College, reredos, photograph of 1872 (see below, 108)

scientific evidence, at least as I read it, does not contradict or endorse this new chronology. The stonework is all of a piece, which points neither one way nor the other. Work on the polychromy is seen as incoherent and protracted, which might favour the 'traditional' interpretation, and some of it is dated by Howe to Chichele's time; but without an absolute timeline for the painters' work, which neither science nor archival research can provide, we cannot say more than that.

The implications of Wilson's chapter reach further. After another wide-angle chapter, from Diarmaid MacCulloch, on the long history of iconoclasm, we come, in my own short note on the next phase in the history of the reredos, to the destruction or removal of the statuary in the reign of Edward VI. (The shocking effect can perhaps best be gauged from the photograph of 1872 that records the medieval reredos as it was first seen after subsequent coverings had been stripped away; see fig. 0.13) Howe's work shows that what was left behind after the iconoclasm was a set of niches with the painted silhouettes of the figures still visible. Wilson's work shows that the destruction was wrought upon a reredos that had been wholly reworked, or at the very least completed, not a century before but only a few decades.

There is then a lull in proceedings, and a corresponding gap between chapters, which really is over a century long. Despite the liturgical and material changes enforced on churches and chapels from the reign of Mary to that of Charles I and on through the Protectorate of Cromwell, the east end of the chapel remained substantially unaltered. Further iconoclasm passed it by; there was no cover-up of the bare niches. In that sense the Gothic history of the chapel sanctuary lasts from the 1440s to the 1660s. Only with the Restoration did everything change.

No one will claim that the painter Isaac Fuller is a neglected master of a high order (see above, page 16, for the present display of his paintings, and below, figs. 7.5 – 8). Yet his *Last Judgement*, which covered the reredos over for the first time and extended along the ceiling on panels placed between the hammer beams, is rightly lauded by Michael Liversidge. It provided an 'extraordinary baroque spectacle on a scale no English painter had attempted before .... Fuller was trying to create a visually and iconographically unified effect – one of the first examples in England of treating a whole interior decoratively in the baroque idiom as a single spatial and thematic entity'.

Perhaps surprisingly, that places the All Souls chapel in the vanguard of taste. In the phase or phases described by Wilson, the College was very much in the swim of current taste in architecture and decoration; but one would not see it as taking the lead. From the Restoration onwards, all that changes. The large-scale decorative schemes that result from the College's patronage first of Fuller (chapter by Michael Liversidge) and then, some half century later, of Thornhill (Richard Johns) put All Souls at the forefront of aesthetic developments. Major indigenous figures are brought in – for the first time since Massyngham. Far more successful and renowned than Fuller, Thornhill was, as Johns puts it below, 'the only English-born painter capable of competing alongside the most prominent foreign artists for the most prestigious projects'. He rose to the challenge of creating, in place of Fuller's 'nakeds' on top of the reredos, a baroque fantasy in which a fifteenth-century archbishop takes his place among the saints as if he were Romulus or Caesar being welcomed by the gods (see fig. 0.14). Thornhill also prompted a redecoration of most of the chapel in the same idiom, from east end

0.14 (8.1) James Thornhill, *Henry Chichele*, from the east wall of All Souls College chapel, 1715–16 (removed 1872), oil on plaster, 320 × 220 cm

to screen and beyond to west-end glass. Into this classicising-baroque interior comes, several decades later, the altarpiece by Anton Raphael Mengs, reckoned by many at the time to be the greatest painter in Europe (Robin Darwall-Smith). Recruiting this progenitor of neoclassicism to enhance the one remaining blank space above the altar is the College's most ambitious act of artistic patronage. It also marks the apogee of the disguising of Chichele's chapel (see fig. 0.15).

There was then another lull. As Johns soberingly notes, Thornhill's work survived in the chapel for over 150 years, longer than any other phase in its history thus far. During this lull, the tide of taste turned against Mengs and the classicising baroque style and in favour of revived Gothic. Yet the tearing down of the Thornhill, the re-exposure of the reredos for the first time since the 1660s, and the reinsertion of sculpted figures into the niches, might, as S. J. D. Green shows, never have happened. The College was bitterly divided on what if anything to do about the chapel's deterioration. Only the astute machinations of Warden Leighton and the proffered munificence of the senior fellow,

0.15 (9.2) East end of All Souls chapel with the Mengs altar painting, Thornhill fresco and larger decorative scheme, lithograph by G. Cooper, 1817

Lord Bathurst, ensured the factional triumph that would lead eventually (after the ignominious sacking of Henry Clutton) to the arrival on the scene of George Gilbert Scott. Scott was after all the most eminent Gothic revival architect of the day. He was also a client of Bathurst (Michael Hall). The College was once again securing the services of the best. What Scott and his sculptor Edward Geflowski wrought on the reredos is – despite the changes of taste already evident when Scott was at work, and despite continuing divisions within the College – what we see there today. (Proposals in the 1990s to reintroduce the Mengs to stand somehow in front of the Victorian reredos were, after further internal dissension, rejected.)

0.16 Cenotaph of Sir William Anson (d. 1914) against the north wall of the chapel sanctuary; figure by the 'British Rodin', John Tweed

The architectural history of the chapel sanctuary ends, Green reminds us, not in fact with Scott but with the cenotaph of Warden Sir William Anson installed against the north wall in 1915 (see fig. 0.16). I would add one further footnote to the history of the east end: the placing there of a movable organ in the present century, the first such instrument to be heard in the chapel since the reign of Elizabeth I. Among the many changes to which Chichele's chapel and its east end have been subjected, it is probably one of the few of which he would have approved.

PART I
PROBING — THE NEW SCIENTIFIC DATA

CHAPTER I

THE STONEWORK
OF THE REREDOS

**TIM PALMER
AND RUTH
SHAFFREY**

The stonework in the reredos dates from one or other of two principal episodes of construction, the first medieval and the second Victorian. The first episode dates to the time of the initial construction of the College, starting in 1438 and continuing until late in the fifteenth century or even into the beginning of the sixteenth century.[1] The types of building stone used in the earliest phase of building (1438 – 1443) are all limestones and their identities are made clear from entries in the building accounts that relate to purchase, preparation and transport of both ragstone and freestone from six different localities within Oxfordshire or close to its borders.[2] These are described more fully herein. The records contain references to the figures and niches above the altar, so it is clear that at least some reredos was constructed at the time of the initial building of the chapel. If other architectural features of the reredos date from somewhat later, then the stone would appear to have come from the same sources as were used for the earlier work – particularly those in Headington and in the Windrush valley west of Burford.

The second episode of construction was the restoration of the reredos under the direction of George Gilbert Scott, for which E.E. Geflowski carried out most of the figure carving.[3] The state of the reredos in 1872, before restoration began, can be seen in the photograph that is reproduced as fig. 4.5 in the present volume. The existing full-sized statues of historical and biblical figures, the figures on the Crucifixion and Judgement panels, and the small figures arranged on the mullions date from this restoration. Much repair work to the architectural features within the reredos, particularly the tabernacle work in the niches but also smaller areas of damage that could be mended using insets of new stone, was also undertaken by Scott's

---

1   See Wilson, this volume.
2   *Building Accounts*, xix–xx.
3   See Hall, this volume.

masonry team. Chalk in some of the statue plinths was replaced with new chalk, and the white oolitic limestone that was used by the restorers for so much of the replacement statuary, their supports and the niches, is very similar in superficial appearance to the palest of the oolitic limestone seen in the surviving medieval structure. The nineteenth-century stonework has remained unpainted, in contrast to the surviving surfaces of the medieval work. The fifteenth-century paintwork and metal leaf are still well preserved and only moderately worn, and greatly simplify the matter of distinguishing Victorian replacement stone from original medieval stonework, though their presence interferes with petrographic examination of the latter. There appears to be no surviving documentary evidence for the sources of the freestones favoured by Scott and Geflowski, but close visual study reveals the presence of two limestones that were in wide use during the nineteenth century. These are Painswick stone from north of Stroud, Gloucestershire, and Caen stone from Normandy.

Stonework from the original medieval build of the College

The different sources of stone that were used in the College buildings as reported in the accounts have been summarised previously.[4] There were four main sources of stone, of which two or three played a part in the construction of the reredos and were recognised in our examination (though no samples were taken for petrographic confirmation). The complete stone palette (summarised in fig. 1.1) consisted of: (a) Coral rag from the Corallian hills on the western fringes of Oxford, a ragstone used as rough masonry and rubble fill (not as facing stone) and not encountered during examination of the reredos; (b) Headington stone, a freestone from the Corallian of Headington, brought to the building site in large quantities from a leased quarry and certainly used for walling, for example in the facing stones of the walls in the front quadrangle; (c) fine-quality oolitic freestones used throughout the College for ashlar, dressings and carved work, from the quarries within the Great Oolite up the Windrush valley above Burford – specifically from Upton (Whiteladies / Wychelate quarry), Sherborne and Taynton – but mostly Taynton; and (d) chalk (of Lower Chalk age) from the foot of the Chilterns, probably in the vicinity of Princes Risborough. The stones designated (a)–(c) above were extensively used in high-status buildings in Oxford from medieval to post-Restoration times. The terms Corallian,

---

4   Besides the edition of the *Building Accounts*, see Colvin and Simmons, 6.

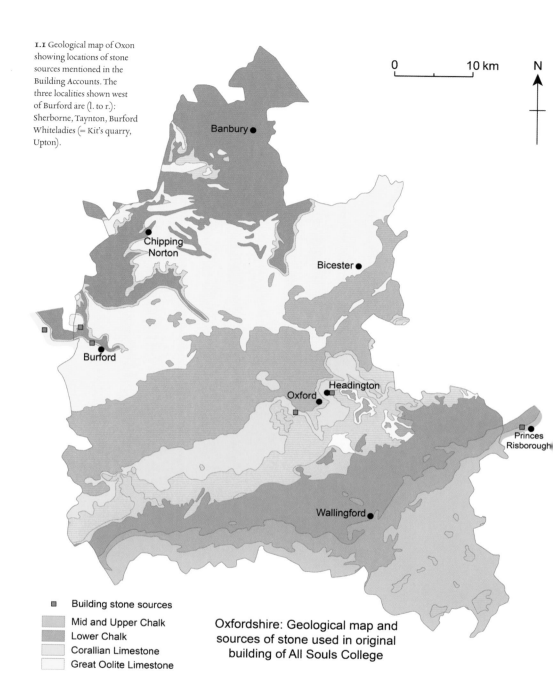

1.1 Geological map of Oxon showing locations of stone sources mentioned in the Building Accounts. The three localities shown west of Burford are (l. to r.): Sherborne, Taynton, Burford Whiteladies (= Kit's quarry, Upton).

0   10 km   N

Banbury ●

Chipping Norton ●

Bicester ●

Burford ●

Headington
Oxford ●

Princes Risborough

Wallingford ●

■ Building stone sources
  Mid and Upper Chalk
  Lower Chalk
  Corallian Limestone
  Great Oolite Limestone

Oxfordshire: Geological map and sources of stone used in original building of All Souls College

46

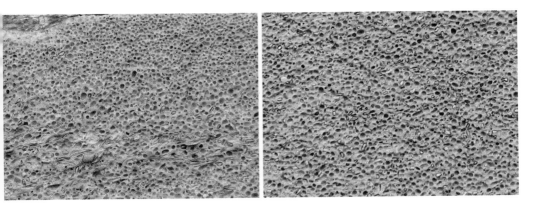

1.2 Pale and dark variants of Windrush Valley freestone (pale Sherborne stone on left: iron-stained Taynton stone on right), also showing characteristic surface textures as a result of ooliths falling away from the cut surface. Width of each view = 10 mm

Great Oolite and Lower Chalk are used in their geological sense. These matters are expanded upon in W. J. Arkell's *Oxford Stone* and *The Geology of Oxford*.[5]

OOLITIC FREESTONES FROM THE BURFORD REGION

In the medieval reredos, it was the oolitic freestones of the Windrush valley that were by far the most extensively used, and much of the carving (but not the major statuary) would probably have been carried out in the masons' yard in Burford. The records show that the Taynton stone came from a quarry rented by the College for the purpose.[6] It would have been about a mile from Burford and presumably both the proximity and the leasing arrangement kept costs down. The Sherborne stone came from three miles further westwards and certainly cost more to transport. Why then was cheaper Taynton not used for the whole job? The answer may lie in aesthetics. The Windrush valley freestones vary in colour (fig. 1.2). Taynton stone veers towards the yellow end of the range: in contrast, Sherborne stone is a much paler colour, verging towards cream. The argument that a whiter stone may have been preferred for some jobs is somewhat undermined by the painting, but maybe not all of the jobs for which a paler stone was favoured were painted. Nor is the amount of Sherborne stone that was used in the whole building project apparent from the accounts, as most of it is compounded with Taynton in individual records. Possibly the volume was quite modest.

5   W. J. Arkell, *Oxford Stone* (London, 1947); *The Geology of Oxford* (Oxford, 1947).
6   *Building Accounts*, xix-xx.

The Windrush Valley limestones are composed of ooliths (spherical grains of the mineral calcite with diameters up to $c.$ 0.7 mm) held together in a crystalline matrix of natural calcite cement. There are also bands a centimetre or two wide, somewhat oblique to the horizontal, that are rich in comminuted shell debris. Such shell fragments also form the central nuclei of some of the ooliths, giving rise to many larger and more elongate grains than is typical. Both types of grain readily fall away from the surrounding cement at the cut surface, leaving concave impressions (fig. 1.2). This property, often useful in distinguishing between different Jurassic oolitic limestones, is well-marked in Taynton and Sherborne limestones.

Also mentioned twice in the accounts (1441 and 1442) are stones from Wychslad or Whychslade quarry, and the first of these records is for the purchase of three large stones (*pro tribus magnis lapidibus*) for niches (*pro hovellis*).[7] These have been taken to be statue canopies.[8] This quarry was in Upton, half a mile west of Burford, and was also known as Whiteladies quarry. It was Burford's closest large quarry. Later, it became the property of Wren's mason, Christopher Kempster, and was known as Kit's Quarry[9] (it still is). The quarry excavations are now completely overgrown and cannot be examined. Plot, however, records it as being white in colour, less hard than Taynton but holding a sharp carved edge, and favoured by masons for fine quality work.[10]

STONE FROM RYSBORGH

Stones from Rysborgh, thought to be Princes Risborough, are itemised in two entries for purchase in the accounts.[11] Both state that they are for images. A third entry refers to the costs of two days' work for a mason to dress the stone, also for use as images.[12] Princes Risborough is built adjacent to the outcrop of Lower Chalk, the fine-grained, white, flint-free variety of chalk that was later used in the Scott restoration (see above) to match original chalk in the Crucifixion panel. It survives as the cross, the back wall of the Crucifixion niche, and as the back walls behind St Mary and St John, where the construction is of large, smooth, close-jointed ashlar blocks laid in courses. Behind Mary Magdalen (nineteenth-century Caen stone) is a stump of original chalk work

---

7   *Building Accounts*, 231, 259.
8   Wilson, this volume, 155.
9   Arkell, *Oxford Stone*, 68.
10 R. Plot, *The Natural History of Oxfordshire*, 2nd edn (Oxford, 1705), ch. 4 para. 26.
11 *Building Accounts*, 96, 164.
12 *Building Accounts*, 110.

(apparently showing drapery) where earlier carving has been removed, but which indicates the site of at least one of the original chalk images that are referred to in the accounts.

We do not agree with the suggestion of Colvin that the stone from Rysborgh might have been Totternhoe Stone, quarried in Bedfordshire.[13] Totternhoe Stone is indeed dug from the Chalk, but it is a lime sand (calcarenite in geological nomenclature), not a fine-grained lime mud like the medieval chalk used in the reredos panel. Furthermore, the record of payment to a mason for two days of scappling (squaring up blocks) in Rysborgh locates him in the quarry there (in *lapidario de Rysborgh*).

WHEATLEY LIMESTONE FROM WHEATLEY OR HEADINGTON
These coarser-grained freestones that were used widely in the construction of the College appear to have formed only a very minor component of the visible parts of the reredos. Although partly covered by original paintwork, one of the courses of ashlar in the back wall of the Crucifixion, behind Mary, is significantly more shelly than the adjacent chalk blocks, and is non-oolitic. We identify it as probably being this stone type.

The painted freestone fragments found in the blocked north doorway that were described by Doggett and inferred to be demolition rubble from the medieval reredos would have been ideal for detailed petrographic inspection, but have not been located. Consequently, no material has been available from which to prepare petrographic samples for microscopy and full identification of the stone used in the earliest building episode.[14]

Stonework of the restoration of 1873–1875

Three different types of stone were used in the nineteenth-century restoration. Over 90% of the work was carried out using a white or light cream-coloured oolitic limestone, in which the ooliths are bound together by a well-developed crystalline calcite cement that filled the space in between them during the early geological history of the stone. This is Painswick stone. For some of the smaller statues, a slightly yellowish, non-oolitic, fine-grained limestone from the environs of Caen

---

13 Colvin and Simmons, 6.
14 N. Doggett, 'Fragments of the Fifteenth-Century Reredos and a Medieval Cross-Head from North Hinksey Discovered at All Souls College Chapel, Oxford and Some New Light on the Nineteenth-Century Restoration', *Oxoniensia*, 49 (1984), 277–87.

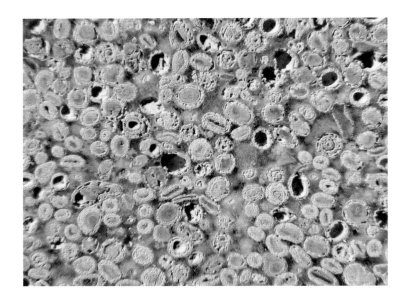

1.3 Painswick stone, the main freestone used for the restoration in 1872–74; cut surface showing truncated ooliths that have not fallen away from the surface (cf. typical texture of Windrush Valley stones shown in 1.2). Width of view = 3 mm

(Normandy) was used (Caen stone). For the visible upper shelf of the plinth beneath the Crucifixion, and maybe for the unseen lower part as well (hidden behind the retable), a fine-grained chalk was chosen to match the medieval chalk work of the cross in the crucifix panel above.

PAINSWICK STONE

This white, even-grained, well-cemented oolitic limestone (oolitic calcarenite in traditional geological terminology) comes from the region round Painswick in Gloucestershire. It was readily carvable, and was worked from medieval times until the middle of the twentieth century. The name is applied to similar stones from a number of different quarries in the locality. Geologically, they occur in the Freestone Beds of the lower part of what used to be known as the Inferior Oolite (now called the Cleeve Cloud Member; Lower Middle Jurassic in age), from which many of the Cotswold limestones were quarried. It is distinguished from other well-known Jurassic limestones by its pale colour, the roundness and even sizes of the constituent ooliths (c. 0.5 mm in diameter), and the small amount of fragmented shell material in the stone. On broken surfaces the ooliths typically break along the concentric layers that compose them, and the nucleus in the centre of each is often somewhat browner than the surrounding layers, due to the presence of small amounts of iron minerals (fig. 1.3). The individual ooliths do not fall away from the natural calcite cement in the stone (as we have seen that they tend to do in Taynton and Sherborne limestone). Painswick stone could thus be worked to a very smooth surface and was popular for internal work in the nineteenth century. However, it was susceptible to weathering and therefore not much used externally. In Oxford, it was used in 1827 for the organ-screen at St Mary's church, where it can still be seen, looking just like the stone in the All Souls reredos.[15]

CAEN STONE

Caen Stone was introduced into southern and south-eastern England soon after the Norman Conquest and has been used intermittently, war and politics permitting, up to the present day. A coarser variety of this limestone has good external weathering properties;[16] the finer-grained variety became very popular for monuments and furnishings in nineteenth-century churches because it was so easily carved. Fine-grained Caen stone was used for the figures on the Crucifixion panel and on some of the other figures, both large and small, in the reredos.

CHALK

Chalk, of Cretaceous age geologically, is a fine-grained limestone and almost white in colour. It has been used widely in building from medieval times, but often not in conspicuous or easily examined places, so the extent of its general use is underappreciated. The Chalk in the reredos contains pale greyish zones and small rusty patches that probably represent burrows in the original sediment. Scott used this stone for the visible upper shelf of the plinth beneath the Crucifixion panel, and also for the plinths underneath Archbishop Chichele and Henry VI to either side. The stone does not contain any flints, and its petrographic characters suggest that the stone came from the lowest levels of the geological unit, the Lower Chalk, as did the medieval 'Rysborgh' stone. The nearest outcrop of these beds is along the foot of the Chilterns, about fifteen miles south-east of Oxford. Because of the uniformity of the Lower Chalk across large distances, a specific source cannot be identified from petrology alone.

15 Arkell, Oxford Stone, 85.
16 T. J. Palmer, 'Understanding the Weathering Behaviour of Caen Stone', Journal of Architectural Conservation, 14 (2008), 43–54.

In the lowermost four feet of the reredos, either side of the altar, there are many small inserts of oolitic freestone which have been let into the surfaces of some of the larger individual blocks of painted medieval stonework. They are unpainted and represent repairs to areas of minor damage. They were probably made at the time of the Scott restoration (some of the damage looks to be visible in the pre-restoration photograph of 1872), but they seem to be Windrush Valley stone, not the Painswick stone that was used for the statues and the major repairs higher up. Both Taynton and Sherborne stones were being worked and would have been available in the late nineteenth century.

Discussion

The surviving medieval reredos screen was mostly made from oolitic limestones from the Windrush valley. It is impossible to be sure what the destroyed figures were carved from but the evidence from some surviving plinths indicates that both oolitic limestone and chalk were used for the plinths. The survival of part of Mary Magdalen is certain evidence that chalk was used for at least some of the figures in the Crucifixion scene – but not all. Original oolitic limestone remains behind the top left angel, for example. Because little material from original plinths survives, it is not possible to be sure what they were made of, but we have assumed either oolitic limestone or chalk.

We note the care with which much of Scott and Geflowski's replacement stone was selected to match the medieval stonework. The white oolitic Painswick stone that was used by the restorers for so much of the replacement statuary, their supports and the niches, is very similar to the oolitic limestone seen in the surviving medieval structure.

All the figures in the Crucifixion scene are carved from Caen stone but the small sections of the crouched figure of Mary Magdalen that survive in chalk suggests that Caen stone may have been chosen to mimic the similarly fine-grained nature of the original chalk figures. The plinth of Bishop Goldwell (statue 3, south bottom tier) was originally of chalk and was replaced in chalk, presumably a deliberate choice, since no other plinths of individual figures were restored in this material. However, such decisions were not entirely consistent. A small portion of the figure originally in the place of the top left angel in the Crucifixion scene survives. The original figure was of Windrush valley oolitic limestone but the replacement angel is of Caen stone. This choice may reflect a desire for the restoration to establish consistency of appearance in the central scene, which is close to the ground and conspicuous. On the other hand, matching the original stonework may not have been the sole determinant of stone choice. Quite why some of the smaller figures are in Caen stone and some are in Painswick stone is unclear. It is possible that Geflowski simply used stone that was to hand at the time of the works and that there was no particular reason behind stone choices for individual figures at higher levels. If, alternatively, he selected Caen stone to replace original statues made of finer-grained stone such as chalk, then this would only be determinable by closer (and destructive) investigation.

Acknowledgements

We are very grateful for the help given to us by Gaye Morgan, Norma Aubertin-Potter, the late Bronac Holden and Philip Powell.

CHAPTER 2
THE MEDIEVAL POLYCHROMY

EMILY HOWE

Introduction

It is hard to appreciate, faced with the pale limestone of Gilbert Scott's restoration, how Chichele's reredos might originally have looked when the chapel at All Souls was consecrated in 1442. Indeed, there is strong evidence that work on the monument – a significant part of which can be attributed to the renowned London sculptor John Massyngham[1] – continued well into the late fifteenth century and perhaps even beyond.[2] Given the vicissitudes suffered by the reredos over the ensuing decades, it is astonishing that what survives of the medieval structure retains so much of its original painted decoration. Evidence pertaining to the purchase of painting materials for the reredos is, however, scarce and much less still is known about the identity of those responsible for its decoration. There is a brief and specific entry in the accounts rolls for 1440, a payment for pigments and gold leaf purchased for painting an image of 'the Trinity' (for the carving of which Massyngham also receives payment),[3] and, some sixty years later, three further payments to unnamed individuals for the painting of the reredos and its associated statuary.[4] Whether those sculptors working at All Souls were in the practice of painting their own work is unclear. There is certainly evidence that 'kerveres' of some distinction were accustomed to

---

1 Massyngham, along with his son, John, and his assistant, Thomas Whitlock, make regular appearances in the building accounts in the period between 1438 and 1442 (*Building Accounts*). Massyngham receives especially frequent mention, most often under the subheading 'kerveres', during the summer of 1439 (July–October), and then again in 1440 (April–November). While they were apparently absent from site in 1441, the period between January and September 1442 seems to have been one of considerable productivity and Massyngham and Whitlock are cited weekly on the payroll.

2 Doggett cites evidence for statues being commissioned for the reredos as late as the 1490s; N. Doggett, 'Fragments of the Fifteenth-Century Reredos and a Medieval Cross-Head from North Hinksey Discovered at All Souls College Chapel, Oxford and Some New Light on the Nineteenth-Century Restoration', *Oxoniensia*, 49 (1984), 277–87, at 278 and nn. 3–4. Wilson, this volume, examines evidence for a much more extensive remodelling of the reredos.

3 See *Building Accounts*, 81, f. 51.

4 These later payments have only recently been unearthed by Christopher Wilson in the Computus and Expense rolls for 1510–11. See p. 99 below.

painting not only their own creations but also pre-existing monuments. Sculptural polychromy undertaken by Massyngham's own son at Winchester Cathedral and its neighbouring college is a case in point,[5] and it is not unreasonable to conjecture that he might have performed similar tasks when he and his father were working at All Souls. It is a source of deep frustration that the mutilation suffered by the reredos in the years following its completion is so much better chronicled than its making.[6] In fact, it is not until the reredos is ultimately uncovered, in 1872, that we catch our first glimpse of its original decorative scheme, 'richly coloured with blue, red and gold'.[7]

The painting scheme

Scientific examination of the reredos, undertaken in 2017, was commissioned with the aim of recording, for the first time, the extent and condition of its surviving medieval polychromy, most of which is located on the backs of the niches and on the undersides of the canopies (fig. 2.1). Following careful in situ examination, thirty minute paint samples were taken with the aim of more fully characterising the painting materials and techniques employed.[8] Microscopic analysis has revealed an astonishingly lavish scheme of decoration on the chapel's east wall. The range of pigments employed was extensive

---

5   See J. Harvey, *English Mediaeval Architects*, 2nd edn (London, 1984), 200, who details various commissions undertaken by Massyngham's son; also E. A. Gee, 'Oxford Masons, 1370–1530', *Archaeological Journal*, 109 (1953), 54–131 at p. 71.

6   The destruction of the reredos is treated by Horden, this volume.

7   The words of Warden Leighton; the restoration of the reredos is treated at length by Green and Hall, this volume.

8   The samples were examined under a binocular microscope (10× to 40× magnification) and their stratigraphy documented. A portion was then mounted as a cross-section in polyester embedding resin (Tiranti™ clear casting resin) and examined with a Leica DMRX optical microscope (100× to 500×) in both visible light and under ultraviolet illumination in order to characterise the materials and painting stratigraphy. The microscope was equipped with Leica 10× and 20× PL Fluotar™ objectives and a 50× PL Apo™ objective. For UV examination, excitation filter BP340-380 nm, dichroic mirror (RKP 400 nm) and suppression filter LP 425 nm was used. Photomicrographs were taken with a Canon EOS 1100 camera at 50× to 500×. Several of the paint layers were subsequently examined in dispersion in Meltmount™ (n=1.662), and their behaviour in incident and plane polarised transmitted light, and under crossed polars, recorded. Where confirmation of inorganic components proved necessary, microchemical tests were undertaken to identify characteristic metal ions and functional groups. For some samples SEM-EDX analysis was undertaken using a Jeol JSM-6480LV high-performance, Variable Pressure Analytical Scanning Electron Microscope with a high resolution of 3.0nm, along with EDS (Energy Dispersive System) and EBSD (Electron Backscatter Diffraction) using the Oxford Link system. The presence of organic binding media was assessed using histochemical tests capable of detecting oil- and protein-based media (Sudan Black B and Acid Fuchsin). It is hoped that more specific characterisation of these materials will be achieved through further analysis including Fourier Transform Infrared spectroscopy (FT-IR) and gas chromatography coupled with mass spectrometry (GC-MS).

2.1 Surviving polychromy in the niches on the north side of the first register, with Geflowski's later figures

2.2 Schematic of the reredos, based on the drawing of 1873 produced by the office of Gilbert Scott (fig. 11.3 below), annotated to show the nomenclature and numbering conventions used in the course of this study. Registers are numbered bottom upwards (1 to 4), sections identified as north, centre or south (N, C, S), and niches numbered left to right (I to IV). Thus 'S2.III' is the third niche from the left on the south side of the second register etc.

and extravagant. High quality, coarsely ground azurite blue features prominently, along with the plant-derived colorant indigo, a copper green, vermilion, red lead and lead-tin yellow, as well as more commonplace iron oxide pigments, charcoal black and large quantities of both lead and calcium carbonate white. Furthermore, examination has brought to light an unprecedented array of embellishment, ranging from silver leaf to sumptuous gilded tin relief fashioned to emulate luxurious brocade textiles, an innovative form of applied decoration that was being developed just around the time Chichele's reredos was commissioned.

Aside from its obvious technical sophistication, what is particularly striking about what survives of the reredos is that, in contrast with its highly organised hierarchy of niches, its scheme of painted decoration is neither coherent nor integrated. On the first (or lowest) register in particular (see fig. 2.2 which details the nomenclature and numbering system used to reference the various elements of the reredos), polychromatic treatment varies greatly between the niches, and it is only in the second and third registers that the coloration becomes systematic. At the very base of the reredos is an array of plinths, uniformly painted in dark green with tracery picked out in red (fig. 2.3). The intricately

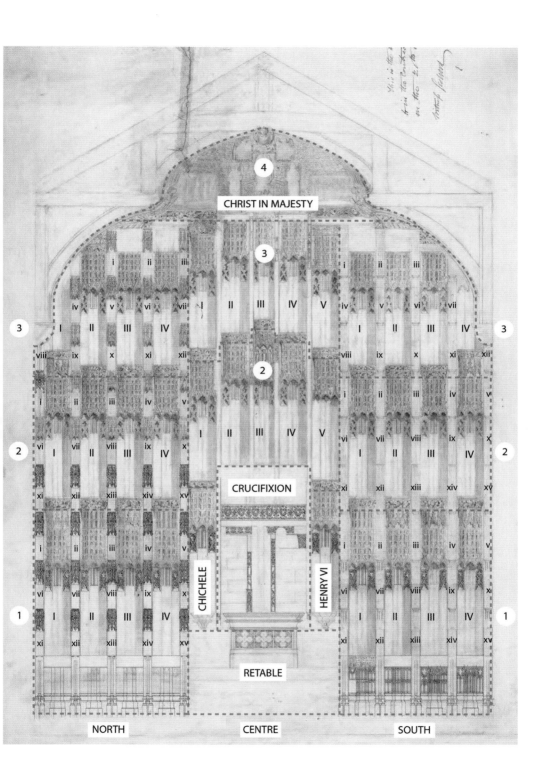

CHRIST IN MAJESTY

CRUCIFIXION

CHICHELE

HENRY VI

RETABLE

NORTH — CENTRE — SOUTH

57

carved, canopied niches which surmount the plinths are painted in a manner altogether less well-ordered. Whereas the majority of the vaults and recesses on the north side of the first register are rendered in rich blue, with red tracery and ribs, in the third niche the vault is painted olive green (see Catalogue below, Register 1: North). On the south side, by contrast, hardly any blue is used. While niches I and IV are coloured a deep iron oxide red with dark green tracery and ribs, this colour scheme is reversed in niche III, and in niche II an altogether different scheme is adopted in which the vault is a more opaque green and the tracery picked out in blue (see Catalogue, Register 1: South).

There is further disunity in the central section featuring the patronal figures of Chichele and Henry VI. Whereas the former niche is painted royal blue with red tracery, that in which the young king now stands is scarlet with dark green ribs (see Catalogue, Register 1: Centre). The overwhelming impression is that the decoration of this register was almost certainly undertaken by more than one painter and that those involved were given the liberty to vary their treatment as much as the sculptors who carved them. While the loss of the figurative components from the central Crucifixion panel deprives us of insight into its original form and colour scheme, a good amount of paint does survive on the remaining bands of tracery which run horizontally and vertically, framing Geflowski's new cross (see Catalogue, Register 1: Crucifixion).[9] The application of painted decoration in these areas seems to have been undertaken with a great deal more care than in the adjacent niches, and was perhaps entrusted to a more accomplished colourist. The tracery is consistently rendered in red, with the front surfaces picked out in gold, and green and blue used in the recesses. The patchy black material which surrounds the figure of Christ belies the beauty of an opulent 'cloth of honour' of which it is the remains.[10]

The painted decoration of the second register is far more consistent in its approach. Here deep blue vaults are bisected by bright red ribs and tracery (see Catalogue, Register 2). The third register of niches would appear to have been treated in a manner almost identical to the second, save for the central five niches which are painted, conversely, with red vaults and blue ribs (see Catalogue, Register 3). Analysis of the blackened coating on the ribs in these two registers reveals that these areas, like the supporting corbels and central boss motifs, were originally picked out

---

9   For Geflowski see Hall, this volume.

10 Scant traces of green grass are also visible on the masonry to which the base of the original crucifix was attached. For the cloth of honour see further Wilson, this volume.

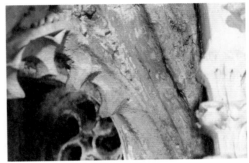

2.3 Detail of a plinth on the north side of the reredos with original red and green polychromy

2.4 Detail of niche S2.III, with corroded silver foil in the tracery recess

2.5 Detail of surviving colour on the hood moulding of niche S1.IV

in gold, and that the recesses behind the traceried lights – the surfaces of which also appear black and are disfigured by extensive flaking – were originally gilded with silver, possibly coated with a coloured glaze to evoke stained glass (fig. 2.4). These variations aside, the reredos scheme is lent some degree of unity by the fact that the inside of each niche is rendered in the same dark iron oxide red. There is also broad consistency in the coloration used on the outsides of the canopies, the mouldings of which are picked out in bands of red, green and gold (fig. 2.5) (or red, *blue* and gold on the second and third registers), and in the treatment of the finials and pinnacles that surmount each niche. The traceried strips which run vertically throughout the reredos are, likewise, consistently rendered in red and blue.[11]

The surviving medieval components of the Last Judgement scheme, which forms the uppermost register of the reredos, are rendered in colours close in character to those found at the lower levels of the

---

11 In many places the blue paint layer has been lost, revealing an underlying black ground layer. In some of those areas where the blue does survive it has partially altered to green (on which see the following note).

2.6 Niches S1.II-IV on the
south side of the first register,
with residual iron oxide
decoration

monument (see Catalogue, Register 4). The background field, which
is carved with a distinctive reticulated 'cloud' motif, is painted bright
azurite blue (now altered in places to green).[12] Surviving foliate detail
is picked out in an opaque copper green against a background of iron
oxide red, and the rainbow upon which Christ sits is coloured in bands
of green, red and blue (now altered to black).[13] Traces of a dark brown
material in the interstices of the supporting angels' wings point to the
fact that these, and probably much of the original figure of Christ, were
originally embellished with metal leaf.

Careful examination of the reredos has afforded a fresh
understanding of the order in which the monument was painted. The
insertion of Geflowski's new statuary has not altogether obscured the
painted silhouettes of the previous incumbents and it seems clear that,
even if the statues themselves were painted in the workshop prior

---

12 The alteration of azurite, which can also be observed in some niches on the lowest register, is generally
    thought to be caused by environmental conditions such as elevated relative humidity and the presence
    of chloride ions, resulting in the transformation of copper carbonate to copper chloride; on this
    deterioration mechanism see H. Howard, *Pigments of English Medieval Wall Painting* (London, 2003), 49;
    D. Scott, *Copper and Bronze in Art: Corrosion, Colorants, Conservation* (Los Angeles, 2002), 110–11; also D.
    Saunders and J. Kirby, 'The Effect of Relative Humidity on Artists' Pigments', *National Gallery Technical
    Bulletin*, 25 (2004), 62–72.

13 As with the alteration of azurite to green discussed in the previous note, the pigment's alteration to black
    tenorite (copper (II) oxide) has been associated with humid, alkaline environments.

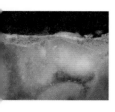

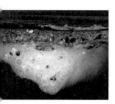

to their installation, the niches in which they were placed remained unpainted until the point of occupation. Quite clearly, the dark red background was applied around the figures following their installation (fig. 2.6). Furthermore, on the basis of the subtle inconsistencies observed in the coloration of the registers, it seems reasonable to conjecture that the reredos was not painted in one single phase, but over a period of time, quite probably by different workshops or painters. This hypothesis would seem to be corroborated by the variations in painting materials and techniques observed across the monument, and it is to these that we now turn.

Painting materials and techniques

PAINTING SUPPORT

The majority of the stone sourced for the reredos and its statuary, came – as Palmer and Shaffrey have detailed – from quarries around the Windrush Valley and Burford region.[14] Traces of this pale buff limestone can be seen on many of the paint samples taken in the course of this survey (fig. 2.7). By contrast, the back wall of the Crucifixion, and quite possibly much of its original associated statuary, appear to have been made of chalk (fig. 2.8).[15] Being workable to a much smoother surface finish, chalk seems to have been selected specifically for the most important, detailed carving, amongst which those figures undertaken by Massyngham.[16]

PREPARATORY TECHNIQUES

On the whole, the use of a ground – that is to say a layer which would have been applied in order to seal the porous stone substrate prior to painting – is limited, with most instances being observed in the lowest register of niches. A white priming layer, comprising chalk bound in oil, has been found beneath localised areas of colour as well as areas that were to be gilded (fig. 2.9). This layer does not, however, seem to have been uniformly applied across the first register. Indeed, in almost half of the locations sampled, coloured paint layers were applied directly

14 See Palmer and Shaffrey, this volume; also English Heritage, *Strategic Stone Study: A Building Stone Atlas of Oxfordshire* (Oxford, 2011), 5.

15 This is believed to have come from near Princes Risborough; see Palmer and Shaffrey, this volume; also their unpublished report to All Souls, 'The Stonework of the Reredos at All Souls College, Oxford' (2017), 5, which observes that chalk was used for 'the cross, the back wall of the Crucifixion niche, and also…the back walls behind SS Mary and John', as well as for the original plinth surviving under Geflowski's new figure of Bishop Goldwell.

16 *Building Accounts*, 264, f. 81.

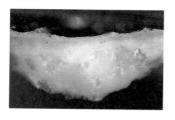

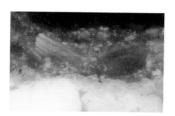
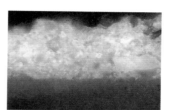
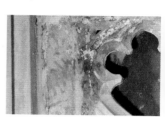

2.9 Cross-section of sample 21, taken from an area of gilding on the first register, showing a white chalk ground layer applied over the limestone substrate

2.10 Cross-section of sample 8, taken from the third register, with finely ground azurite applied directly to the oolitic limestone

2.11 Cross-section of sample 10, taken from the vault of a third register niche, comprising a bright red admixture of vermilion and red lead, applied over a pale blue underlayer of indigo mixed with chalk

2.12 Cross-section of sample 13, with niche S1.III, with copper green applied over a lead white ground

2.13, 14 Cross-section of sample 12 (niche N1.III), where copper green has been combined with lead-tin yellow to achieve an opaque olive green; the same lead-tin yellow was used for the foliate motif painted on the splays of niche S1.III (detail)

to the stone, and there would not appear to be any systematic logic to the decision of whether or not a ground was required.[17] The absence of such preparatory layers is still more conspicuous in the second and third registers, where – with the exception of those areas to be gilded – coloured paint layers are more commonly applied directly to the stone (fig. 2.10). In the uppermost register, however, a white priming layer appears to present beneath the azurite blue of the clouds. The inconsistency with which grounds have been employed is surely significant – not only is it indicative of differing painting practices, but it potentially also accounts for the badly deteriorated state of large areas of original colour in the second and third registers of the reredos.

PIGMENTS AND PAINT STRATIGRAPHY

As a general rule, most of the pigments used across the reredos have been applied in admixtures designed to modify their hue or improve their depth of colour. Intense, rich reds are achieved in all registers using an admixture of red lead combined with smaller amounts of coarsely ground vermilion (fig. 2.11). On the lowest register of the reredos, three different hues of green – ranging from deep emerald to an opaque olive colour – are achieved using the same copper-based pigment mixed with varying proportions of lead white and lead-tin yellow

17 Whereas, for example, samples taken from two locations on the north and south sides feature copper green layers applied directly to the vault (samples 12 and 14), another sample taken from one of the southern vaults shows a copper green layer applied over a thick lead white ground (sample 13).

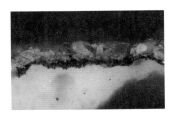

2.15 Cross-section of sample 3, taken from niche N1.I on the lower register, where coarsely ground azurite is applied over a layer of charcoal black

2.16 Detail of niche N2.III on the second register, where a rich blue is achieved by applying azurite over a grey-blue ground

2.17 On the southern niches of the third register (S3.III), a much paler blue results from applying more finely ground azurite directly to the stone substrate. See fig. 2.10 above, for a cross-section taken from this location

(figs 2.12 and 2.13).[18] Elsewhere, on the south side of the lowest register, this same yellow is used on its own to effect a foliate motif (see niche S1.III, fig. 2.14) and a striped effect on the red bands on one of the hood mouldings (niche S1.II).[19]

Throughout the reredos, high quality, coarsely ground azurite blue is applied unadulterated, but often with coloured underpaint used to modify its hue. On the lowest register it is applied over black, grey and sometimes red layers, on the second register over a pale grey comprising indigo mixed with lime white (figs 2.15 and 16). Such techniques were a means of compensating for the pigment's relatively poor covering power. An underlayer would help to reduce light scatter from the stone substrate, ensuring intense colour without having to invest in multiple layers of this expensive pigment. Indeed, it is interesting to note that the absence of such a underlayer on the south side of the third register has resulted in in much greater light scatter and a dramatically paler hue (fig. 2.17).

---

18 While further instrumental analysis such as FTIR would be required to identify the green more precisely, it is most likely verdigris (a form of a copper acetate) applied in an oil medium to produce a translucent copper oleate. On copper green pigments used in England around this time see M. van Eikema Holmes, 'Verdigris Glazes in Historical Oil Paintings: Recipes and Techniques', *Zeitschrift für Kunsttechnologie und Konservierung*, 15 (2001), 163 – 95; also Howard, *Pigments*, 87.

19 On lead-tin yellow and its wider use in this period, see Howard, *Pigments*, 159 – 63; also E. Howe, 'An Investigation of the Polychromy on the Lady Chapel Reredos, Gloucester Cathedral', unpublished report (2012), 87 – 8.

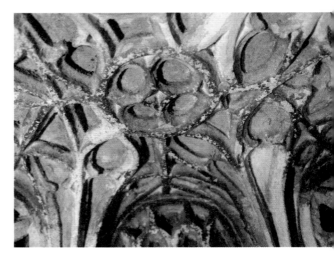

2.18 Gilded decoration on the boss on a second register canopy (N2.IV)

2.19 Detail of the salmon-pink mordant layer on an area of formerly gilt tracery (niche S1.II)

2.20 Detail of deteriorated 'part-gold' used to gild the ribs of the vault, the silver content of which has now oxidised and blackened (niche S3.III)

GILDING EFFECTS AND APPLIED RELIEF DECORATION

An incredibly broad range of gilded surface effects has also been used to embellish the reredos. Gold leaf is used throughout all four registers to highlight elements such as hood mouldings on the niche canopies, as well as crockets on the finials, floral decoration on buttresses, corbels and bosses (fig. 2.18). Many areas that were clearly originally gilt, such as the fronts of the tracery in each niche, have since lost this surface embellishment and retain only their salmon-coloured mordant layer, now grey with dirt deposits (fig. 2.19).[20] On the lowest register of the reredos, a simple oil-based mordant has been used to apply gold leaf over a layer of chalk.[21] This would have served the dual purpose of sealing the porous stone as well as providing a cushioned surface upon which to apply the delicate metal leaf. On the second register, by contrast, gold leaf has been applied directly to the stone using a much thicker, medium-rich mordant which has shown itself to be more susceptible to deterioration and loss.[22]

---

20 Traces of such gilding can, nevertheless, be found on tracery in the better protected upper registers; see, for example, samples 27 and 28 in E. Howe, 'Examination of Surviving Polychromy on the Reredos in the Chapel of All Souls College, Oxford', unpublished report (2017).

21 The metal leaf was adhered using a mixture of red and white lead and chalk bound in linseed oil mixed with small amounts of pine resin and animal fat (tallow); see samples 19, 21 and 22, and instrumental analysis of the latter by Dr Brian Singer in Howe, 'Examination... All Souls', appendix 1.

22 The mordant was found to comprise a mixture of linseed oil, pine resin and egg, and contained a much lower proportion of pigment than the mordant used on the lower register; see Singer's analysis of sample 25 in Howe, 'Examination... All Souls', appendix 1, and also sample 20.

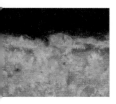

2.21 Cross-section of sample 25 (from niche N2.IV), showing the gold component of the surface treatment which survives intact beneath the oxidised silver layer (imaged at 500×)

2.22 Cross-section of sample 30 (from niche C3.II), showing the oxidised layer of silver leaf applied over a mordant comprising lead white, chalk and yellow iron oxide (imaged at 500×)

Also notable exclusively on the second and third registers is the widespread use of 'part-gold', a composite metal leaf fashioned from silver and gold leaves beaten together.[23] This material was used to gild the ribs on each of the vaults (fig. 2.20). Interestingly, however, the manner in which the part-gold has been adhered varies noticeably between registers. Whereas, on the second register, the gilding is attached directly to the stone with a thick layer of medium-rich mordant containing very small quantities of lead-based pigments, doubtless added for their siccative properties (fig. 2.21), on the third register the leaf has been applied over a far more stable mordant which is pigment-rich and therefore less prone to deform and detach from its substrate. While the oxidisation of the silver content in the metal leaf means that these areas are now uniformly blackened across the registers, the original appearance of this embellishment must have been exceptionally opulent. The use of such alloys was not necessarily motivated by budgetary constraints, but a choice born of the desire for a particular surface effect, or working properties better suited to its application in inaccessible locations.

Another important discovery has been the extensive use of pure silver leaf, which would seem to have been used exclusively for adorning the recesses of niches in the second and third registers (see fig. 2.4). It is not clear whether the silver was originally glazed with colour, to resemble stained glass, or simply burnished, but in the better-protected corners the edges of the now blackened leaf stand out against the red-brown ground. It is particularly noteworthy that comparable areas on the lowest register of the reredos are not gilded in this way, but treated in colour. The silver leaf used on the higher registers was applied over a ground of iron oxide red, or sometimes indigo blue, using a complex mordant system containing pigments to aid drying (fig. 2.22).[24] Without exception these areas are now blackened and flaking.

The most complex form of gilded decoration employed is a form of applied tin relief – the technique used to evoke the sumptuous cloth of gold behind the Crucifixion (figs 2.23 and 2.24). Close examination reveals the edges of rectangular leaves of tin featuring dianthus flowers, a symbol of Marian devotion. This type of embellishment was the height

23 On the production and use of 'part-gold' in England in the Middle Ages see J. Nadolny, 'The Techniques and Use of Gilded Relief Decoration by Northern European Painters, *c.* 1200-1500', unpublished PhD thesis, Courtauld Institute of Art (London, 2001), 159 – 64.

24 Interestingly, the stratigraphy of the paint and mordant layers which underlie the silver foil is almost identical in the second and third registers; see samples 29 & 30. For analysis of the mordant, which comprises a relatively simple admixture of non-heat-bodied linseed oil and a small amount of pine resin, see Howe, 'Examination… All Souls', appendix I (sample 30).

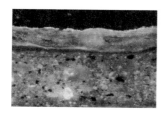

2.23 Cross-section of sample 23, taken from the Crucifixion scene, showing the stratigraphy of the tin-relief decoration, including (bottom to top) the medium rich filler, corroded tin foil, fine yellow mordant layer and gold leaf

2.24 Detail of the applied tin-relief decoration used to evoke a cloth of honour behind the Crucifixion

of fashion among high-status commissions at around the time the chapel at All Souls was being completed.[25] The relief would usually have been manufactured in the workshop, by pressing tin leaf into moulds incised with an intricate design. The tin was backfilled with a relief mass, in this instance lead pigments and chalk bound in an oil-based system.[26] When gilded, the striated surface was intended to give the impression of the raised threads of a brocade textile.

Technological context

That no expense was spared in the adornment of Chichele's collegiate chapel is clear, yet, in both its concept and its making, the All Souls reredos was very much a creation of its time and place. The statutes for New College, founded by William Wykeham at the close of the fourteenth century, and upon which All Souls and its chapel were modelled, made provision for a very similar reredos painted in a near identical palette.[27] Indeed, not long after Chichele's own reredos was completed, a third such monument was commissioned by Waynflete at Magdalen. It is quite astonishing, given the catalogue of interventions

25 Nadolny, 'Gilded Relief Decoration', 159 – 64; also I. Geelen, D. Steyaert et al., *Imitation and Illusion: Applied Brocade in the Art of the Low Countries in the Fifteenth and Sixteenth Centuries* (Brussels, 2011), 25 – 39, on the use of applied brocades specifically.

26 While histochemical tests suggest the presence of oil, further instrumental analysis is required to fully characterise the binding media. On the techniques of making tin-relief textiles see Geelen and Steyaert, *Imitation and Illusion*, 65ff; also J. Nadolny, 'Documentary Sources for the Use of Moulds in the Production of Tin Relief: Cause and Effect', in E. Hermens and J. H. Townsend (eds), *Sources and Serendipity: Testimonies of Artists' Practice. ICOM-CC Working Group on Art Technological Source Research* (ATSR) 3rd International Symposium, Glasgow University, Scotland, 12–13 June 2008 (London, 2009), 39 – 49.

27 Records from the campaign of restoration undertaken by Wyatt between 1789 – 94 attest that the back wall in the upper ranges of niches retained their original painted decoration in colours almost identical to those at All Souls, with areas of 'deep ultramarine blue' and carved elements that were 'richly gilt'; see Doggett, 'Fragments', 286. The iconography of the New College reredos is discussed in detail by Wilson, this volume.

2.25 Detail of the Marian miracles in Henry VI's chapel at Eton College, c. 1477-87 (south wall, scene 1)

it has suffered, that the All Souls reredos retains so much of its original decoration, and deeply regrettable that no other polychromed example survives against which to compare it, those at New College and Magdalen being almost entirely restorations.[28] In terms of the decorative materials employed, however, the palette identified at All Souls is very much in keeping with those used on other high-status schemes commissioned around this time, including the elaborate, though slightly earlier, Warwick chantry chapel in Tewkesbury Abbey (c. 1423).[29] Further similarities can be drawn with the technique of the exceptional Marian wall paintings in Henry VI's ambitious new chapel at Eton College (c. 1477–87) (fig. 2.25).[30] A similar range of oil-bound pigments has been documented in studies of contemporary painted figural sculpture, amongst which statuary from the Great Screen at

---

28   Colvin and Simmons, 52, 58–9, and figs. 40 and 49. See further Wilson, and Hall, this volume.

29   See E. Howe, 'An Investigation of Polychromed Statuary from the Warwick Chantry Chapel, Tewkesbury Abbey', unpublished report (2014).

30   For which see E. Howe et al., Wall Paintings of Eton (London, 2012), part 1.

Winchester (*c.* 1470–76),[31] the funerary effigy of Joan Nevill at Arundel (*c.* 1470–80), and polychromed figures from the west front of Exeter Cathedral (*c.* 1460–80).[32]

Viewed in the context of such a painting tradition, the relative absence of ground layers from the All Souls scheme distinguishes it as remarkable and, it might be argued, technically deficient in a period in which polychromy on walls, statuary and microarchitecture was customarily applied in an oil-based system over a lead-white priming layer.[33] The purpose of such layers was to prevent the absorption of the painting medium into the substrate and thus ensure the cohesion of overlying paint layers. It is noteworthy that analysis undertaken by Broderick and Darrah has revealed a similarly unmeticulous approach to the preparation of the substrate of statuary from the Winchester screen, the painting of which Massyngham's son has been associated with.[34] Whereas lead-based grounds were used under almost all areas of polychromy examined, in a few locations colour was found to have been applied directly on to the stone, without the application of a preparatory layer.[35] The much more widespread absence of such a technically important element of the painting system at All Souls is however, puzzling and unexpected, not least because Chichele's reredos is simultaneously remarkable for the sophisticated range of gilded embellishment it features. Applied gilded tin-relief decoration emulating rich brocades of the type used on the All Souls Crucifixion features on another, much more modest reredos made in around 1480 for the Lady Chapel of St Peter's Abbey, Gloucester (now Gloucester Cathedral) (fig. 2.26).[36] While perhaps more refined in its execution, this

---

31 Whereas Lindley dates the screen to the 1470s (P. Lindley, 'The "Great Screen" of Winchester Cathedral. Part II: Style and Date', *Burlington Magazine*, 135 (1993), 796–807), C. Wilson proffers an earlier date, 120 below.

32 For which see A. Brodrick and J. Darrah, 'A Description of the Polychromy on the Fragments of Limestone Figure-Sculpture from the Great Screen at Winchester Cathedral', *Burlington Magazine*, 131 (1989), 615–17; A. Brodrick and J. Darrah, 'The Fifteenth-Century Polychromed Limestone Effigies of William Fitzalan, 9th Earl of Arundel, and his Wife, Joan Nevill, in the Fitzalan Chapel, Arundel', *Church Monuments*, 1 (1986), 65–94; and E. Sinclair, 'The West Front: II. The West Front Polychromy', in F. Kelly (ed.), *Medieval Art and Architecture at Exeter Cathedral*, British Archaeological Association Conference Transactions 11, 1985 (Leeds, 1991), 116–33.

33 See Howard, *Pigments*, 178–9.

34 Entries in the cathedral's Compotus rolls for 1469–70 cite 'Messyngham' being paid the sum of £26 13s. 4d. and an additional reward of £2 for his work on the 'images of the chapel reredos' over a period of 16 weeks; see Harvey, *English Mediaeval Architects*, 200.

35 See Brodrick and Darrah, 'Description of the Polychromy on the Fragments of Limestone Figure-Sculpture from the Great Screen at Winchester Cathedral'; I am most grateful to Professor Paul Williamson for bringing this to my attention.

36 See D. Welander, *The History, Art and Architecture of Gloucester Cathedral* (Stroud, 1991); also Howe, 'An Investigation of the Polychromy on the Lady Chapel Reredos, Gloucester Cathedral', unpublished report (2012), 11–12.

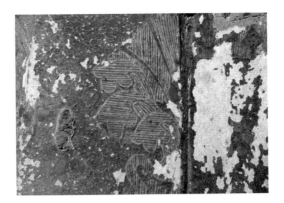

2.26 Detail of applied relief decoration on the reredos in the Lady Chapel at Gloucester Cathedral, *c.* 1480

example dates from the later part of the century, by which time such techniques had become supremely fashionable and were much more widely evoked.[37]

Considered in this wider context, the All Souls reredos was in many ways exceptionally lavish and technologically advanced for its time, and this may go some way towards accounting for the failure of the silver-based gilding techniques used in its second and third registers. It is conceivable that, in these relatively early days of experimentation, the risks inherent in using such materials may not yet have been well understood. Although the use of silver leaf in English medieval mural decoration is known from at least the late fourteenth century,[38] most of the legislation proscribing the use of silver for such purposes does not start to appear in England until somewhat later. In her seminal study of gilded relief decoration in northern Europe, Nadolny cites a statute of

37 See Nadolny, 'Gilded Relief Decoration', 333–42, who discusses the regulation of tin-relief embellishment by the painters' guilds in the fifteenth century. Also Geelen and Steyaert, *Imitation and Illusion*, on the use and social significance of applied brocade relief in the Low Countries around this time. For examples of tin-relief decoration on contemporary wooden statuary see M. S. Frinta, 'The Use of Wax for Appliqué Relief Brocade on Wooden Statuary' (including analytical appendix by J. Mills and J. Plesters), *Studies in Conservation*, 8 (1963), 136–49, and more recently the contributions of Bucklow and Wrapson to S. Bucklow, R. Marks and L. Wrapson (eds.), *The Art and Science of the Church Screen in Medieval Europe: Making, Meaning, Preserving* (Woodbridge, 2017), 38, 67–9, on its use on fifteenth-century East Anglian rood screens.

38 See, for example, H. Howard, 'The Chapel of Our Lady Undercroft, Canterbury Cathedral, and the Relationship of English and Bohemian Painting Techniques in the Second Half of the Fourteenth Century', *Technologia Artis*, 3 (1993), 31–4, on the use of silver leaf to decorate the vault of the chapel of Our Lady Undercroft in Canterbury Cathedral in the late fourteenth century. Silver was also used to evoke glass windows in the fourteenth-century murals commissioned by Edward III for St Stephen's Chapel, Westminster (for which see E. Howe, 'Divine Kingship and Dynastic Display: The Altar Wall Murals of St Stephen's Chapel, Westminster', *The Antiquaries Journal*, 81 (2001), 259–303). An entry in the accounts roll TNA, E 101/471/6 cites 'iijc foliis argenti emptis pro pictura cuiusdam fenestre contra facturam vitro [*sic*] precij cne viij d.: ij s.'), an observation kindly brought to my attention by Professor Tim Ayers.

2.27 Diagram indicating possible phases of painting on the All Souls reredos, as evidenced by differences in the painting technology (based on the 1873 drawing by Sir Gilbert Scott's office)

1466 from the Painters of the Guild of St Luke in London, prohibiting the use of 'or parti' unless expressly requested by the patron.[39] While some guild ordinances from the second half of the fifteenth century go so far as prohibiting the use of silver and part-gold altogether, others require the varnishing of these materials with a coloured glaze or 'vermeil' to prevent tarnishing. If such a protective coating was applied at All Souls, no trace of it survives. It would seem that in their eagerness to satisfy their patron's desire for prestige, those entrusted with the decoration of the reredos embraced innovative – but technically precarious – methods of embellishment.

Conclusion

Despite its badly compromised condition and extensive restoration, the technical significance of what remains of the All Souls reredos is plain to see. Analysis has revealed the considerable range of painted and applied embellishments employed to adorn a monument which formed the devotional focus of Chichele's new foundation. Discrepancies observed in the materials employed across the scheme have raised important questions about the way in which the reredos was decorated, and by whom. Whether the structure that survives today was painted, at least in part, by Massyngham and his assistants is hard to tell and, in the absence of the scheme's original statuary, we cannot form an opinion about whether the same people were responsible for painting the microarchitectural framework within which such figures stood. In respect of the polychromy that does remain, however, the differences observed in the techniques used are almost certainly indicative of work undertaken by different people or workshops, most likely in multiple phases of work undertaken over a period of time (see fig. 2.27). This is evidenced not only in the way in which the coloration becomes more systematic as we move up the registers, but also by the dramatic contrast in the condition of these different parts of the scheme, in particular in the upper registers where extensive deterioration and loss corresponds with the use of innovative and unstable silver-based gilding techniques, adhered with mordants which proved inherently susceptible to

---

39   See Nadolny, 'Gilded Relief Decoration', 162–5, and appendix 3 (section 5.3).

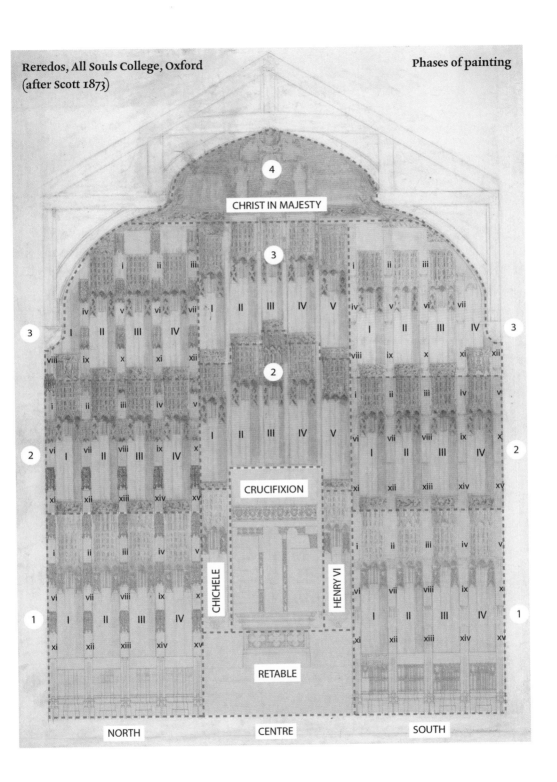

Reredos, All Souls College, Oxford
(after Scott 1873)

Phases of painting

CHRIST IN MAJESTY

CRUCIFIXION

CHICHELE

HENRY VI

RETABLE

NORTH

CENTRE

SOUTH

deformation.[40] It takes a leap of the imagination to visualise what the completed monument must have looked like, with its imposing ranks of figures, enlivened with colour and enshrined within a structure which scintillated with silver and gold. As befitted the elevated status of the foundation's patron, the reredos scheme was at once ambitious and opulent, and affords us an invaluable insight into the most sophisticated painting practices being used in England on the eve of the Reformation.

Acknowledgements

I am extremely grateful to the Very Revd Dr John Drury for approaching me to undertake the survey of the reredos, and to Gaye Morgan for her invaluable assistance in navigating the College archives. I am also indebted to the Conservation of Wall Painting Department, Courtauld Institute of Art, for affording access to their analytical facilities, to Jim Davy (Earth Sciences Department, UCL) for his help with SEM-EDX analysis, and to Dr Brian Singer (University of Northumbria) for undertaking organics analysis for the study.

---

40 For detailed analysis of the gilding mordants, see Howe, 'Examination… All Souls', appendix 1. The north sides of the second and third registers are particularly badly affected by flaking and there is a great deal of material which has detached from the substrate and is vulnerable to loss. The north side of the reredos also seems to have fared particularly badly in terms of the survival of the original masonry; much of the stonework in these canopies is not original. For a more detailed condition overview, see Howe, 'Examination… All Souls', 72 – 6.

CATALOGUE

The catalogue comprises a photographic survey of all four registers of the reredos, including surviving polychromy on the undersides of each of the niche canopies and polychromed details from the Crucifixion and Last Judgement panels. The nomenclature and numbering system used follows that set out in the caption to fig. 2.2 of Chapter 2, with registers numbered from bottom to top and niches from north to south.

REGISTER I: NORTH

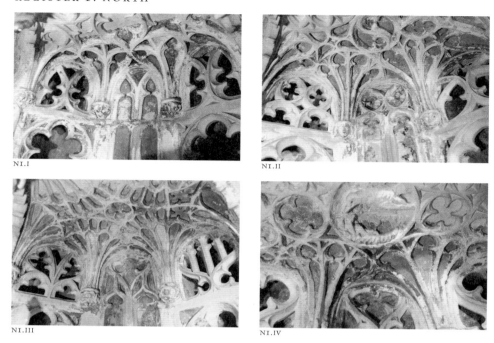

NI.I

NI.II

NI.III

NI.IV

REGISTER I: SOUTH

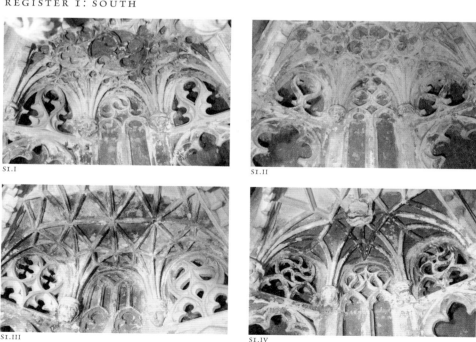

SI.I

SI.II

SI.III

SI.IV

CI. CHICHELE

CI. HENRY VI

CI. CHICHELE

CI. HENRY VI

REGISTER I: CRUCIFIXION

REGISTER 2: NORTH

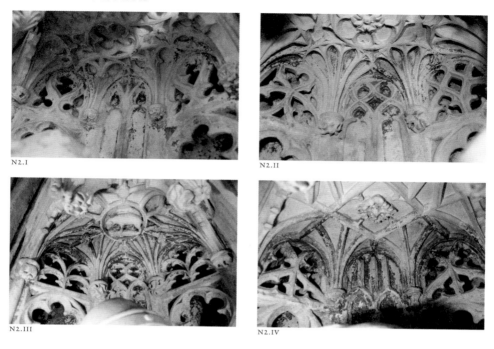

N2.I

N2.II

N2.III

N2.IV

REGISTER 2: SOUTH

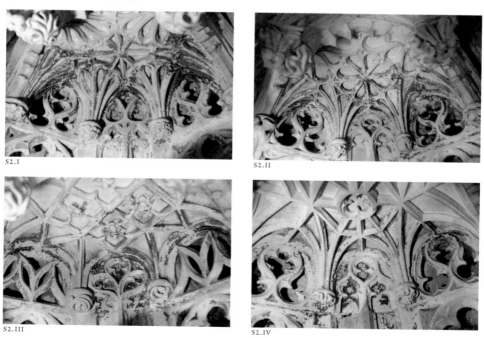

S2.I

S2.II

S2.III

S2.IV

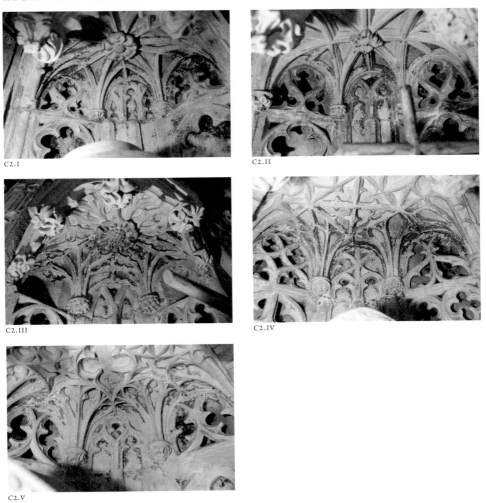

C2.I

C2.II

C2.III

C2.IV

C2.V

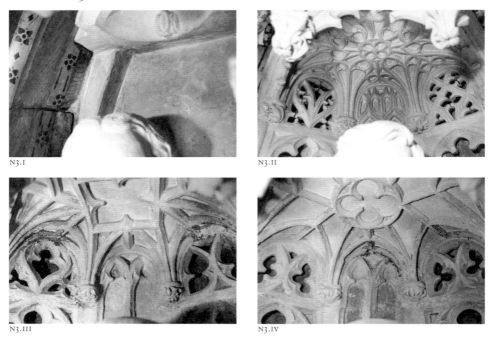

N3.I

N3.II

N3.III

N3.IV

REGISTER 3: SOUTH

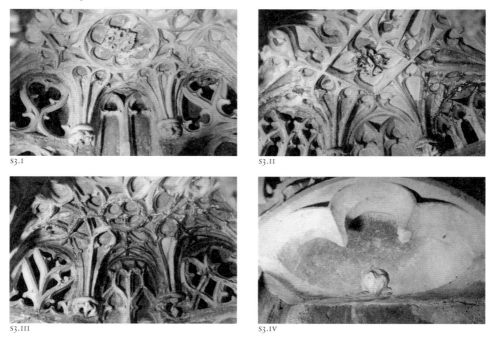

S3.I

S3.II

S3.III

S3.IV

C3.I

C3.II

C3.III

C3.IV

C3.V

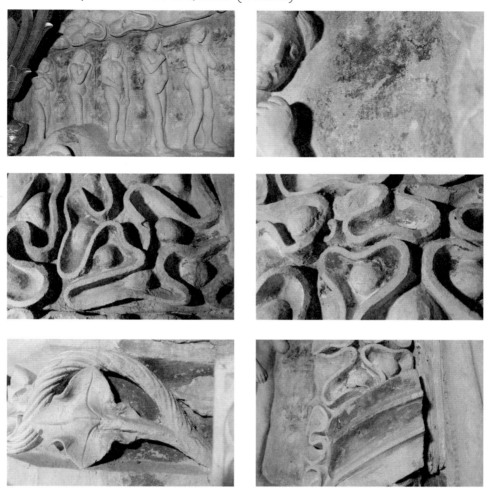

PART 2
MAKING

CHAPTER 3
THE RELIGIOUS CONTEXT

EAMON DUFFY

The religious historiography of the age of has been dominated by interest in the spread and then forcible suppression of Lollardy, the native heresy derived ultimately from the teaching of that disagreeable Oxford academic, John Wycliffe. Wycliffism began as a dissident intellectual tradition within the University: it would ultimately wither into a straggling popular movement, sustained but also limited by its strong familial and regional embedding. But at the turn of the fourteenth and fifteenth centuries the movement seemed vital, well-patronised and menacing enough to convince contemporaries then, and historians ever since, that it posed a major threat to the religious and political stability of Lancastrian England.[1] The passing of the Act *De haeretico comburendo* in 1401 can be seen as signalling the Lancastrian dynasty's adoption of a zero tolerance policy towards religious dissent, and Henry Chichele was undoubtedly a vigorous exponent of that policy: we have an account of him in the late 1420s riding round Kent in pursuit of Lollards who 'in many parts of England, as in Bohemia, were craftily scheming and working greatly to rage and rebel against the Christian faith'.[2]

---

1   For an influential presentation of Lollardy as a formidable and coherent intellectual movement, see above all A. Hudson, *The Premature Reformation: Wycliffite Texts and Lollard History* (Oxford, 1988). By way of contrast, R. Rex, *The Lollards* (Basingstoke, 2002). For some recent discussions of the nature of fifteenth-century Lollardy see R. Lutton, *Lollardy and Orthodox Religion in Pre-Reformation England* (Woodbridge, 2006); J. Patrick Hornbeck II, *What Is a Lollard? Dissent and Belief in Late Medieval England* (Oxford, 2010), and the article by R. Swanson, '"Lollardy", "Orthodoxy" and "Resistance" in Pre-Reformation England', *Usuteaduslik Ajakiri*, 64 (2013), 12–26, available at https://usuteadus.ee/wp-content/uploads/2013%20(64)/Swanson.pdf (accessed 16 Aug. 2020).
2   P. Horden, 'The Origins of "All Souls" and its Significance for Henry Chichele', in C. M. Barron and C. Burgess (eds), *Memory and Commemoration in Medieval England* (Donington, 2010), 292–308; the reference to Chichele's heresy hunt at p. 305. For the wider early fifteenth-century campaign against Wycliffism which provides the context for Chichele's activities, Ian Forrest, *The Detection of Heresy in Late Medieval England* (Oxford, 2005). See also J. H. Arnold, 'Lollard Trials and Inquisitorial Discourse', in C. Given-Wilson (ed.), *Fourteenth-Century England*, II (Woodbridge, 2001), 81–94.

The positive complement of that concern about heresy was the promotion of what the late Jeremy Catto has characterised as 'a national public religion … a standard orthodox doctrine imposed by regular inquisitorial procedure, a unified and explicitly national liturgy … and an official spirituality … encapsulated in authorized devotional books and expressed in liturgical prayers and settings by the royal chapel musicians'.[3] That is a helpful insight into the mindset and intentions underlying Chichele's foundation here at All Souls, so long as it is not taken to imply a rather greater degree of political management of the very varied energies that made up early fifteenth-century religious orthodoxy than could be or was actually the case. This was, after all, the England of Margery Kempe, that uninhibited Lynn equivalent of the Wife of Bath, who in middle age took to celibacy and set up as a professional pilgrim and B-celebrity mystic. As her career suggests, orthodox religious belief and practice could be as unruly, and as resistant to management, as Lollardy itself.[4]

However that might be, the first half of the fifteenth century was certainly a religious boom-time. Opinions differ about the nature of the impact of Archbishop Arundel's repressive *constitutiones* on the religious creativity of the period.[5] There is no doubting the widespread twitchiness about heterodoxy that Lollardy provoked, but the Church of John Capgrave, Thomas Netter and William Lyndwood, all of them staunch defenders of the Lancastrian status quo, cannot be considered intellectually moribund, just as the haunting religious music of John Dunstaple and Leonel Power argues for a sensitivity and creativity which royal patronage might certainly encourage and promote, but could not create. Early fifteenth-century England had no equivalent to the kind of revivalism represented in Italy by St Bernardino, and England proved resistant to the austerities of the Observant movement more generally. But Henry V's Brigittine and Carthusian foundations

3   J. Catto, 'Religious Change under Henry V', in G. L. Harriss (ed.), *Henry V: The Practice of Kingship* (Stroud, 1985), 97–115; idem, 'The World of Henry Chichele and the Foundation of All Souls', in *Unarmed Soldiery*, 1–13.

4   J. H. Arnold, 'Margery's Trials: Heresy, Lollardy, and Dissent', in J. H. Arnold and K. J. Lewis (eds), *A Companion to The Book of Margery Kempe* (Cambridge, 2004), 75–94. For a (not entirely persuasive) argument for the essentially subversive character of *The Book of Margery Kempe*, L. Staley, *Margery Kempe's Dissenting Fictions* (University Park, PA, 1994).

5   N. Watson, 'Censorship and Cultural Change in Late-Medieval England: Vernacular Theology, the Oxford Translation Debate, and Arundel's Constitutions of 1409', *Speculum*, 70 (1995), 822–64, and the essays in response in V. Gillespie and K. Ghosh (eds), *After Arundel: Religious Writing in Fifteenth-Century England* (Turnhout, 2011).

of Syon and Sheen at Isleworth would prove to be spiritual powerhouses which were very much more than mere props of state religion.[6]

And if the clergy and laity of early fifteenth-century England showed little of the revivalist fervour sweeping Italian cities, they were nevertheless receptive to new as well as older expressions of piety. The early fifteenth century saw a burgeoning of lay investment in the fabric of religion, in both the literal and metaphorical senses, investment which owed at least as much to local initiative as to any central promotion by crown or hierarchy – all over England wealthy laity and clergy like William Cannynges II, who became sheriff of Bristol in the year All Souls was founded,[7] were lavishing money on the rebuilding and adornment of their churches, and staffing them with auxiliary clergy. These were the years in which great urban churches like St Peter Mancroft in Norwich, and almost equally majestic rural churches like Salle, set amid the sheep ranges of north Norfolk, were going up.

Some of the newer forms of devotion owed something to royal patronage, like the growing popularity of the passion prayers known as the Fifteen Oes, associated with Brigitta of Sweden. But much of it had no discernible debt to official sponsorship or management. For example, the early fifteenth century saw the proliferation of highly emotive images of the Pietà in parochial and monastic churches as well as in private churches and chapels, and in the iconography of devotional books and rolls. These were also the years in which votive masses for Christocentric cults like that of the Holy Name of Jesus and the Five Wounds, native English products which differed significantly from their European counterparts, began to multiply in calendars and the *sanctorale* sections of breviaries and missals. And in these same decades the public veneration of the Blessed Sacrament in solemn Corpus Christi processions was observed throughout England, and Corpus Christi play cycles established themselves as integral parts of the civic and religious life of great cities – Coventry, York and Chester.[8]

6 The influence of Syon is particularly well studied: for a discussion of its widespread medieval impact see the introduction and chs 1–4 in E. A. Jones and A. Walsham (eds), Syon Abbey and its Books: Reading, Writing and Religion c.1400-1700 (Woodbridge, 2010); T. Bude, 'The Myth of Retrospection: Syon Abbey and the Futurity of Lancastrian Legitimation', The Chaucer Review, 51 (2016), 227–47; N. Beckett, 'St Bridget, Henry V, and Syon Abbey', in J. Hogg (ed.), Studies in St. Birgitta and the Brigittine Order, 2 vols (Salzburg, 1993), ii, 125–50.

7 For Cannynges, see the brief biography in the History of Parliament, http://www.histparl.ac.uk/volume/1386-1421/member/canynges-william-1396 (accessed 16 Aug. 2020), and E. E. Williams, The Chantries of William Cannynges in St Mary Redcliffe, Bristol (Bristol, 1950).

8 R. W. Pfaff, New Liturgical Feasts in Late Medieval England (Oxford, 1970); M. Rubin, Corpus Christi: The Eucharist in Late Medieval Culture (Cambridge, 1991), 271–87.

The Holy Name or the Five Wounds were Christocentric cults, but as the multiple niches of the All Souls reredos suggest, the cult of the saints was central to mainstream religion.[9] The steady proliferation of sacred images in parish churches over the course of the fourteenth century had led to the emergence of hundreds of minor regional image shrines with their own territories of grace and their own often multitudinous clientele, while pilgrim numbers at the established major shrines had grown measurably after the Black Death.[10] Chichele's pontificate coincided with the high point of this striking expansion of the cult of the saints. The Canterbury Jubilee of 1420 saw spectacular numbers of pilgrims converging on Becket's shrine, with a surge in offerings which recalled the earliest days of the cult – amazingly, over £360 was collected that year.[11]

In the 1430s Henry VI himself publicly endorsed this recourse to the saints by an extended stay in the Abbey of Bury St Edmunds. His visit triggered the commissioning of Lydgate's immense *Life of St Edmund*, a text which was itself to exert a long-term influence on the course of vernacular hagiography in England. All this led to the luxurious growth of the iconography of the saints.[12]

From at least the late thirteenth century it had been *de rigueur* to have images of the saints above or flanking the high altar on the east wall, in every case at least images of the Virgin, and of the patronal saint or saints of the church. That expectation was often elaborated during the fourteenth century, and in many great churches large multi-niched screens appeared behind the high altar: the Neville screen in Durham cathedral, erected in 1380, supported the images of 107 saints.[13] The screens at New College and Magdalen did not, as the screens in Durham, Winchester and St Albans did, divide the sanctuary from a major shrine space, but they obviously belong both to this elaboration of eucharistic worship and the efflorescence of the cult of the saints.

---

9   See also Wilson, this volume, 132–42, on the likely programme of the sculpted figures.

10   The multiplication of images in the late Middle Ages is explored in Richard Marks, *Image and Devotion in the Late Medieval England* (London, 2004). For the importance of the proliferation of local saints' cults in late medieval England, E. Duffy, 'The Dynamics of Pilgrimage in the Late Middle Ages', in Duffy, *Royal Books and Holy Bones: Essays in Medieval Christianity* (London, 2018), 205–20; for the growth in pilgrim numbers after the Black Death, B. Nilsen, *Cathedral Shrines of Medieval England* (Woodbridge, 1998), 144–82 (discussion), 210–42 (tables and graphs).

11   Nilsen, *Cathedral Shrines*, 211–15.

12   S. McKendrick, J. Lowden and K. Doyle (eds), *Royal Manuscripts: The Genius of Illumination* (London, 2011), 158–9.

13   For Durham's Neville Screen, D. Brown (ed.), *Durham Cathedral: History, Fabric and Culture* (New Haven, 2015), 153–4. For a discussion of the issues round the visual impact of screens and reredoses, Nilsen, *Cathedral Shrines*, 81–91.

The cult of the dead was, however, the aspect of early fifteenth-century religion which might be thought most pertinent to Chichele's foundation. The commemoration of All Souls, originating in the monastic practice of intercession for deceased brethren, had spread gradually from great houses like Cluny into general observance over the course of the eleventh, twelfth and thirteenth centuries, a period during which theological and imaginative speculation about the nature of the post-mortem purgation of souls flourished. By the fourteenth century, intercession for the dead was one of the central preoccupations of western Christendom. There formed round it multiple forms of institutionalized piety, in the form of chantry foundations, guilds whose key activities included intercession for deceased members, and of course indulgences, those spiritual lollipops earned by prayer, penance, pilgrimage or other good works, including alms in the form of money donations, and which were believed to remit the temporal punishment still due after sin had been repented and absolved.

And this was the great age of Purgatory. The most famous of all medieval evocations, Dante's *Commedia*, presents the suffering of souls in Purgatory as essentially therapeutic. Dante's Purgatory is a mountain rising by terraces towards Paradise: guarded by angels, no demons can enter it, and the souls who suffer there are eager participants in their own cleansing, in a place of hope and renewal. But that was *not* at all how medieval English people imagined it. In the burgeoning late medieval English literature on Purgatory, Purgatory was conceived in a much more Boschean fashion as essentially punitive, a kind of infernal concentration camp where the guards and torturers are gleefully sadistic demons, permitted to do whatever they fancied to suffering souls. A representative example here is the early fifteenth-century vision attributed to an anonymous holy woman, and supposedly experienced on 10 August 1422.[14] In this vision Purgatory was a pit filled with three great fires, one leading out of the other, the central fire 'so horrible and stynkande that all the creatures in the world might never tell the wicked smellynge thereof'.

Those in the fire 'had so grete paynes that for drede I might not describe them', but they included having their hearts and bowels torn out and raked with sharp irons, or being nailed up in barrels full of

14 I have used the text in C. Horstman, *Yorkshire Writers*, 2 vols (London, 1895), i, 383–92. There is a modern scholarly edition by M. P. Harley, *A Revelation of Purgatory by an Unknown Fifteenth-Century Woman Visionary: Introduction, Critical Text, and Translation* (Lewiston, NY, 1985). For the context and early distribution of the vision, M. Erler, 'A Revelation of Purgatory (1422): Reform and the Politics of Female Visions', *Viator*, 38 (2007), 312–83.

poisonous snakes. The objective of such ferocious and terrifying visions of the afterlife was to impress on the living the urgent obligation to pray for the dead. As the soul of the nun Margaret cries out to the visionary, 'Cursed mote thou be and wo worth thee bot if thou haste thee to be my helpe'. It was integral to the whole cult of Purgatory that it was the almost inescapable destination not only of penitent great sinners, but of all the spiritually mediocre, which, of course, meant almost everyone – 'alle manere of crystene mene and womene that hath lefed here in this werlde of what degree thay were'. And so to pray for the holy souls, all souls, and not just one's relatives, friends and benefactors, was a transcendently good work. In the English rendering of Brigitta of Sweden's *Liber Celestis*, produced in the early 1420s, Brigitta declares that

> Than were ther herd many voices oute of purgatory saynge, 'Lord Jesus Criste, ryghtwyse domesman, send thi charite to thame that has spiritall power in the world, that we may be holpyn of their syngyn, redynge and offerynges'. Bot above the place where there voyces were herde where other voyces of many, and saide, 'Mede be unto thame of Gode that sendes us helpe in our need'.[15]

The first and most important reason for establishing intercessory institutions, whether single altar chantries or colleges like All Souls, was to secure intercession for one's own soul. Chichele's tomb in Canterbury cathedral, with its helpless cadaver image intended to evoke pity for the piteous soul in God's prison, encapsulates that concern. But a wider and less egocentric value placed on intercession for the nameless multitudes of the dead rather than primarily oneself or one's relatives, patrons and friends was considered a meritorious work deserving 'great mede' or reward. It is captured in a story that the late fourteenth-century English homelist John Mirc recycled from the *Golden Legend*, of a man who dwelt by a churchyard. As he passed through the graveyard every day his custom was to recite, for the repose of all those buried there, the *De profundis* psalm (number 129 in the Vulgate), then as now the centrepiece of the church's liturgy of the dead. Then came a day when the man was pursued through the churchyard by murderous enemies: fleeing for his life, he nevertheless paused and knelt to say his usual *De profundis*:

---

15   R. Ellis (ed.), *The Liber Celestis of St Bridget of Sweden*, vol. 1 (Text), Early English text Society (Oxford, 1987), 260.

And anone therewith alle this chyrch-yorde rose ful of bodyes, vchone with an instrument in hys hond of hys crafte, and dryvon azeyne hys enemyes… and he was evere aftur the more devoute preying for soules.[16]

In an age which was, like Eliot's Webster in 'Whispers of Immortality', so much possessed by death, you might well think that we need look no further for a rationale for Henry Chichele's foundation of an academic chantry offering prayers on behalf of the souls of the multitudes who had perished in England's French wars. But Peregrine Horden has shown just how unusual Chichele's chosen 'dedication' to the Holy Souls was: though intercession for the dead was a universal practice, there are almost no other English examples of religious institutions specifically dedicated to intercession for All Souls, rather than primarily for specific family members or benefactors, with intercession for all the faithful departed added as a subsidiary and perhaps largely formulaic concern. So Horden comments, though Chichele 'might be thought to have ample precedents for his collegiate quasi-dedication' he was in fact 'being rather more unusual and creative'.[17]

I think that is right, so long as we do not look for too much else in the way of creativity in the religious regime that Chichele prescribed for his foundation. Every member of the College was expected to begin the day appropriately with a short prayer – 'Animae omnes fidelium defunctorum, per misericordiam Domini nostri Jesu Christi Nazareni crucifixi, in pace requiescant', followed by the Psalm 'Levavi oculos meos ad montem', and they were to end the day with an advent compline hymn and the De profundis psalm.[18] But these prescriptions were entirely conventional – formal prayers for the dead, invariably including the psalm De profundis, will have been routine for evening in all colleges. With the single exception of the short prayer 'Animae omnes', the intercessory regime imposed on Chichele's fellows and scholars, including its weekly collegiate requiem mass and office for the dead, was derived almost entirely from the statutes of New College, and was in fact considerably shorter, less circumstantial and less demanding than those laid down for New College: fellows and scholars of All Souls, for example, like those of New College, were required to attend Mass in the chapel every day unless legitimately hindered, but they were not required, as William of Wykeham's scholars were, to recite the rosary while they were there.

---

16 S. Powell (ed.), John Mirk's Festial, Early English Text Society, 2 vols (Oxford, 2009, 2011), ii, 242.
17 Horden, 'Origins of "All Souls"', 308.
18 Statutes of the Colleges of Oxford, 3 vols (London, 1853), i, 'Statutes of All Souls' College, Oxford', cap. 23, pp. 7–8.

There are other ways in which Chichele's religious intentions strike one as entirely conventional. It is sometimes suggested that a prime consideration in establishing the College was concern about Lollardy, and as we have seen Chichele, ably assisted by William Lyndwood, had vigorously pursued suspected heretics. His choice of the Four Latin Doctors – Ambrose, Augustine, Gregory and Jerome - as patrons of the chapel certainly points towards a similar concern with orthodoxy, representing as they did not only the fountainheads of the Western Church's theology, but also encapsulating in their various offices and conventional visual emblems the Church's hierarchical structure – Augustine a mitred bishop, Ambrose an archbishop with cross, Jerome a cardinal in his hat and Gregory a pope with triple tiara.[19] But nowhere in the statutes is there any hint of the existential angst about heresy that seems to have driven Richard Fleming just a few years earlier in the establishment of Lincoln College. We get no hint in Chichele's provisions of anything approaching Fleming's fervent evocation of the dreadful apocalyptic signs of the last days, chief among them the festering of heresies and poisonous opinions, which seemed to Fleming to threaten the 'precious pearl' of the gospel. Though, as Ian Forrest has shown, lawyers were of course crucial to the fifteenth-century campaign against heresy, the pre-eminence of the study of law over theology at All Souls suggests a very different and much cooler understanding of the nature of the 'unarmed militia' of the clergy the times required, and a very different feel from Fleming's urgent promotion of the study of theology as queen of the sciences, 'omnium imperatrix et domina facultatum'.[20]

There is little in Chichele's liturgical prescriptions, or in the known iconography of the chapel, to indicate much in the way of religious individuality. The cult of the saints in early fifteenth-century England was dynamic, with new saints featuring in both popular and elite piety. One element in that dynamism was the Hundred Years War: members of the English aristocracy might adopt military and chivalric cults, or develop devotion to the loc al saints of the parts of France in which they fought – the prayer book of John Talbot, in the Fitzwilliam Museum, for example, includes unusual *memoria* of local French saints as well as petitions for deliverance in battle, alongside more conventional pieties.[21] But if Chichele had

19 On the cult of the Four Doctors in the late Middle Ages, Duffy, *Royal Books and Holy Bones*, 275 – 88.

20 *Statutes of the Colleges of Oxford*, i, 'Statutes of Lincoln College, Oxford', *Praefatio*, p. 8.

21 Talbot's book is discussed in E. Duffy, *Marking the Hours: English People and their Prayers 1240 – 1570* (New Haven, 2006), 67 – 80.

personal devotional favourites, he seems not to have imported them into his foundation. The days to be kept solemnly by all members of the house were the standard *festa ferianda* kept in every other religious institution, including of course New College – Easter, Christmas, Pentecost, the feasts of the Virgin and the Apostles, a handful of other major saints like Mary Magdalen, Nicholas, Catherine, venerated everywhere in the late Middle Ages. The only mildly distinctive observances were the commemoration of All Souls, which in this context needs no comment, the feast of St David, whose celebration as a solemn day in the College perhaps echoes Chichele's extension of the feast day of St David to the general calendar in 1415, and the feast of St Frideswide, Oxford's patron. Naturally, the feast days of the Four Doctors, the chapel's patrons, were also to be solemnly kept: the Four Doctors featured on the College seal presenting Henry VI and Chichele himself to the enthroned Christ (fig. 4.30 below), and presumably they will also have featured prominently on the reredos, maybe looking something like the doctors on the pulpit of All Saints, Trull, in Somerset a generation or so later – it would have been highly irregular for the chapel's patrons not to be represented prominently around the altar, their presence in the chapel glass notwithstanding. And the chapel glass, with its rows of apostles, virgin martyrs, kings and archbishops of Canterbury, suggests piety ordered by the shelfful rather than fine-tuned or custom made. Surprise presences, like the Exeter St Sidwell, probably represent the devotional preferences of the first warden of the College, a Devonian.[22]

A final word about what else might have been represented on the reredos. The statutes of New College describe their reredos there as supporting 'imago sanctissimae ac individuae Trinitatis, patibulum sanctae Crucis cum imagine crucifixi, beatissimae Mariae Virginis, sanctorumque aliorum plurium imagines', a description which would have applied equally to the All Souls reredos.[23] But we know that there was a painted image of the Trinity in the chapel, presumably on the reredos, and we can speculate that it looked something like the representations of the Trinity of the type art historians often refer to as 'Bosom of Abraham Trinity', in the late Middle Ages often called the image of All Saints.[24] Ultimately derived from the parable of Dives and Lazarus, and representations of Abraham with Lazarus in his bosom, the souls in the sheet on God the Father's breast were often taken to be the

22 F. E. Hutchinson, *Medieval Glass at All Souls College* (London, 1949), for Sidwell pp. 34–7.

23 *Statutes of the Colleges of Oxford*, i, 'Statutes of New College, Oxford', cap. 63, p. 99.

24 See further Wilson, this volume, 139–40.

souls of the redeemed, hence the title, All Saints.[25] But approximations to this Trinity type also feature in fifteenth-century illustrations to the office for the dead, where they clearly represent not All Saints but All Souls — as in the miniature of God the Father holding souls in a napkin at the beginning of the office of the dead from a book illuminated in London by Hermann Scheere round about 1420, and now in the Huntington Library, or an illumination by an unknown artist from a book of hours associated with the Beaufort family, and dating from the early 1420s.[26] Chichele's self-conscious orthodoxy would almost certainly have bridled at the latter book's representation of the Trinity, not as God the Father holding a crucifix but, with much more dubious orthodoxy, as three separate chaps. Nevertheless, the context makes it clear that here, as in the less problematic representation by Hermann Scheere, the souls in God's napkin are the holy souls in Purgatory, not the blessed in Heaven. I take it that this is how representations of the Bosom of Abraham Trinity were often read. It would have been entirely appropriate if something like this figure once formed the centrepiece of the All Souls reredos.

---

25 Four fifteenth-century examples in alabaster are illustrated in F. Cheetham, *English Medieval Alabasters: with a catalogue of the collection in the Victoria and Albert Museum* (Woodbridge, 2005), nos 226–9, discussed on p. 196.

26 K. L. Scott, *Later Gothic Manuscripts 1390–1490*, 2 vols (London, 1996), i, nos 87, 192; ii, 157–8, 846–8.

CHAPTER 4

ARCHBISHOP CHICHELE'S REREDOS AND ITS EARLY TUDOR REWORKING

CHRISTOPHER WILSON

Discussions of the All Souls reredos in print are remarkably few and slight, and they amount to little more than jejune descriptions and factually deficient summaries of the documentary evidence.[1] This state of affairs is perhaps not altogether surprising, for the scholarly literature on Perpendicular architecture as a whole is very sparse, and the same is true of the monumentally treated church fittings that are a salient feature of the period.[2] But if the general disfavour shown towards Perpendicular by architectural historians is likely to be the single most important reason for the neglect of the All Souls reredos, there are two aspects of the reredos itself which will have had the effect of inhibiting discussion: the seemingly contradictory evidence for its dating, and the uncertainty regarding the accuracy of the extensive restoration that it underwent after its mutilated remains were uncovered in 1871. These aspects represent potentially insurmountable barriers to any attempt to situate the reredos in the development of the visual arts in late medieval England and for that reason they need to be considered first.

---

1   See, for example, the entry on the reredos by Nikolaus Pevsner in J. Sherwood and N. Pevsner, *The Buildings of England, Oxfordshire* (Harmondsworth, 1974), 93: 'Original also, and marvellous, is the REREDOS, or at least much of its architectural framework. It was restored by Scott. The figures are by E. C. [*sic*] Geflowski, 1872. The framework is of 1447 and as thoroughly covered with decoration as are the *retablos* of Spain, but it has the dry, repetitive logic of the English Perpendicular, the very opposite of the wild exuberance of Spanish Late Gothic. Spun-over with ornament are the uprights, the bases or brackets of figures, and the big canopies.' Pevsner's dating of 1447 appears to be based on a misunderstanding of a document published (and misdated) by E. F. Jacob, for which see n. 4. His view that the reredos is typically Perpendicular contrasts with the discussion presented below, which stresses atypical and exotic characteristics. Critical thinking has been applied to the architecture of the reredos in just one publication: N. Doggett, 'Fragments of the Fifteenth-Century Reredos and a Medieval Cross-Head from North Hinksey discovered at All Souls College Chapel, Oxford and some New Light on the Nineteenth-Century Restoration', *Oxoniensia*, 49 (1984), 277–87.

2   J. Harvey, *The Perpendicular Style, 1330–1485* (London, 1978), the only ambitious account of Perpendicular ever written, excludes from consideration the architecture of Henry VII and Henry VIII's reigns and most of the period's major architecturally treated church fittings, including the All Souls reredos. Exceptions to the general dearth of recent writing on major church fittings: C. Tracy, *English Gothic Choir-stalls, 1400–1540* (Woodbridge, 1990); idem, *Britain's Medieval Episcopal Thrones: History, Archaeology and Conservation* (Oxford, 2015); D. T. Ollmann, 'The Origin and Development of the English Reredos, 1000–1540', unpublished PhD thesis, University of Cambridge, 2001.

The documentary dating evidence

Six documentary references have been applied to the making of the All Souls reredos. The three earliest occur in the accounts for the building of the College between 1438 and 1442 at the expense of the founder, Henry Chichele, archbishop of Canterbury (1414–43). In 1440 two separate payments were made for colours and gold leaf used for the painting and gilding of an image of the Trinity. The exact nature and location of that image are not given in the accounts, but it has generally and reasonably been assumed that it belonged to the reredos, and if the building of the chapel had kept pace with that of the other buildings of the College, which there is every reason to think was the case, the fitting out would have begun in 1440. In the accounts for late January 1442 there is a payment to the London-based sculptor John Massyngham and an assistant for 'making large images of stone situated above the high altar'.[3] The latest mid-fifteenth-century reference occurs in a list dated 17 October 1446 of disbursements made from the sum of 1000 marks which Chichele had bequeathed to the College: £14 13s. 4d. paid 'in connection with the reredos at the back of the high altar'.[4] After an interval of almost 50 years comes the next known reference, that in the will drawn up on 10 April 1493 for Robert Este, chapter clerk of York Minster and one-time fellow of All Souls: a bequest to the College of £21 13s. 4d. 'for the fashioning of certain images which are to be made at the back of the high altar

---

3   'Et pro coloribus emptis pro pictura ymaginis Trinitatis'; 'Et pro auro foliato pro pictura ymaginis Trinitatis emptis'; 'Et solut' eodem die [27 January 1442] Johanni Massyngham kervere locato cum famulo suo per ebdomadam faciendo magnas ymagines lapideas situat' super summum altare dicti Collegij ut patet viij s.'; *Building Accounts*, 167, 264. The amounts spent on colours and gold leaf for the Trinity image are not apparent, as the accounts give only the costs of these items together with others. The 1439 accounts contain three payments for stone to be used for making images (ibid., 95–6), some of which will have been destined for the reredos as distinct from the gatehouse facing the High Street. For the incorrect statement, repeated several times by later writers, that an entry elsewhere in the building accounts shows that the number of images for which Massyngham and his assistant were paid was two and that they were located above the Trinity image see J. Gutch (ed.), *The History and Antiquities of the Colleges and Halls in the University of Oxford by Antony Wood*, M.A., 2 vols (Oxford, 1786–90), i, 288 n. 114.

4   'Et de xiiij^{li} xiijs iiijd circa reredoc[e] in fronte magni altaris'; ASC, unnumbered receiver's account for 2 November 1445–1 November 1446, dorse. This document is presumably the second mentioned of the 'six rolls of receivers' accounts, dated '23, 24, 25, & 29 Hen. VI' which make up no. 216 in CTM, 393. The list is misdated to 1447 and is misleadingly said to be 'attached' to the receiver's account (which is also misdated) in E. F. Jacob, 'The Building of All Souls College, 1438–1443', in J. G. Edwards, V. C. Galbraith and E. F. Jacob (eds), *Historical Essays in Honour of James Tait* (Manchester, 1933), 121–35, at 131 n. 7. The 1447 dating is followed in A. H. M. Jones, 'All Souls College, Site and Buildings', in VCH: *Oxfordshire*, iii (1954), 173–93 at 183 n. 8. For an explanation of the translation of the phrase 'in fronte' as 'at the back' see n. 31 below. On 10 August 1454 5s. 3d. were paid for 14 ells of canvas for 'muro supra summam altare', perhaps protection for dossals made out of precious textiles from moisture exuded by the still fairly new masonry of the east wall; CTM, 416, Computus and Expense roll, 1453–4.

there, in accordance with what was begun by the founder of the same altar'.[5] The latest reference to have reached print is a receipt issued on 31 July 1504 by the warden of the College to Nicholas Goldwell, archdeacon of Suffolk, younger brother and chief executor of the will of James Goldwell, bishop of Norwich from 1472 to 1499. The warden was acknowledging that Nicholas had paid £50 out of the late bishop's goods in connection with the building of the high altar.[6]

When these references are fleshed out a little, they establish four major points. Firstly, the high altar of Chichele's chapel was equipped from the outset with a reredos incorporating large polychrome stone figures carved by and under the direction of John Massyngham, who is documented at All Souls from 1438 onwards. Secondly, work of an unknown nature was being carried out on the reredos four years after the first celebration of mass at the high altar, which took place in June 1442. Thirdly, Robert Este left money in 1493 for further figures conforming to those that had been provided by Chichele. The nature of their conformity is not spelt out but presumably it concerned dimensions and stylistic character. Fourthly, the reconstruction of the architectural part of the reredos was either in progress or newly completed when the executors of Bishop Goldwell handed over £50 for the building of the high altar in the summer of 1504. The use of the word 'edificatio' in the receipt issued to Nicholas Goldwell strongly suggests that the architecture of the reredos was a new structure.

Confirmation that important work on the reredos was taking place at the start of the sixteenth century is provided by a handful of previously unpublished entries in the College's internal accounts, the Computus and Expense rolls. The earliest of these, which occurs in the roll for 1501–2, is a payment of 43s. 4d. to 'the carvers', and the next earliest, in the roll for the following year, is a part payment of 6s. 8d.

---

5   'Collegio Animarum et Omnium Christi Fidelium Defunctorium Oxoniae xxjˡⁱ xiiijs iiijd ad fabricationem certarum imaginum in dorso magni altaris ibidem faciendarum, secundum quod inchoatum est per fundatorem ejusdem altaris'; J. Raine, J. Raine Jr and J. W. Clay (eds), Testamenta Eboracensia or Wills Registered at York, Illustrative of the History, Manners, Language, Statistics, &c., of the Province of York, from the Year MCCC. Downwards, 6 vols, Surtees Society, 4, 30, 45, 53, 79, 106 (1836–1902), iv, 85. The citing of this bequest in Gutch (as n. 3), 289, gives the amount left as £1 too much, does not note who Robert Este was, and, like all subsequent discussions of the reredos that make mention of this bequest, fails to include the clause stipulating that the new sculptures were to accord with those produced for the founder. For Este see A. B. Emden, A Biographical Register of the University of Oxford to A.D. 1500, 3 vols (Oxford, 1957–9), i, 648.

6   The payment is said to be 'circa edificationem summi altaris'; ASC, Warden's MS 1, f. 49. The earliest mention in print of Bishop Goldwell's subvention is in Gutch (as n. 3), i, 262, where no source is given.

towards the cost of one of the 'heads of the high altar'.[7] This can only mean one of the heads or canopies of the niches of the reredos, for the heads of the images would never have been paid for separately, and although it might seem a little odd to speak of the reredos behind the high altar as if it were the high altar itself, that was clearly normal usage at All Souls in the early sixteenth century. The 1502–3 payment was made to an individual whose known career will be discussed in the last section of this paper and who may well have been the same as the unnamed 'principal mason' paid 4s. in the account for 1504–5 for a purpose that is not stated.[8] It seems likely that all of these payments are no more than stragglers from a lost set of accounts devoted specifically to the manufacture of the components of the reredos. The next Computus and Expense account to mention the reredos is that for 1510–11, which includes a payment of £4 for the 'fabricatio' of the high altar made to a single unnamed mason and no fewer than three payments totalling £45 7s. 1d. for the painting of the reredos, including one of £5 10d. specifically for the painting of images. No mention is made of the number or the names of those who painted the reredos. Given that it occurs in the same account as the painting, the payment for 'fabricatio' can only refer to the installation of the completely carved components of the architectural stonework and statuary, and the round sum involved indicates that it was a figure agreed in advance between the College and the setting mason hired to do the work. If one assumes that the mason was to take 6d. per day for each of six working days in an ordinary week that would give a period of slightly more than 23 weeks, but the time allowed for could have been significantly less than

---

7   'Et de xliijs iiijd solutis ly Carvars'; 'Et de vjs viiid solutis eidem [John Fustyngs] in parte solutionis pro uno capite summi Altaris'; CTM, 416, Computus and Expense rolls, 1501–2, 1502–3. The fact that there appear to be no other examples of the use of the word 'caput' to denote the canopy or head of a niche is not necessarily problematic, for words deriving from Latin 'pes' such as 'pedestallus' were not infrequently applied in the late Middle Ages to the other main component of niches. For other instances of architectural terms currently known only from single examples see n. 62. The general characteristic of inconsistency in the use of architectural terminology in late medieval texts is well exemplified in documents relating to building at All Souls: 'hovellus' and 'caput' both meaning 'canopy', in 1441 and 1501–2 respectively (n. 62 and above); 'reredoce' and 'summum altare' both meaning 'reredos', in 1445–6 and in the first decade of the sixteenth century respectively (nn. 4, 6, 9); 'in fronte magni altaris' and 'in dorso magni altaris' both meaning 'at the back of the reredos', in 1445–6 and 1493 respectively (nn. 4, 5); 'edificatio' and 'fabricatio' both meaning 'setting up' or 'installation', in 1504 and 1510-11 respectively (nn. 6, 9). A comparable instance of referring to a decorative architectural adjunct as if it were the thing dignified by the adjunct is the regular mentions of the bishop's throne in the fourteenth-century fabric accounts of Exeter Cathedral when what is actually being referred to is the canopy which stood over the throne; A. M. Erskine, The Accounts of the Fabric of Exeter Cathedral, 1279–1353, 2 vols, Devon & Cornwall Record Society, new series, 24, 26 (1981, 1983), i, 71 and passim.

8   Computus and Expense rolls, 1502–3. 'Et de iiijs datis Bursario pro solutione principali latamo'; ibid., 1504–5.

that if, as seems likely, the mason had to find the wages of at least one labourer to assist him. The same account shows that 2s. 6d. was spent on metal hooks for use in the reredos and there can be little doubt that these were needed to secure the 84 small, separately carved figures that adorned the ten uprights in the side sections of the reredos. It is not obvious why there should have been an interval of around half a decade between the making of the components of the reredos and their installation and painting, especially as the total spent on the latter processes amounted to £49 9s. 7d., a sum remarkably close to the £50 that had been made available by Nicholas Goldwell for the 'edificatio' of the reredos in 1504.[9] Robert Este's bequest of 1493 to the making of additional imagery for the reredos does not indicate whether that work was a completion of Chichele's work or an extension of it, but the closeness in time of that bequest to the early sixteenth-century references makes it virtually certain that it was the latter and that all the documentary references to the reredos dating from the decades to either side of 1500 were generated by a single programme of work.

This interpretation is radically different from that which is implicit in the ultra-laconic comments of earlier writers. In 1872 James Parker, the son of the architectural author and publisher John Henry Parker, made some remarks after a lecture on the medieval buildings of All Souls to the effect that Robert Este's bequest proved that the niches were filled not all at once but in instalments.[10] The clear implication of

---

9 Ibid., 1510–11, in the 'Capella' section: 'Et de 2s 6d pro hamis in summi altaris'; last entry in the 'Reparationes Infra' section: 'Et de iiij^{li} pro fabricatione summi Altaris solutis latamo'; added (in the hand of William Broke, Warden of All Souls 1504–24) after the statement of the total expenditure for the year: 'De qua summa [Bursarii] solverunt pictoribus summi Altaris per manus Magistri Godfrey xix^{li} et in peccunijs minuatis per eiusdem Magistrum Godfrey xxi^{li} vjs iijd. Et de cs xd solutis custodi & in manibus eiusdem ad picturiam [sic] imagines [sic] per manus Magistri Gyfforde.' The total amount of money said to have been spent in 1510–11 evidently includes the costs of erecting and painting the reredos, which suggests that an entry for these items had been accidentally omitted. An instance of the common late medieval practice of using metal hooks to secure small sculptures within their architectural settings is the head of the door of the mid-fifteenth-century choir screen in Canterbury Cathedral. A possible explanation for the interval of approximately half a decade between the making of the components for the reredos and its installation is that the College was concentrating its efforts on the completion of the structure of the cloister, which is documented in ibid., 1509–10, in the 'Reparationes Infra' section.

10 J. Parker thought it was possible that when the chapel was consecrated in 1442 'there were few if any figures there at all, but that they were gradually added from time to time, as funds were forthcoming'; Proceedings of the Oxford Architectural and Historical Society, new series, 3 (1872–80), 50. It is possible that this interpretation was suggested by the slow rates of execution evident in some of the large assemblages of sculpture adorning the west fronts of English cathedrals, for example those of Salisbury and Exeter, the latter of which incorporates a mid-fourteenth-century image screen completed only in the early years of the sixteenth century. Whether or not that was Parker's thinking, drawing such a parallel would take insufficient account of the reality that the adornment of the high altars of major English churches will normally have been much more important to the clergy than the provision of sculpture for west fronts, a process that was often allowed to languish.

those observations was that the existing reredos dated from Chichele's time. Parker's view found an echo in the only reference to the reredos made by Howard Colvin in the published version of his 1986 Chichele Lecture on the building of the medieval College. After noting the 1442 payment for large stone figures over the high altar, Colvin suggested that these could have been 'the first instalment of the array of saints that was eventually to fill the niches that covered the windowless east wall of the Chapel'. It may be suspected that Colvin realised that there was an unresolved problem about the dating of the reredos and chose not to address it. He will of course have known E. F. Jacob's article of 1933 on the building of the College, the only publication to state explicitly that the 1493 and 1504 references preclude dating the existing reredos to the 1440s.[11]

The essence of the story as preserved in the documentary record is that Chichele's chapel possessed a reredos incorporating statuary, that it was still being worked on three years after his death in 1443, and that in the early 1490s the sculptural programme of his reredos was being expanded in advance of the imminent renewal of its architectural structure. In the following section of this paper the testimony of the documents will be confirmed but also clarified by the identification of two phases of work in the remaining late medieval fabric. In the penultimate section, that devoted to the sources drawn on in the design of the architecturally treated main part of the reredos, the impossibility of a dating earlier than the last decades of the fifteenth century will be reinforced. For the sake of clarity and brevity, the reredos created in the 1440s along with the chapel and the rest of the College will be referred to hereafter as Reredos I and the reredos as reworked c. 1493–1511 will be referred to as Reredos II.

The artefactual dating evidence

The architecturally treated part of Reredos II, which ends at the level of the hammer-beams in the roof of the chapel, is undoubtedly the product of a single campaign of work. The detailing of the niches in all three tiers is consistent with their having been made at the same time and the sizes of the constituent blocks of the niches within each course

---

11   Colvin and Simmons, 5; Jacob (as n. 4), 130–1. Presumably an attempt to take account of Jacob's comments is the non-committal 'mid to late fifteenth-century' dating offered in RCHM, *An Inventory of the Historical Monuments in the City of Oxford* (London, 1939), 18. There is no mention of Bishop Goldwell's money in the catalogue entry on the All Souls reredos in Ollmann (as n. 2), 207–8, where the sources cited are Sherwood and Pevsner (as n. 1), RCHM (as above) and Jones (as n. 4).

or layer are standardised except at the very top of the seven central niches of the uppermost tier (fig. 4.1). The treatment of the canopies of this group of niches is made asymmetrical by irregularities in the roof, the easternmost truss of which defines the top of the trefoil-arched field occupied by the reredos. The asymmetry of the roof trusses, which reveals itself most clearly in the disparate levels of the hammer-beams on the north and south sides, is due to the fact that the windows and roof corbels of the south wall have been inadvertently set higher than their counterparts in the north wall.[12] Bounded by the arched central part of the easternmost truss is a tympanum showing Christ in Judgement flanked by two pairs of angels and by advancing processions of the dead in their newly resurrected bodies, the whole set against a background of boldly stylised clouds indicating that the action takes place in the highest heavens (fig. 4.2). The asymmetry of the roof affects the levels of the two groups of risen dead and the strips of ground along which they walk.

The treatment of the tympanum as a single field devoid of any architectural subdivisions and built up from a series of eighteen comparatively thin slabs makes a strong contrast with the main part of the reredos below. But whereas this disparity arises entirely from the demands of traditional iconography, at the junction between the tympanum and the top of the architecturally treated part of the reredos there are several anomalies that cannot be ascribed either to iconographic needs or to the asymmetry imposed by the easternmost roof truss. The first of these anomalies is the fact that the four buttress-like uprights flanking and separating the central niches in each tier rise to different heights and terminate abruptly without any kind of capping element. The second is that the lower faces of two of the lowest slabs making up the tympanum, which ought of course to be totally invisible, can be glimpsed to either side of the canopy of niche 6 (fig. 4.3). The third is the single violent undulation in the ground under each group of resurrected dead, which is clearly an ad hoc alteration occasioned by the need to accommodate figures standing on the uprights separating the central niches from the rest. As a result of this alteration the lower legs of some of the dead are truncated, an unfortunate feature but one

---

12 This discrepancy has not previously been noticed in print. The elevation drawing dated 1873 from the office of Sir Gilbert Scott (fig. 11.3) does not show it, even though some of the asymmetries at this level in the reredos itself are indicated. In the roof truss against the east wall the asymmetry of the arch between the hammer-beams and the collar is quite effectively masked by the angels at the terminations of the hammer-beams, although in the southern angel the lower part of the single wing shown is significantly smaller than in its northern counterpart.

4.3 All Souls College, reredos, overhanging lower edge of tympanum and canopies of niches 5–7 of tier 1, showing original rear parts retaining polychromy (in the captions and footnotes the tiers are numbered from the top downwards and the niches are numbered from left to right)

4.4 All Souls College, reredos, tympanum, left-hand group of the resurrected dead

whose existence is only obvious when seen from a scaffold (fig. 4.4).[13] All of these anomalies become explicable if one assumes, firstly, that the tympanum is a survival from John Massyngham's work on Reredos I and, secondly, that the setting mason responsible for the installation of the niches of Reredos II in 1510–11 encountered difficulties in achieving a neat junction with the retained tympanum. The very thorough defacing of the figures in the tympanum in Edward VI's reign frustrates any attempt to validate the attribution to Massyngham by making stylistic comparisons with the three surviving sculptures carved by him and his assistants for the gatehouse facing the High Street (figs 4.29, 35, 36).[14]

The accuracy of the nineteenth-century reconstruction of the architecture of Reredos II

An unsharp photograph taken in 1872 (fig. 4.5) is the only known visual record of what was found when the remains of Reredos II were exposed following the removal of the boarding on which Isaac Fuller's *Last Judgement* had been painted in the early 1660s. The damage was immense, for in addition to the mid-sixteenth-century defacing of all the imagery of the tympanum and the Crucifixion tableau above the altar and the removal of the 122 images which occupied the main part of the reredos, all of the architectural components which projected further forwards than the fronts of the uprights in the side sections of the reredos had been dressed back in order to accommodate the boarding. The main casualties of this latter process were the 34 large image niches, whose hexagon-plan canopies lost most of their three forwards-projecting sides. The gablets decorating these sides were cut away almost entirely and all the delicate openwork tracery behind and above the gablets was shattered. On the pedestals most of the carving on the uppermost parts was chopped back. The canopies and pedestals to the 84 small figures on the fronts of the uprights in the side sections of the reredos were dressed off in order to make the uprights present

---

13   Observed by the writer when the reredos was scaffolded in July 2017. The undulations are visible in the 1872 pre-restoration photograph in the Bodleian Library (fig. 4.5). The 1873 elevation drawing from the Scott office eliminates them, presumably reflecting a proposal for their removal.

14   The rendering of the tympanum in the Scott office drawing of 1873, which seems to be for the most part a reliable record of the pre-restoration state, indicates that only very small portions of the original figures had survived before the installation of the present figures. Of these only the wings of the standing angels flanking Christ are still extant and visible today. Although the accounts for the building of the College from 1438 do not mention the sculptures on the gatehouse, they provide no grounds for doubting that Massyngham was the chief sculptor with overall responsibility for stone imagery.

4.5 All Souls College, reredos, photograph of 1872 (Bodleian Library, G. A. Oxon. a. 48, p. 61)

continuous flat surfaces.[15] The pedestals of the second tier of niches were obliterated by the cutting of a horizontal channel which ran across the entire width of the east wall. A short distance above this was a similar

15   The total of 122 images in Reredos II excluding the tympanum and the Crucifixion tableau is reached by adding the 34 large standing figures in the niches that make up most of tiers 1–3, the 84 small figures on the fronts of the uprights in the outer sections of the reredos, the two figures standing on the innermost of those uprights and the two figures in the small niches at the outer edges of tier 1. If one includes the fifteen figures in the tympanum, the wooden angel bust at the top of the tympanum, the minimum of eight figures in the Crucifixion tableau, the two small figures of angels marking the lower limit of the uprights flanking the Crucifixion tableau, and the pairs of small shield-bearing angels decorating five of the pedestals of the niches in tier 3, the total comes to a minimum of 158. The 1872 photo (fig. 4.5) shows that the small figures on the fronts of the outer uprights must have been made from separate pieces of stone. See also n. 9. In the restoration the replacement figures were made integral with the uprights.

but shallower channel. It is possible that the purpose of the channels was to allow the introduction of timber beams supporting the boarding on to which Fuller painted his *Last Judgement*.

When the architecture of the reredos is examined at close quarters it becomes clear that its restorer in the 1870s, Sir Gilbert Scott, went to great lengths to ensure that surviving original work guided the form of the additions needed to replace what had been destroyed in the 1660s. Scott's decision to leave untouched the polychromy of all the retained original parts and to refrain from adding colour to the new masonry makes it a simple matter to distinguish between original and nineteenth-century work. The distinction is most obvious in the vaults inside the canopies of the niches (fig. 4.6), but careful examination of the rearmost parts of the exterior faces of the canopies shows that they too are original and that they provided Scott and his team with clear evidence to follow (fig. 4.3). The profile of the pedestals under the small figures on the fronts of the uprights in the side sections would doubtless have remained traceable even after they had been dressed back, and the form of the canopies there could be recreated on the basis of detached fragments, a few of which were incorporated into the new masonry (fig. 4.7). This reuse of original fragments bears witness to the desire both to achieve accuracy and to demonstrate that it had been achieved,

4.7 All Souls College, reredos, reused portion of original canopy in upright between niches 3 and 4 of tier 3

4.8 All Souls College, reredos, reused original pedestal to niche 8 of tier 2

4.9 All Souls College, reredos, 1870s repairs to pedestals of niches 1 and 2 of tier 3 and reused portion of lowest part of upright between niches 1 and 2 inserted into renewed plinth

and the same practice can be seen in other of Scott's restorations.[16] Further examples in the All Souls reredos are a substantial portion of the pedestal of niche 8 in tier 2 (fig. 4.8) and several of the continuations into the plinth of the central elements of the complex uprights in the side sections (fig. 4.9). It appears that quite a few small fragments of the original canopy work which Scott's team could not integrate into the new stonework were preserved by building them into the blocking of the door to the vestry on the north side of the sanctuary. They were rediscovered in October 1983, but they were not recorded and have since disappeared. In the published account of their finding it was noted that many of them authenticated the detailing of the new masonry added under Scott.[17]

The only sector of the architectural design not successfully recreated by Scott is the uppermost portion of the compartment occupied by

16   Compare, for example, the tracery in the choir clearstorey of Chester Cathedral and the easternmost image socle of the north transept porches of Westminster Abbey, both restored by Scott in the 1870s. The detached original fragments reused in the restoration of the All Souls reredos will have been available because they had been treated as fill for the image niches in the early 1660s.

17   For the observation that the fragments included several finials from the gablets on the external faces of the niche canopies which were larger than their counterparts in Scott's canopies see Doggett (as n. 1), 282. In the absence of the fragments themselves it is difficult to know what Doggett's grounds were for writing that 'although a mid to late fifteenth-century date seems likely for the mouldings, the decorative fragments (from the canopied niches and crocketed finials) can be tentatively assigned a date between 1480 and 1520[, suggesting] that further embellishment took place when statues were added to the niches in the 1490s' (ibid., 283).

4.10 All Souls College,
reredos, Crucifixion tableau

4.11 Wells Cathedral, canopy
over altar in chantry of
Bishop Bubwith

the Crucifixion tableau. No part of the original treatment here had
remained in place after the cutting of the larger of the two mid-
seventeenth-century horizontal channels mentioned earlier (figs 4.5,
10). The highest part of the tableau still in situ today is a band of
blind tracery set immediately above the arms of the cross. Into the
gap above this feature Scott inserted two elements: a continuation of
the blind tracery which turned the design into a series of large and
very nearly symmetrical quatrefoils, and above that a trio of canopies
whose lowness puts them at odds with those in the rest of the reredos.
There can be little doubt that the principal feature of this sector of
the tableau was a forwards-projecting coving, a larger version of what
can still be seen above the sites of the figures that flanked the crucifix.
Such covings made from stone or wood will once have been a common
feature of late medieval English altars, although very few remain. Two
stone examples which have survived because they are integral parts of
larger structures are those in the chantry chapels of Bishop Nicholas
Bubwith (died 1424) in Wells Cathedral (fig. 4.11) and of Prior William
Bird (died 1525) in Bath Abbey. Postulating that the coving at All Souls
sprang forward from the upper limit of the original blind tracery still in
place offers an explanation for the unique and bizarre motif of encircled
quatrefoils set within the outline of shields: the horizontals forming
the tops of the quasi-shields would originally have read as fragments
of a continuous horizontal line marking the level of the springing. The
coving would have had to project far enough to enable it to support the
pedestals of the three niches immediately above. One of the fragments
recovered from the blocking of the vestry door in 1983 was 'a miniature
hanging boss' whose formal traits were evidently closely akin to those

4.12 Wells Cathedral, canopy over altar in chantry of Bishop Bekynton

of the miniature vaults in the image niches of the reredos. Very small-scale pendants are incorporated into the vaulted coving above the altar serving the chantry of Bishop Thomas Bekynton (died 1465) in Wells Cathedral, which is said to have been recently completed in 1452 (fig. 4.12). The designer of the architecture of the All Souls reredos could well have known the Bekynton chantry altar and he could also have been aware of the fact that in some ambitious early fifteenth-century reredoses that incorporate numerous image niches the special status of the central image was reinforced by giving its canopy a pendant such as no other canopy possessed.[18]

Those who ordered the concealment of the reredos in the early 1660s will have been unconcerned by the damage caused to something which they will have assumed was being consigned to oblivion. Those who took the decision to embark on a complete restoration in the early 1870s exhibited remarkable self-confidence and resolve, and there is nothing to indicate that any of them allowed themselves to be daunted by the spectacle of devastation confronting them when the boarding was removed. Gilbert Scott was Victorian England's foremost specialist in the restoration of medieval churches, and it seems likely that he would have seen this as an opportunity to advertise his prowess in this field. What is

---

18   Ibid., 282. For the dating of Beckington's chantry chapel see L. Stone, *Sculpture in Britain: The Middle Ages* (Harmondsworth, 1955), 214. The early fifteenth-century reredoses in which pendant vaults are used only in the central niches are those in the Lady Chapel of Christchurch Priory and the north transept of St Cuthbert's church in Wells. No traces remain of the junctions between the coving above the All Souls Crucifixion tableau and the inner faces of the uprights flanking the tableau because the masonry of the latter at this level belongs to Scott's restoration. Contemporary viewers of the All Souls reredos will have been familiar with covings not only above altars but also in the halls of major houses, where they served to honour those sitting at the high table on the dais.

certain is that the outcome, notwithstanding the reservation expressed in the preceding paragraph, represents a triumph of painstaking research and skilled craftsmanship.

The architectural patronage of Bishop James Goldwell

Bishop Goldwell's will, which is dated 15 February 1499 (new style), contains no indications of his support of the remaking of the All Souls reredos or indeed of any kind of artistic patronage.[19] It is possible that he had made subventions in his lifetime and there could have existed some kind of informal agreement with his brother Nicholas and his other executors that he wished to support the project if funds were available after the bequests itemised in his will had been fulfilled. Be that as it may, the 1504 payment of £50 towards the building of the reredos was clearly not a random choice on the part of the executors, for the bishop was a former fellow of All Souls, and a chantry was in the process of being established there for his soul and for that of Nicholas Goldwell.[20] In the 1490s he had contributed towards the building of the cloister at All Souls, and at an unknown date he paid for a rood screen which presumably replaced totally that provided by Archbishop Chichele in the early 1440s. The new screen bore Chichele's arms besides Goldwell's, and after the latter's death verses were added which spelled out that he was the donor.[21] The western face of the screen will have incorporated altarpieces for the two altars which flanked the central entrance, but whether Goldwell was involved in their making is not known. In fact he was a considerable patron of architecture, among his other benefactions being the addition of a stone vault to the presbytery of Norwich Cathedral (fig. 4.13) and the rebuilding of the choir of Leeds Priory in Kent. Leeds is very close to Great Chart, whose simply detailed late fifteenth-century parish church

---

19 TNA, PROB 11/11/487. For Goldwell's career see Emden (as n. 5), ii, 783–6.

20 Mentions of the chantry occur in ASC, CTM, 416, Computus and Expense rolls, 1498–9, 1501–2, 1502–3 etc, and also in an undated and badly damaged draft letter written to Nicholas Goldwell by William Broke, warden 1504–24 (ASC, CTM, 297, no. 1). Broke's letter thanks Goldwell for a variety of gifts including plate, and I am grateful to Bronac Holden for her suggestion that at least some of the references to his munificence here might be related to the donation of £50 for the building of the reredos from Bishop Goldwell's estate. From 1497 Nicholas Goldwell was a confrater of All Souls, an honour which seems not to have been bestowed on his brother; Emden (as n. 5), ii, 786.

21 'Hoc circiter tempus collegii claustra aedificantur impensis partim collegii partim Jacobi Goldwell episcopi Norvic. Mri. Thomae Colfoxe et aliorum'; Colvin and Simmons, 16 n. 29, citing 'entry in sixteenth-century College Register under 1491'. The register in question is the unpaginated first register of admissions to the College: ASC, MS 402a. For the arms and verses on the rood screen see Gutch (as n. 3), i, 287–8.

was at least partly built and glazed at the bishop's expense.[22] A reredos of the 'high wall' type defined in the next section of this paper had been installed in the presbytery at Norwich by the time of his successor and there is a possibility that Goldwell was responsible for that as well as the vault above it.[23] Robert Este's bequest proves that Goldwell was not the sole patron of the reconstruction of the All Souls reredos, but there can be no doubt that the fellows of the College considered his munificence to be exceptional, for they counted him among their founders. It is not impossible that Goldwell's patronage of All Souls had been influenced by the fact that the next building on the High Street to the west of the College, the imposing chancel of St Mary's church, had been built and glazed in the early 1460s at the cost of his predecessor in the see of Norwich, Walter Lyhert (1446–72) (fig. 4.19).[24]

The pre-existing English tradition of reredos design

The pioneering phase in the development of the English late medieval reredos occurred in the early fourteenth century when two new types came into being. The more complex type, now represented only by the high altar reredos installed in Durham Cathedral in the 1370s, comprises a low wall surmounted by a linked sequence of open-sided, multi-stage tabernacles containing images.[25] The other type consists of a solid wall rising through most of the height of the interior, on whose western face imagery is housed in niches arranged in stacks. By the third quarter of the

---

22   For the suggestion that Goldwell was also patron of the stone spire on the crossing tower see E. Fernie, *An Architectural History of Norwich Cathedral* (Oxford, 1993), 191–3. He is credited with commissioning the eastern parts of the choir stalls at Norwich in Tracy (as n. 2), 32–6. For the choir of Leeds Priory see T. Philipott, *Villare Cantianum; or, Kent Surveyed and Illustrated*, 2nd edn (Kings Lynn, 1776), 214; P. J. Tester, 'Excavations on the Site of Leeds Priory. Part II – The Claustral Buildings and other Remains', *Archaeologia Cantiana*, 94 (1978), 75–98 at 97. For Goldwell's involvement at Great Chart, where his family held a manor, see E. Hasted, *The History and Topographical Survey of the County of Kent*, 4 vols (Canterbury, 1778–99), iii, 246, 250.

23   Although the point seems never to have been made in print, postulating the existence of a high-wall reredos is effectively the only way of explaining why the lower storeys of the Romanesque main apse were left alone when the lateral elevations of the east arm were extensively remodelled in the time of Bishop Richard Nix (1501–35). A comparandum is the largely Gothic eastern arm of Llandaff Cathedral, which retains in its east wall a large and richly decorated Romanesque arch which survives only because it was obscured by the early fourteenth-century high wall reredos (for which see n. 25).

24   The bishop of Norwich, clearly meaning Goldwell, is one of four persons listed as founders who were commemorated on the Feast of Relics; CTM, 416; Computus and Expense roll, 1504–5. For the chancel of St Mary's, whose east window formerly contained an inscription recording Bishop Lyhert's patronage and the completion of the glazing in 1462, see T. G. Jackson, *The Church of St Mary the Virgin, Oxford* (Oxford, 1897), 113–4, 213; Harvey (as n. 2), 195–6.

25   For the antecedents of this type and the three known examples of it see C. Wilson, 'The Neville Screen', in N. Coldstream and P. Draper (eds), *Medieval Art and Architecture at Durham Cathedral*, British Archaeological Association Conference Transactions, iii (Leeds, 1980), 90–104.

century the 'high wall reredos' was beginning to predominate and it had given rise to a variant, the reredos formed of stacked niches decorating the east wall of a single-cell chapel and rising all the way to the roof. This is the category to which the All Souls reredos belongs. The earliest known example of a high wall reredos is that in the collegiate church of Ottery St Mary, which was founded in 1339 by the long-serving bishop of Exeter, John Grandisson, jointly with his sister Catherine (fig. 4.14). Catherine's husband was Thomas Montagu, first earl of Salisbury, whose family had long been the principal patrons of Christchurch Priory in Dorset, where the next earliest surviving example is to be found (fig. 4.15).[26] The Christchurch reredos appears to date from the 1350s and its

---

26   For the patronage of Christchurch Priory by the Montagu family see K. Stöber, *Late Medieval Monasteries and their Patrons: England and Wales, c. 1300 – 1540* (Woodbridge, 2007), 151 – 2 and passim. The Christchurch reredos now forms part of the wall terminating the early sixteenth-century central vessel of the east arm. That it was originally a freestanding structure like the reredos at Ottery St Mary is effectively proved by the existence to either side of the high altar of doors whose east sides are still

4.15 Christchurch Priory, Hampshire, high altar reredos

design was clearly influenced by the emerging Perpendicular style, not so much in its detailing as in its approximation to an all-over grid of similarly sized compartments linked by strong verticals, a concept whose outstanding contemporary expression was the east window of St Peter's Abbey, Gloucester. Continuity with the Ottery scheme is evident in the way in which stacks of large and small image niches alternate. In the side

visible. For the ex-situ lowest tier of the early fourteenth-century high altar reredos of Llandaff Cathedral, which is likely to have been broadly similar to that at Ottery St Mary, see the drawings of the west elevation and details made in 1883 by H. A. Prothero; *The Spring Gardens Sketch Book*, viii (London, 1890), plates 15–16. For a rather basic description of this reredos in 1717, when it still retained all of its three tiers, see B. Willis, *A Survey of the Cathedral-Church of Landaff* ... (London, 1719), 19–20, where a late fifteenth-century date is advanced fallaciously. The earliest known evidence of the existence of the word 'reredos' is the use of the Latinised 'retrodorsum' in a reference of 1347 to the cleaning of the high altar reredos of Exeter Cathedral (which is called a 'tabulatura' in the account for its making in 1318–19); A. M. Erskine (ed.), *The Accounts of the Fabric of Exeter Cathedral, 1279–1353*, 2 vols (Devon & Cornwall Record Society, new series, 24, 26, 1981–3), i, 110; ii, 276. The fact that reredoses and altarpieces of all kinds were not deemed to be part of altars in canon law is likely to have worked against the emergence of a standard terminology.

sections of the reredos at All Souls the general disposition of the images was similar except that the small images were attached to buttress-like uprights rather than being set in stacked niches.

Beyond reasonable doubt the most splendid example of the high wall reredos ever created was that in Winchester Cathedral (fig. 4.16). Unfortunately no documentary evidence for its making has survived, but the style of its architecture indicates a date during the middle decades of the fifteenth century, and there must be a possibility that its design was drawn up at the behest of the famously opulent Cardinal Henry Beaufort, occupant of the see of Winchester from 1404 to 1447.[27] In its original state this reredos must have been quite exceptionally magnificent, for its stonework was polychrome and gilt and the main images at its centre were of massive sheet gold encrusted with gems. Even today, shorn of its original imagery and extensively restored in the nineteenth century, this almost certainly episcopally patronised reredos makes a striking contrast with the unambitious fourteenth-century architecture of the presbytery in which it stands, the product of the grudging and dilatory patronage of the monks of the cathedral priory.[28] The contrast is of interest in relation to All Souls, as every high wall reredos automatically became a cynosure, reducing its architectural container to a kind of backdrop. At

---

27 The features of the canopy work of the Winchester reredos indicative of a mid-fifteenth-century date are the harking back to the heavy reliance on late thirteenth-century-style Geometric tracery forms found in the earliest works of Perpendicular in south-east England and the incorporation of comparatively low upper stages into the canopies over the lowest rank of large images. Both traits are present in important works of the early 1440s, most notably the Beauchamp Chapel at Warwick (including the oratory on its north side) and the chantry chapel of King Henry V and the high altar reredos in Westminster Abbey. Evidence that Beaufort was the posthumous patron and that the design had been formulated to some extent in the mid-fifteenth century is the record that in 1451 the prior was shown a design for the 'new altar frontal of gold and silver with six images and other things', the making of which was provided for in Beaufort's will; translation in J. Greatrex (ed.), *The Register of the Common Seal of the Priory of St Swithun, Winchester, 1345–1497*, Hampshire Record Series, 2 (1978), 102–4. I am very grateful to John Crook for sending me his transcription of the Latin text of this document. The 'frontal' can only have been a retable for the high altar, and it is very unlikely that it was a separate project rather than a subsidiary part of the new reredos. The patronage of Beaufort's successor William Waynflete is suggested and a date of before 1476 advanced in P. Lindley, 'The "Great Screen" of Winchester Cathedral, Part II: Style and Date', *Burlington Magazine*, 135 (1993), 797–807 at 798–801. Lindley is undoubtedly correct in assigning a date in the second half of the fifteenth century to the fragmentary stone sculptures that he attributes to the niches of the reredos. See also R. Marks and P. Williamson (eds), *Gothic: Art for England, 1400–1547*, catalogue of exhibition, Victoria and Albert Museum (London, 2003), 356.

28 P. Draper and R. K. Morris, 'The Development of the East End of Winchester Cathedral from the thirteenth to the sixteenth century', in J. Crook (ed.), *Winchester Cathedral: Nine Hundred Years, 1093–1993* (Chichester, 1993), 177–92 at 182–9. A clear indication of the perceived inadequacy of the fourteenth-century architecture of the presbytery is the enormous amount of work done to embellish it under Bishop Richard Fox (1501–28).

St Albans Abbey the staid architecture of the late thirteenth-century presbytery is unlikely to have received much attention once the high wall reredos closely modelled on Winchester had been installed early in the abbacy of William Wallingford, which lasted from 1476 to 1492 (fig. 4.17). The *Book of Benefactors* compiled at St Albans contains a passage in its section on Wallingford which captures some of the enthusiasm that a newly completed project of this kind could engender: 'Moreover let us add that most ornate, sumptuous and lofty reredos of the high altar, which greatly beautifies the church, graciously feeds the eyes of beholders, and is to all those who gaze upon it the most perfect mirror of the divine to be found in this kingdom'.[29] The competitive element here is important and, as will emerge presently, it recurred at All Souls.

The architecture of All Souls College was strongly influenced by that of William of Wykeham's Oxford foundation, begun in 1379, the New College of St Mary of Winchester, and this is hardly surprising for Chichele was a New College man. The debt which is of particular relevance here is the windowless treatment of the east wall of the chapel, the result of its being butted up against the hall (figs 4.18–19), but whereas at All Souls the hall was set at right angles to the chapel, the analogous buildings at New College form a single range, just as they do in Edward III's remodelling of the Upper Ward of Windsor Castle in the 1350s and 1360s (figs 4.20–21). The indebtedness of New College to Windsor is easily explained, for Wykeham had served as clerk of works to that project, the costliest of the English Middle Ages, and William Wynford, the architect whom Wykeham placed in charge of New College and his many other architectural projects, had been functioning during the 1360s as a kind of adjutant to the ageing original architect of Edward III's Windsor. The New College reredos (fig. 4.22), which occupies the full height of the east wall of the chapel, was almost certainly anticipated some two decades earlier by the reredos in the chapel in the Upper Ward at Windsor, which is

29 'Addimus praeterea illam ornatissimam et sumptuosissimam alte erectam summi altaris faciem, quae multum venustat ecclesiam, et pascit oculos intuentium gratiose, et cunctis inspectantibus speculum hujus regni divinissimum'; H. T. Riley (ed.), *Registrum Abbatiae Johannis Whethamstede, Abbatis Monasterii Sancti Albani*, 2 vols, Rolls Series, 28 (1872–3), i, 477. The use of the term 'facies' invites comparison with the other quasi-anatomical term applied to reredoses, namely 'frons', for which see n. 31. A dating of the St Albans reredos to the late 1470s or early 1480s is strongly suggested by the presence of a single example of Edward IV's rose-en-soleil badge in the carved decoration on the base of one of the apostle figures in the panel above the dossal.

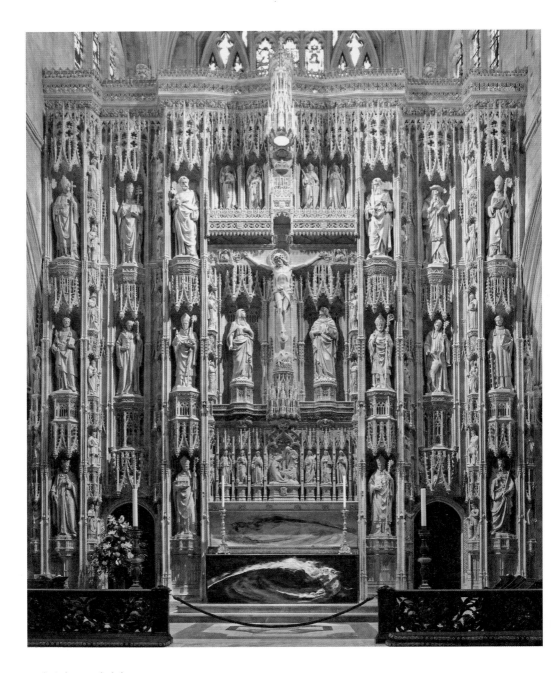

4.16 Winchester Cathedral,
high altar reredos

4.17 St Albans Abbey,
high altar reredos

4.20 Windsor Castle, Upper Ward, south range of royal lodgings block, ground-floor and first-floor plans from C. Wilson, 'The Royal Lodgings of Edward III at Windsor Castle: Form, Function, Representation', in L. Keen and E. Scarff (eds), *Windsor: Medieval Archaeology, Art and Architecture of the Thames Valley* (British Archaeological Association Conference Transactions, 25, 2002), 22–3

4.21 Windsor Castle, chapel and hall of Upper Ward (detail of etching by Wenceslaus Hollar in E. Ashmole, *The Institution, Laws & Ceremonies of the Most Noble Order of the Garter* (London, 1672))

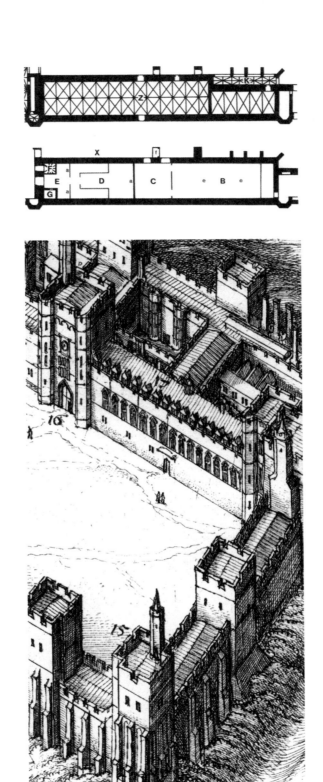

known to have incorporated a sumptuously painted and gilded retable and a large amount of figure sculpture. There is no way of ascertaining whether the architectural setting of that sculpture foreshadowed New College's strongly demarcated tiers of close-packed niches, but there must be a good chance that it did. It is safe to assume that all the reredoses mentioned in this section were once fully polychrome, but the extent of the original colour still surviving at All Souls is exceptional.[30]

A reconstruction of the architecture of Reredos I

As will emerge later in this section and in the section which follows it, Reredos I seems to have resembled the rest of Chichele's work at All Souls in being significantly indebted to New College, yet it must have been in some respects an eccentric design. The main requirement of any hypothetical reconstruction of the lost parts of Reredos I is that it take account of the evidence already cited that Reredos II possessed a larger number of standing images housed in niches. The form that a reredos incorporating fewer images is most likely to have assumed is several short rows of niches occupying all the wall space between the dossal of the high altar and the tympanum. Some support for that hypothesis is provided by the already mentioned reference of 1446 to Reredos I, in which it is said to be 'in fronte magni altaris'. Counter-intuitive though it may seem, the noun 'frons' in this context signifies not the front of the high altar but rather the wall or wall-plane *behind*

---

30   For an overview of the destruction, rediscovery and restorations of the reredos see V. Decker, *William of Wykeham als Collegegründer und Bauherr. Architektur und Glasmalerei zur Zeit Richard II* (Kiel, 2017), 148 – 53. Neither Decker nor any other student of the architecture of New College has noted that the reredos retains enough original late-fourteenth-century masonry to validate the main lines of the design. In 1986 Howard Colvin observed that 'All Souls must have been the only religious establishment in England where the beer was kept immediately underneath the high altar', but at Windsor the situation was even odder in that it was the need for space below the chapel to store the royal household's drink which had given rise to the decision to make the reredos of the chapel from timber; Colvin and Simmons, 9; C. Wilson, 'The Royal Lodgings of Edward III at Windsor Castle: Form, Function, Representation', in L. Keen and E. Scarff (eds), *Windsor: Medieval Archaeology, Art and Architecture of the Thames Valley*, British Archaeological Association Conference Transactions, xxv (Leeds, 2002), 15 – 94 at 38 – 9. The polychromy of the Windsor reredos will no doubt have concealed from the great majority of its viewers the fact that it was made from wood. At New College the niches were found to have been painted 'a deep ultramarine blue, and the exterior edges of the shafts of the niches richly gilt'; A. Chalmers, *A History of the Colleges, Halls and Public Buildings attached to the University of Oxford…* (Oxford, 1810), 135. Although no traces of paint seem to be recorded at St Albans, at Winchester, as Dr John Crook kindly pointed out to me, substantial amounts of architectural polychromy were uncovered during the recent cleaning.

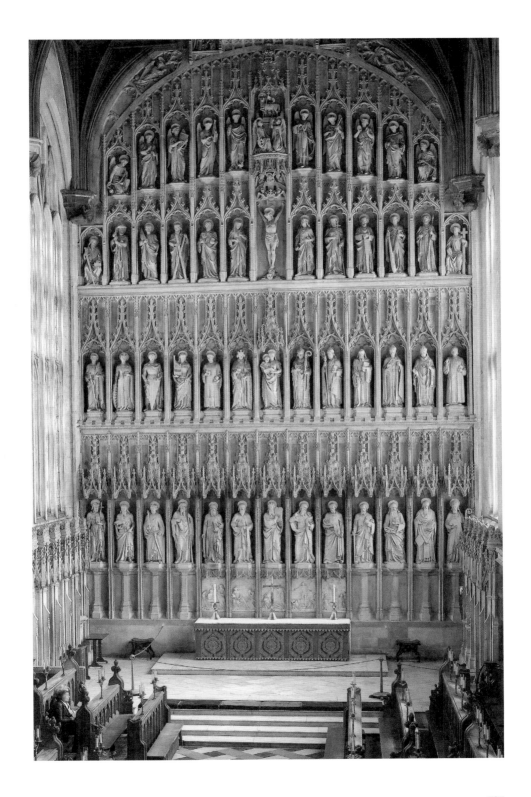

it.[31] Once that is grasped the force of the preposition 'in' becomes clear: Reredos I, unlike Reredos II, did not occupy the full width of the east wall. To either side of the reredos there would have been substantial areas of walling treated either as plain masonry or, more probably, as blind tracery. The number of niches in each tier is likely to have been seven and there were probably three tiers, as in Reredos II. The dossal immediately above and behind the high altar of Reredos I probably rose no higher than the pedestals carrying the images in the lowest tier, as in the New College reredos. If, as is highly likely, the altar had the same width as that provided for in Reredos II there would have been just single image niches to left and right (fig. 4.23). An arrangement broadly similar to this is to be found in the east wall of the chancel of Adderbury church in north Oxfordshire, where there is a low reredos flanked by single niches with very elongated pedestals (fig. 4.24). This exceptionally elegant building, which was constructed in 1408 – 18 at the expense of New College and to the designs of Richard Winchcombe, the outstanding architect working in Oxford and its vicinity during the first three decades of the fifteenth century, is quite likely to have

31 See n. 4. Medieval English texts concerned with architecture sometimes make use of the word 'frons' and its French and English cognates to denote an external façade, but these terms can also denote the structure or the internal face of the east wall of a church; O. Lehmann-Brockhaus (ed.), *Lateinische Schriftquellen zur Kunst in England, Wales und Schottland vom Jahre 901 bis zum Jahre 1307*, 5 vols (Munich, 1955– 60), nos 645, 704, 805, 1318, 1683, 3762 – 3, 4808; H. R. Luard (ed.), *Annales Monastici*, 5 vols, Rolls Series 36 (1864 – 9), iv, 415. In the mid-thirteenth century Matthew Paris applied the term to two eastern terminations of complex plan, that of Edward the Confessor's church at Westminster Abbey and that of Salisbury Cathedral; K. Y. Wallace (ed.), *La Estoire de Seint Aedward le Rei* (London, 1983), 65– 6; F. Madden (ed.), *Matthaei Parisiensis Monachi Sancti Albani, Historia Anglorum*, 3 vols, Rolls Series, 44 (1866 – 9), iii, 260. In the late thirteenth century and the late sixteenth century the eastern transept (Nine Altars Chapel) of Durham Cathedral was referred to as the front of the church; Lehmann-Brockhaus (as above), nos 1485, 1488; J. T. Fowler (ed.), *Rites of Durham*, Surtees Society, 107(1902), 1. The meaning intended in the 1447 reference to the reredos at All Souls is closely paralleled in several nearly contemporary texts including Thomas Rudborne's mid-fifteenth-century *Historia Major Ecclesiae Wintoniensis*, which refers to a large cross of precious materials given to the high altar of Winchester Cathedral more than 400 years earlier, 'quae stat in fronte summi altaris'; Lehmann-Brockhaus (as above), no. 4700. For Winchester Cathedral's mid-fifteenth-century gold 'frontal', in reality a retable, see n. 27. Other examples of the use of the term 'frontal' to signify a dossal or a retable are given in Ollmann (as n. 2), 15. That the term 'front' was fairly widely used of reredoses in late medieval England is suggested by a bequest of 1361 to Lichfield Cathedral 'pro fronte facienda ultra magnum altare', by the use of the word in the contract of 1471 for the still partly surviving reredos in the south transept of St Cuthbert's church, Wells, and by the record of a payment to the carver John Hill in 1480–1 for 'the making of a new front otherwise called a reredos' which was to possess three image niches and stand above the altar of St Thomas of Canterbury in All Saints' church, Bristol; Raine, Raine and Clay (eds) (as n. 5), i, 73; T. Serel, *Historical Notes on the Church of St Cuthbert in Wells* (Wells, 1875), 26; J. Harvey, *English Mediaeval Architects: A Biographical Dictionary down to 1540*, rev. edn (Gloucester, 1984), 145; C. Burgess (ed.), *The Pre-Reformation Records of All Saints' Church, Bristol*, 3 vols, Bristol Record Society Publications, 46, 53, 56 (1995–2004), ii, 102. There seems little doubt that all these usages were rooted in the original meaning of 'frons' as 'forehead' and were intended to convey the idea that worshippers were confronted by the westwards-facing sacred imagery incorporated into east walls and windows and by that placed immediately above high altars.

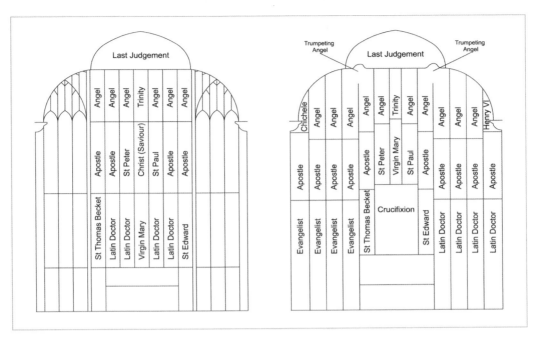

Left diagram (Reredos I):

Last Judgement

St Thomas Becket	Apostle		Angel
Latin Doctor	Apostle		Angel
Latin Doctor	St Peter		Angel
Virgin Mary	Christ (Saviour)		Trinity
Latin Doctor	St Paul		Angel
Latin Doctor	Apostle		Angel
St Edward	Apostle		Angel

Right diagram (Reredos II):

Trumpeting Angel — **Last Judgement** — Trumpeting Angel

| Chichele | | | | | | | | | | Henry VI |

Evangelist	Apostle		Angel					Apostle	Latin Doctor	
Evangelist	Apostle		Angel		St Peter	Angel		Apostle	Latin Doctor	
Evangelist	Apostle		Angel	St Thomas Becket	Virgin Mary	Trinity	St Edward	Apostle	Latin Doctor	
Evangelist	Apostle		Angel		St Paul	Angel		Apostle	Latin Doctor	
					Crucifixion					

4.23 All Souls College, diagrams showing reconstructed iconography of imagery in Reredoses I and II, drawn by Stuart Harrison

4.24 Adderbury church, Oxfordshire, interior of east wall of chancel

4.25 All Souls College, chapel, south side of sanctuary with sedilia

been known to those responsible for formulating the architectural design of Reredos I.[32]

Confirmation that the original east wall at All Souls incorporated substantial amounts of blind tracery is provided by the presence of this kind of decoration on the south wall of the sanctuary next to the sedilia (fig. 4.25). The blind tracery and the sedilia both belong to the primary phase of work on the chapel designed by Chichele's master mason Richard Chevynton. In all probability the north side of the sanctuary was treated similarly before the original wall surface was removed in the course of early eighteenth-century alterations. That Chevynton did not

---

32 T. F. Hobson (ed.), *Adderbury 'Rectoria'. The Manor at Adderbury, Belonging to New College, Oxford: The Building of the Chancel, 1408 – 1418: Account Rolls, Deeds and Court Rolls*, Oxfordshire Record Society, 8 (1926), viii–xxiii, 28 – 43; Harvey (as n. 31), 336 – 7.

think of the blind tracery east of the sedilia merely as a dado forming part of the regular bay design is evident from its two-tier format and from the absence of anything similar in the western parts of the chapel.[33] The most satisfactory explanation for the presence of blind tracery on one or both of the lateral walls of the sanctuary and on much of the east elevation must be that it was conceived as a way of expressing the greater status of the sanctuary vis-à-vis the rest of the chapel. If Reredos I did indeed occupy no more than the central part of the east wall, that would almost certainly have been its undoing. It would have appeared modest by comparison with New College's east wall entirely given over to enriched imagery, and that inferiority would have been felt more acutely after 1474, when a further full-width reredos was installed in the chapel of Magdalen College. A cheaper option for Reredos II would have been to add further niches in place of the side sections of Reredos I, and the fact that that was not done suggests that there was something about the architectural character of Chichele's reredos which was disliked and thought incapable of correction. The aspect most likely to have dissatisfied late fifteenth-century observers is the treatment of the niches, which will almost certainly have been much less elaborate than those of Reredos II.[34]

---

33 In the north and south parts of the antechapel the wall surface below the windows is totally plain and below the great west window there is blind tracery formed of single lights enclosed in upright rectangular panels, a form of dado frequently encountered in Perpendicular architecture. The singular two-tier format of the dado in the Beauchamp Chapel at Warwick could well have been influenced by the sanctuary dado at All Souls.

34 The main source for the remains of the architecture of the Magdalen College reredos is a pencil and watercolour sketch and an accompanying note, both made by the architectural and antiquarian draughtsman J. C. Buckler in July 1828, after the removal of the painting of the Last Judgement which had occupied the east wall of the chapel since the late seventeenth century; BL, MS Add 27964, f. 14. The sketch is reproduced in L. W. B. Brockliss (ed.), *Magdalen College, Oxford: A History* (Oxford, 2008), pl. 17A. Buckler's evidence makes clear that the principal survival was two tiers of thirteen image niches extending the full width of the east wall. The lower tier, whose base was set approximately level with the sills of the lateral windows, is likely to have contained an image of the Virgin flanked by saints, and the upper tier is likely to have contained an image of Christ flanked by apostles. In the lunette above the upper tier there was a single niche which was 'larger and more sumptuous' than the niches below it. Almost certainly this contained an image of the Trinity. Buckler's note indicates that the other decorations at this level, which 'had been savagely mutilated', were high reliefs. The repetitive pattern shown in this part of his sketch suggests that the Trinity was flanked by angels. Below the two rows of thirteen niches and very close to the lateral walls was a pair of doors leading to the former sacristy. The rest of this level was taken up with 'tabernacle and panel work' which had been dressed back to a depth of six or seven inches. The images of St Mary Magdalen and St John the Baptist said in a late fifteenth-century source to have stood beside ('juxta') the altar (W. D. Macray, *Register of the Presidents and Other Members of Magdalen College, Oxford: New Series – Fellows 1458–1915*, 8 vols (London, 1894–1915), i, 6) will have been above the altar and next to its north and south ends. The restoration of the east wall by L. N. Cottingham from 1829 was presented as an attempt to reconstruct the original architectural design (R. Darwall-Smith, 'The Monks of Magdalen, 1688–1854', in Brockliss (as above), 253–386 at 363), even though some elements mentioned by Buckler were omitted and others not mentioned were included. See further Hall, this volume.

4.26 All Souls College,
tympanum of reredos, detail
of drawing from the office
of Sir Gilbert Scott dated
20 October 1873 (British
Architectural Library)
(contrast enhanced)

A reconstruction of the iconography of Reredos I

The tympanum is the only part of Reredos I still remaining, but
its fifteen high-relief figures are restorations of the 1870s by E. E.
Geflowski, who took account of the outlines that remained after the
defacing ordered early in Edward VI's reign (figs 4.2, 5, 26). Many
of the iconographic choices made in the 1870s represent departures
from the original conception, which was a Last Judgement placing
heavy emphasis on the Passion of Christ yet lacking several important
components that one would expect to find in any large-scale late
medieval rendering of this subject. The most obvious omissions are
representations of the dead in their newly resurrected bodies climbing
out of their tombs, figures of St Mary and St John the Baptist kneeling
to either side of Christ and interceding for those facing judgement,
and groups of the judged walking towards the gates of heaven on
Christ's dexter side or being consigned to the jaws of hell on his
sinister side. A further standard element almost certainly not included
originally was a pair of angels blowing their trumpets to wake the
dead. The large figure of Christ at the centre of the composition was
shown fully clothed by Geflowski, but in the original image Christ
will have exposed the wound in his right side as well as the piercings
of his hands and feet, thereby reminding those he is about to judge
of what he had suffered on the cross for the sake of their redemption.
Five angels surround him, their number matching that of his principal

4.27 All Souls College, angel bust above tympanum of reredos

wounds. Originally, all will have carried instruments of the Passion. Directly above Christ's head is a partly original wooden bust of an angel which belongs structurally to the roof but which will have been visually part of the tympanum if, as seems certain, it was originally polychrome rather than gilded, as it is now (fig. 4.27). The cloth held by this angel must originally have extended down to the still-existing border formed by inclined and slightly curved bands in the stonework behind Christ's head. Proof that the cloth was the veil of St Veronica, another instrument of the Passion, is provided by the carved light beams that radiate out from the border. The Scott office drawing of the reredos dated October 1873 (see fig. 4.26) shows the angel bust holding the veil much higher, but this design would have entailed destroying substantial original parts of the bust and was presumably abandoned for that reason. The freestanding head of the original figure of Christ in Judgement was set not far forward of the veil and it seems likely that it took the place of the head normally painted on St Veronica's veil.[35] There appear to be no surviving parallels for this arrangement, and the same can be said of the form of the rainbow on which Christ sits, a depressed trefoil arch or bow which echoes in miniature the easternmost arched truss of the roof (fig. 4.2). The half-length angels

---

35   The original function of the inclined bands behind Christ's head was presumably not apparent to the Victorian restorers of the reredos, who confused matters by adding above them extensions to the light rays below, which are original work (fig. 4.27).

4.28 *The Last Judgement,* preceding the first of the seven penitential Psalms, from the *Hours of Henry Beauchamp,* earl of Warwick (Morgan Library & Museum, New York, MS M. 893, f. 44v)

who hover to either side of Christ's head are shown blowing trumpets, but their fifteenth-century predecessors will have borne the two smallest instruments of the Passion, the crown of thorns and the nails. The full-length angels standing to either side of Christ are shown as mere attendants, whereas the original figures will have carried some of the larger instruments, including the cross and the column of the flagellation and possibly also the spear and the rod with the sponge soaked in vinegar.

An almost certainly correct guess by the nineteenth-century restorers is the installation of trumpeting angels on top of two of the uprights of Reredos II. As was noted earlier, the introduction of the figures originally in this position by the makers of Reredos II necessitated making room by introducing single deep undulations into the ground along which the resurrected dead walk at the base of the tympanum, and the readiness to resort to such a dubious expedient would make sense if there had been a feeling that the lack of trumpeting angels in the sculpture of the original tympanum represented a serious deficiency. The makers of Reredos I probably considered that the absence of angelic trumpeters was adequately compensated for by the inscription in large gold letters on the roof collar which commands the dead to rise up and approach the seat of judgement (fig. 4.2). The second part of that command is enacted by nearly symmetrical groups of five naked figures who walk in single file towards Christ. Geflowski chose to make some of the figures on Christ's sinister side express anxiety about their fate in relatively restrained ways, but the still-surviving parts of the outlines of the original figures on both sides suggest that all maintained a decorous demeanour with no signs of the kind of rejoicing or despairing gestures which differentiate the saved and the damned in some other abbreviated Last Judgements of similar date. If such gesturing had been part of the original concept it would have needed to be very obvious to be readable, for the tympanum is rather dimly lit most of the time and its base is set around 11 m above the floor of the sanctuary. The overall impression created by the balanced and self-contained images in the tympanum is likely to have been remarkably static and emotionless.[36]

Although several components of the iconography of the tympanum are not paralleled in any other extant late medieval work of art, it is entirely possible that there once existed earlier large-scale examples of the same or similar iconography that have not survived. Abbreviated Last Judgements are not uncommon in illuminated manuscripts, and there are considerable numbers of them in books of hours, where they often function as a kind of bookmark indicating the beginning of the seven penitential Psalms (fig. 4.28). Approximately life-sized paintings of Christ in Judgement unaccompanied by ancillary figures appeared on the undersides of the testers incorporated into the elaborate temporary hearses or catafalques which by the mid-fifteenth century had become a regular feature of the funerals of the most elevated members of English society. In his lifetime Chichele will have seen for himself several of these

---

36   The rediscovery of the inscription *Surgite mortui venite ad judicium* on the collar of the easternmost roof truss is reported in H. Clutton, *A Narrative and Correspondence relating to the Restoration of All Souls College Chapel, Oxford* (privately printed, 1872), 4, 11. In an image of the Last Judgement preceding the penitential Psalms in a book of hours of the use of Rheims dating from c. 1460 (Walters Art Gallery, Baltimore, MS W.269, f. 60r) there are extraordinarily many inscriptions, including two reading 'leves vous mors' and one reading 'venes a vostre jugement', all three placed so as to suggest that they are being voiced by the trumpet-blowing angels. Examples of the dead rising on Christ's sinister side who are despairing of their fate can be seen in the Last Judgement in the Walters manuscript, in the similarly abbreviated versions of the iconography found in, for example, the Rohan Hours (Paris, Bibliothèque Nationale, MS latin 9471, f. 194r) and in the probably mid-fifteenth-century wall painting at the east end of the nave of St Mary's church at Lutterworth, Leicestershire; J. E. Ashby, 'English Medieval Murals of the Doom: a Descriptive Catalogue and Introduction', unpublished MPhil thesis (University of York, 1980), 306. Continental abbreviated Last Judgements of late medieval date in which the risen dead on Christ's sinister side exhibit fear seem invariably to incorporate images of the judge blessing with his right hand and waving dismissively with his left hand. As is indicated below, the Christ in the All Souls tympanum was probably of the 'even-handed' type. The term 'abbreviated Last Judgement' is the coinage of Ashby (as above), 399–403 and passim. The iconographically unique features of the All Souls tympanum are not noted anywhere in the meagre literature on the reredos.

so-called 'majesty cloths', including those on the hearses of royalty, and it is quite likely that his own hearse incorporated one.[37]

John Massyngham and his team created a further and still more heavily abbreviated Last Judgement for the front of the gatehouse over the main entrance to the College. Its central image of Christ, destroyed in the mid-seventeenth century, is likely to have been very similar to that on the tympanum of the reredos, but in the far more restricted space available it was expedient to portray the resurrected dead as a single group rising from their tombs below Christ's feet (figs 4.19, 29). The still-surviving carving forming this part of the ensemble shows no sign of any attempt to differentiate between the risen dead on the sinister and dexter sides of the judge. The general design of the images of Christ formerly on the gatehouse and reredos is probably reflected fairly closely in the central image of the virtually contemporary seal of the College (fig. 4.30), but a better idea of their three-dimensional character can perhaps be gained from what might well be the only undefaced sculpture of Christ in Judgement to have survived from mid-fifteenth-century England, that on a wooden roof boss near the east end of the nave of St Peter Hungate in Norwich (fig. 4.31).[38]

---

37 One of the very few extant parish church doom paintings which is likely always to have been an abbreviated Last Judgement (i.e. not accompanied by portrayals of heaven and hell on the side walls of the nave) is that over the chancel arch of Lutterworth church, Leicestershire (for which see also n. 36). For examples of Christ in Judgement and variously abbreviated Last Judgements in English fourteenth- and fifteenth-century manuscript painting see R. Marks and N. Morgan, *The Golden Age of English Manuscript Painting*, 1200–1500 (London, 1981), 80–1; L. F. Sandler, *Gothic Manuscripts 1285–1385*, 2 vols (London, 1986), i, ill. 315, ii, 27, 95, 96, 114, 115, 134, 136, 139, 168, 177; K. L. Scott, *Later Gothic Manuscripts 1390–1490*, 2 vols (London, 1996) i, ills 50, 222, 225, 343; ii, 383. Some of the different options available to book painters portraying the Last Judgement are discussed in M. Twycross, 'Doomsday as Hypertext: Contexts of Doomsday in Fifteenth-Century Northern Manuscripts, 1: The "Bolton Hours"', in N. Morgan (ed.), *Prophecy, Apocalypse and the Day of Doom*, Proceedings of the 2000 Harlaxton Symposium (Donington, 2004), 377–90. Images of Christ in Judgement incorporated into hearses are only attested from the late fifteenth century onwards, though all the indications are that they followed long-established usage. The possibility that such images formed part of hearses in the fourteenth century is suggested by the painted images of Christ in Majesty above the tomb effigies of Bishop Walter Stapeldon (died 1326) at Exeter Cathedral and John Lord Harrington (died 1347) at Cartmel Priory, the image of the Trinity painted on the tester above the tomb of Edward, Prince of Wales (died 1376), at Canterbury Cathedral, and the low-relief sculpture of Christ in Judgement on the vault above the site of the destroyed tomb of Bishop John Grandisson (died 1369) at Exeter Cathedral. For documented royal examples of hearses with 'majesty cloths' see A. F. Sutton and L. Visser-Fuchs, *The Reburial of Richard Duke of York, 21–30 July 1476* (London, 1996), 34–5; eidem, *The Royal Funerals of the House of York at Windsor* (London, 2005) 21, 25, 37, 46 and passim. The fact that Chichele's hearse in Canterbury Cathedral was surmounted by a three-dimensional effigy of the archbishop probably implies that it also incorporated a 'majesty cloth', as the hearse of Archbishop William Warham (died 1532) certainly did; C. Wilson, 'The Medieval Monuments', in P. Collinson, N. Ramsay and M. Sparks (eds), *A History of Canterbury Cathedral* (Oxford, 1995), 451–510 at 480, 487.

38 For the All Souls seal matrix, which was almost certainly made in 1443, see Marks and Williamson (as n. 27), 176, 237. For the arguments in favour of dating the nave of St Peter Hungate to before 1451 see the detailed discussion of the church in B. Ayers, C. Haynes, T. A. Heslop and H. Lunnon, *The Parish Churches of Medieval Norwich: City, Community and Architecture* (Donington, forthcoming).

4.29 All Souls College, relief of the resurrected dead from High Street front of gatehouse

4.30 Modern wax impression of seal matrix of All Souls College

4.31 St Peter Hungate, Norwich, nave roof boss

The reredos installed at New College in the late fourteenth century lacked any counterpart to the tympanum at All Souls, but there can be little doubt that its imagery exerted a very important influence on Reredos I (figs 4.22–3). In rubric 63 of the statutes which William of Wykeham compiled for New College in 1400, the playing of ball games in the hall was prohibited lest balls bounced against the wall separating the hall from the chapel cause damage to the reredos on the other side, and by way of spelling out what was potentially at risk Wykeham noted that the reredos contained images of the Trinity, Christ crucified, the Virgin Mary and many other saints, all of them skilfully fashioned and ornamented with varied colours.[39] The named images will all have been on the central vertical axis, as befitted their christological and hierarchical significance, and the order of their naming clearly corresponded to the height of their placing on the reredos. But Wykeham's reredos incorporates four tiers of imagery and therefore one of the central images has been omitted from rubric 63 of his statutes. The positions of the images of the Trinity and Christ crucified can be regarded as certain, not least because the latter required a niche wider than the rest, and the image of the Virgin Mary must have been directly above the high altar, which was dedicated to the Annunciation and had a dossal showing the Five Joys of the Virgin which still survives in part.[40] The central image not mentioned in rubric 63 must have been a standing figure of Christ, and it is likely that he was shown as Salvator Mundi with the globe of the world in his right hand. The figures in the central niches provide the key to the identity of the occupants of the other niches in the same tiers. In the topmost tier the Trinity will have been accompanied by angels,[41] and in the next tier down Christ crucified will have been flanked by the Virgin Mary and St John the Evangelist. The small and simply detailed niches of the outer edges of this tier are likely to have contained kneeling images of King Richard II and Wykeham approximating to those included in the stained glass of the east window of Winchester College, the bishop's other great foundation, and to the sculptured figures of Wykeham kneeling in adoration before sacred figures which are still to be seen on the exterior of New College (fig. 4.32). The remaining eight niches of this tier could well have contained further angels, especially as these and the ten niches in the tier above provided the right number for two representatives of each of the nine orders of angels. In the third tier the two groups of six niches flanking Christ would have housed the apostles and in the lowest tier the Virgin Mary holding the infant Christ in her arms will have been flanked by major saints to whom Wykeham was specially devoted.

Evidence that the figures in the central niches of Reredos I were iconographically closely related to those of the New College reredos is

---

39 *Statutes of the Colleges of Oxford*, 3 vols (London, 1853), i, 'Statutes of New College, Oxford', cap. 63, pp. 99−100. When the plaster concealing the New College reredos was removed in 1695 'old broken statues' were discovered; A. Clark (ed.), *The Life and Times of Anthony Wood, Antiquary, of Oxford, 1632−1695, Described by Himself*, 5 vols, Oxford Historical Society, 19, 21, 26, 30, 40 (1891−1900), iii, 488.

40 Examples of horizontally compressed crucifixes in stained glass can be seen in the west window of the south nave aisle of York Minster (c. 1339) and the east window of the north transept of Edington church, Wiltshire (probably 1360s). For the heavily defaced sculptures of the Five Joys of the Virgin (Annunciation, Nativity, Resurrection, Ascension and Assumption) from the dossal of the New College reredos, currently in the song room adjacent to the chapel, see Decker (as n. 30), 151−3.

41 The biblical source for the angels surrounding God's throne is Revelation 5: 11.

4.32 New College, Oxford, figure of William of Wykeham on west face of Muniment Tower

4.33 Bosom of Abraham Trinity, alabaster, English, early 15th-century (Museum of Fine Arts, Boston, Mass.)

the fact that traces of a very similar arrangement remain in Reredos II, although one must allow for the theoretical possibility that Reredos II had been influenced directly by New College rather than via Reredos I. If the image of the Trinity mentioned in the All Souls building accounts for 1440 formed part of Reredos I, as can fairly safely be assumed, it must have occupied the central of the topmost tier of niches there and in Reredos II. Confirmation that this image was an example of the so-called Seat of Mercy Trinity, the most favoured type in late medieval England, is provided by the extra-tall pedestal in Reredos II, without which the head of the seated figure of God the Father would have been at a lower level than the heads of the standing images in the adjacent niches. There must be a very good chance that the All Souls Trinity was a Bosom of Abraham Trinity, a variation on the Seat of Mercy type in which God the Father holds a napkin-like cloth enfolding small figures who are representatives of the souls of the saved (fig. 4.33). Some thirty years ago Pamela Scheingorn published a pioneering account of this complex and now rare image, in which she demonstrated that it was peculiar to late medieval

England and that it was regularly used there to represent All Saints, the thinking being that it was the Trinity on which the adoration of the whole community of the saints in heaven was focused. The inclusion of representations of saved souls in the image installed in the chapel in 1440 would have enabled it to be associated not only with All Saints, which was a component of the dedications of both the chapel and the College, but also with All Souls, the comparatively new feast which was closely linked conceptually and temporally to that of All Saints. [42] As one of the executors of King Henry V Chichele must have had some involvement with the

42   P. Sheingorn, 'The Bosom of Abraham Trinity: A Late Medieval All Saints Image', in D. Williams (ed.), *England in the Fifteenth Century*, Proceedings of the 1986 Harlaxton Symposium (Woodbridge, 1987), 273 – 95. The incorporating of the Bosom of Abraham into an image of God the Father on the south side of the canopy of the Percy tomb of *c*. 1340 at Beverley Minster is noted in T. S. R. Boase, *Death in the Middle Ages: Mortality, Judgment and Remembrance* (London, 1972), 53, although the image in question must be a portrayal of the second rather than the first person of the Trinity, on account of being shown wearing the crown of thorns. The pairing of this image with one of Christ in Judgement on the north side of the Percy tomb canopy can be seen as an anticipation of the iconography of the central images in the top two levels of the All Souls reredos as proposed in the present essay. For a discussion of related imagery in more modest funerary monuments see N. Rogers, '"*Et expecto resurrectionem mortuorum*": Images and Texts relating to the Resurrection of the Dead and the Last Judgement on English Brasses and Incised Slabs', in Morgan (as n. 37), 343 – 55. For an exposition of the theological and liturgical links between the feasts of All Saints and All Souls, see Sheingorn (as above), 290 – 3.

commissioning of the All Saints image which originally occupied the central niche of the reredos in the chapel of the same name forming the upper storey of the king's chantry chapel in Westminster Abbey (fig. 4.34).[43] The probability that the Trinity mentioned in 1440 was the very first image to be installed in any of the niches of Reredos I is evidence that it had a special importance for Chichele, and if it was a Bosom of Abraham Trinity at least part of its significance for him will surely have been its inclusion of representatives of the souls who provided the everyday name for his foundation.

The second tier of images in Reredos I will have been related either to the second or to the third tier of the New College reredos. If it resembled the second tier in having at its centre a crucifix it seems unlikely that such an image was incorporated by the same means, that is by allotting it a niche somewhat wider than the other niches. Unlike New College, where the integrity of the tiers is heavily stressed by uninterrupted cornices, the overall format of Reredos I must have been strongly vertical and it is highly likely that its niches also stressed verticality by being of uniform width and linked by continuous uprights, as they are in Reredos II. A crucifix of normal proportions, not subject to the awkward lateral compression that will have been a prominent feature of the New College image, could only have been accommodated if the uprights between the three central niches had been interrupted or suppressed altogether. The presence here of three separate niche canopies would have been justified by the presence of the flanking figures of the Virgin Mary and St John the Evangelist, but it must be said that such an arrangement has no known parallels in late medieval English altarpieces. If the middle tier of Reredos I was modelled on the third tier at New College in having a central figure of Christ

---

43   It seems not to have been noticed that there must once have been an All Saints image in the central niche of the reredos of Henry V's chantry chapel (fig. 4.34). The full form of the chapel's dedication was the Annunciation of the Blessed Virgin Mary and All Saints; W. H. St John Hope, 'The Funeral, Monument, and Chantry Chapel of King Henry the Fifth', *Archaeologia*, 65 (1913–14), 153, citing the king's will drawn up in 1415. The chapel is referred to as 'nuper [...] de Novo erecta' in July 1445; T. Rymer, *Foedera, Conventiones, Literae...*, 2nd edn, 20 vols (London, 1726–35), xi, 90. The image of All Saints in the central niche will have been removed and destroyed no later than the early years of the reign of Edward VI, as all representations of the Trinity were found particularly obnoxious by Lollards and evangelicals. Its pedestal will have resembled those of the adjacent Annunciation figures in being made very high so as to ensure that God the Father's head was not lower than the heads of the standing figures of saints in the outer niches. Significantly, this chapel succeeded a thirteenth-century chapel on the same site whose dedication was to the Trinity. The suggestion has been made that after the building of Henry V's chantry the Trinity chapel was reinstated further west, but this is at odds with the evidence that no chapel bearing that dedication existed after the building of the chantry and its chapel of All Saints; P. Binski, *Westminster Abbey and the Plantagenets: Kingship and the Representation of Power 1200–1400* (New Haven and London, 1995), 147; W. R. Lethaby, *Westminster Abbey and the King's Craftsmen* (London, 1906), 353.

flanked on each side by apostles none of these difficulties would have arisen. As will become clear presently, Reredos II did not incorporate a central standing figure of Christ but finding a worthy new use for such an image displaced from Reredos I would not have been difficult. On balance, it is more likely that the imagery of the central tier of Reredos I showed Christ and six apostles than a Crucifixion group with four further figures. This iconography would have been much easier to accommodate within the architecture of Reredos I and its strong emphasis on the apostles would have made it appropriate to a collegiate body which resembled all religious communities in having Christ's disciples as its ultimate model.[44]

The lowest tier of Reredos I will have followed New College to the extent that its central image showed the Virgin Mary holding the Christ child. The Virgin was one of the dedicatees of the College and her presence was effectively de rigueur in any assembly of saintly figures. The other four niches above the high altar will have been occupied by saints connected in some special way to the chapel or the College. The strongest candidates must be the four Latin doctors, for it was to them that the chapel was dedicated. By their placing in outer positions and to either side of the altar rather than above it, the first and seventh figures in this tier were made slightly subordinate and there can be little doubt that these were St Thomas of Canterbury and St Edward the Confessor. St Thomas was one of the named patrons of All Souls and he and St Edward were both patrons of the college which Chichele had founded in 1422 at his birthplace, Higham Ferrers in Northamptonshire. These were also the principal patrons of the offices held by Chichele and Henry VI, and their representation here would have invited viewers to relate them to the similarly scaled standing figures of the living king and the archbishop installed during the 1440s in the niches on the front of the gatehouse facing the High Street (figs 4.35, 36).[45] As a martyr St Thomas outranked St Edward and his image will therefore have occupied the dexter position.

---

44 For the significance of the apostles for academic colleges see T. Ayers, *The Medieval Stained Glass of Merton College, Oxford*, 2 vols, Corpus Vitrearum Medii Aevi, Great Britain, 6 (Oxford, 2013), i, pp. lxxxix–xc, 48.

45 Jones (as n. 4), 173. At Chichele's invitation Henry VI accepted the role of titular co-founder of All Souls.

4.35 All Souls College, figure of King Henry VI from High Street front of gatehouse

4.36 All Souls College, figure of Archbishop Henry Chichele from High Street front of gatehouse

A reconstruction of the iconography of Reredos II

The thirteen-figure groups of images which occupied the first and second tiers of Reredos II can be identified with a fair measure of confidence. The central niche of the first tier will have housed, or rather rehoused, the Trinity installed in the analogous niche of Reredos I in the early 1440s. As in Reredos I angels are effectively the only possibility for the full-size niches to either side of the Trinity image, and that identification is corroborated by the clear indications of closed wings in the 1872 photograph's record of the outlines generated by the painting of the backs of the niches when the images were in place (fig. 4.5). At the outer edges of this tier there are very simple canopy-less niches which would have provided suitable settings for kneeling patronal images comparable to those of Richard II and William of Wykeham that are likely to have occupied the analogous niches in the topmost tier of the New College reredos. Henry VI and Chichele must be the strongest candidates for the outer niches at All Souls. The occupant of the central niche in the second tier can be identified by a detail of the canopy: a large boss in the form of a rose, one of the most important symbols of the Virgin Mary (fig. 4.37).[46] The narrowness of the niches occupied by the Trinity and the Virgin compared to all the other niches of Reredos II could well perpetuate a feature of Reredos I, but in hierarchical terms the variation seems anomalous and its significance is not now apparent.[47] The two groups of six niches flanking that which housed the central image of the Virgin can only have contained images of all the apostles, whose accommodation here will have been the principal reason for including thirteen niches in all three tiers. Since the infant Christ would automatically have been present in his mother's arms, this entire row of figures will have been readable to some extent as Christ and the apostles, although late medieval viewers would have been habituated to seeing the Virgin occupying a central place among the apostles in representations of Pentecost, the event which inaugurated the disciples' mission to spread Christ's word throughout the world.[48]

In the next level down the central feature was a retable in the form of a Crucifixion tableau. This was separated from the high altar by a comparatively small area of plain masonry that will have been occupied by a dossal, probably a textile hanging which would have been changed in accordance with the liturgical seasons, like the frontal on the altar itself. Enough of the Crucifixion tableau remains to show that it was a completely new piece of work, and its positioning only a short distance above the high altar was surely influenced by the very large Crucifixion groups which dominated the comparatively recent reredoses at Winchester Cathedral and St Albans Abbey (figs 4.1, 10, 16,

---

46 Of course not every rose-decorated vault boss has an explicitly Marian significance, but this is the only example among the 33 original image niches of the All Souls reredos. A slightly earlier instance of the use of the rose to signal the proximity of a focus of Marian devotion is to be found at Canterbury Cathedral, on the spandrels of the arch leading into the Lady Chapel from the north-west transept.

47 This choice might well have been influenced by the need to centre the niches below the figures of Christ and the standing angels in the tympanum. A nearly contemporary parallel for the narrowness of the central niches compared to those that flank them is to be found in the reredos in the chantry chapel of Prince Arthur at Worcester Cathedral, but there the variation is justified by the small scale of the imagery in the central niche. If one assumes, as is done here, that the high altar at All Souls continued to be that first used in 1442, its width will have been major constraint on the disposition of the niches in the central section of Reredos II.

48 Mary is included among the apostles as a witness to the Ascension in Acts 1: 14. Despite the lack of scriptural authority, representations of Pentecost showing her placed centrally among the apostles are frequent in medieval art; R. Bäumer and L. Scheffczyk (eds), *Marienlexikon*, 6 vols (St Ottilien, 1988–94), v, 188–91.

4.37 All Souls College, reredos, vault of niche 7 of tier 2

17). Flanking the tableau are two niches set considerably higher than the eight niches in the lowest tier and it is reasonable to suppose that they contained John Massyngham's images of St Thomas of Canterbury and St Edward the Confessor. The promotion of these two major English saints to more honoured positions than those allotted to them in Reredos I is perhaps a little surprising, but the change can be attributed to pragmatic considerations arising out of the need to devise a coherent scheme for the eight outer niches which incorporated Massyngham's images of the four Latin doctors. Beyond any reasonable doubt the four new figures showed the evangelists and were placed on the dexter side. The authors of the Gospels and Latin Christendom's principal teachers were frequently associated in late medieval art, and such a grouping had an obvious aptness in an academic college.[49] The inclusion of the evangelists here would have generated some duplication with the apostles on the level above, but a similar repetition is to be seen in the nearly contemporary sculptures in Henry VII's Chapel at Westminster Abbey.[50]

---

49 The Latin doctors are the only saints shown on the College seal made in 1443; Marks and Williamson (as n. 27), 237. See also P. Horden, 'The Origins of "All Souls" and its Significance for Henry Chichele', in C. M. Barron and C. Burgess (eds), *Memory and Commemoration in Medieval England*, Proceedings of the 2008 Harlaxton Symposium (Donington, 2010), 292–308 at 304.

50 J. T. Micklethwaite, 'Notes on the Imagery of Henry the Seventh's Chapel', *Archaeologia*, 47 (1882–3), 361–80 at 362, pl. X.

Unique to Reredos II are the raised position of the five central niches relative to the eight outer niches and the way in which, in the upper two tiers, the three central niches are set higher than the two that flank them (fig. 4.1). The differences in the levels of the central niches will have given scope for a hierarchical ordering of the images occupying those niches. In the first tier there could well have been an attempt to show the orders of angels and in the second tier it can safely be assumed that the images of apostles flanking the central statue of the Virgin Mary were St Peter (on the dexter side) and St Paul, who is routinely shown as an apostle in medieval art. The occupants of the next pair of niches working outwards are most likely to have been St Andrew (next to his brother Peter) and St John.

The Crucifixion tableau is the hardest part of Reredos II to visualise in its original state (fig. 4.10). The obliteration of the imagery in Edward VI's reign was inevitably thorough but enough of the settings of the images remains to show that this ensemble was unique. The feature that most obviously sets it apart from other late medieval representations of the Crucifixion is the asymmetrical placing of the cross, and it cannot now be known what prompted that choice. Possibly the only other example in northern European art of relatively recent date was that in the central panel of the triptych of *The Seven Sacraments* painted in the early 1440s by Rogier van der Weyden (fig. 4.38), and it is conceivable that the source of the asymmetry of the All Souls Crucifixion tableau was a work by Rogier or some now-lost work influenced by that greatly admired artist.[51] The nineteenth-century figure of St Mary Magdalen crouching at the foot of the cross occupies an area of hacking back visible in the 1872 photograph (fig. 4.5), and it incorporates at the rear a very small portion of the original draperies. One can only guess why an abnormally large amount of space should have been provided on the sinister side of the crucifix but it is possible that it was occupied by several figures and not merely a standing figure of St John of the kind normally found in this position. The presence of the Magdalen raises the possibility that, like the central panel of Rogier's altarpiece (and unlike all extant English late medieval Crucifixions), the

---

51 In the central panel of Rogier's triptych the asymmetry of the cross is relative to the picture surface and the logic of its displacement to the viewer's left arises out of its relation to the portrayal of the church interior which is its setting. Careful study of the position of the foot of the cross in relation to the tiled floor of the nave shows that the leftwards displacement has been reduced, presumably to achieve the desired disposition of other elements in the design, and notwithstanding the bizarre consequence that the sinister arm of the cross is made to disappear behind a part of the architecture that is further away than the piers between which the cross stands. These anomalies have no counterparts in the spatially unspecific setting of the All Souls Crucifixion tableau.

4.38 *Triptych of the Seven Sacraments* by Rogier van der Weyden, 200 × 97 cm (Antwerp, Koninklijk Museum voor Schone Kunsten), central panel

space round the cross was relatively densely populated by figures whose individual responses to the sight of the crucified Christ were carefully portrayed.[52] Whatever the details, the imagery here must have differed greatly from the traditional images above the rood screen, through the central door of which the reredos had to be viewed by those not entitled to enter the choir. Quite a few of the still-surviving features of the Crucifixion tableau elude explanation. For example, it is not clear why part of the coving on Christ's sinister side should be more recessed than the rest and endowed with blind tracery, and there is much about the nineteenth-century recreation of the flying angels to either side of Christ which looks awkward and unconvincing.[53]

What was the totality of the imagery in Reredoses I and II meant to convey to its viewers? The imagery in the tympanum would have reminded practically everyone who saw it of the painted dooms installed at the east ends of the naves of countless late medieval parish churches, the great prominence of which was designed to keep the minds of the faithful focused on the inevitability of final judgement. But the comparison only highlights the fact that the All Souls tympanum omits a very high proportion of what contemporaries would have expected to find in any large-scale portrayal of the Last Judgement. It is possible that Chichele considered that minatory iconography was inappropriate in the chapel of a community of theologically sophisticated academics. Another possible explanation centres on the two lines of resurrected dead who calmly approach the throne of judgement, for these were surely intended to represent those whose souls had completed the required time in purgatory (shortened in all or most cases by the prayers of the living), who had been in the place of rest awaiting the day of judgement, and for whom the process of being judged could hardly have amounted to more than confirmation that heaven was their destination. It is reasonable to assume that the tympanum was in place by 1440 when an image of the Trinity was installed in the topmost central niche of Reredos I, and if that was indeed the case, and

---

52 The motif of the asymmetrically placed crucifix is to be seen in two panel paintings, now in the Louvre, which were supplied c. 1389 – 95 by Jean de Beaumetz and his workshop for monks' cells at the charterhouse of Champmol; P. Roelofs (ed.), *Johan Maelwael. Nijmegen – Paris – Dijon. Art around 1400*, catalogue of exhibition, Rijksmuseum (Amsterdam, 2017 – 18), 102 – 3. In both paintings the asymmetry can readily be understood as a consequence of the decision to include the figure of a kneeling Carthusian monk at the same scale at the figures of the sacred personages. The ultimately Italian motif of the Magdalen clinging to the cross was already known to English manuscript painters by around 1330; Marks and Morgan (as n. 37), 78 – 9. However, there appears to be no extant evidence of its currency in English sculpture prior to the making of Reredos II.

53 Still original work, and identifiable as such by the presence of original polychromy, are small parts of the outer flying angel on Christ's dexter side and the inner angel on the sinister side.

if the Trinity was an example of that distinctively English type, the Bosom of Abraham Trinity, as was suggested earlier, it will have been apparent to attentive viewers that there was an upwards progression from the corporealised souls in their place of rest with the Trinity to the resurrected bodies about to be judged and admitted straightaway to heaven. The principal message of the imagery in the upper parts of Reredos I (retained in Reredos II) was surely that salvation was readily attainable by all through God's grace, and it would seem not unreasonable to associate that message with Chichele's unremitting struggle against the Lollards, who scorned both purgatory and prayers for the individual dead. Even if the Trinity mentioned in 1440 was of the standard Seat of Mercy type, it would have performed a not dissimilar function to that attributed here to the postulated Bosom of Abraham Trinity, for by the fifteenth century it had become settled orthodoxy that the souls of those fully cleansed in purgatory experienced the beatific vision of God immediately and did not have to wait until the completion of the Last Judgement.[54]

The main iconographic changes introduced in Reredos II can be seen as augmenting the emphasis in the tympanum of Reredos I on the attainability of salvation. The installation of a quasi-pictorial Crucifixion tableau set not far above the altar highlighted the redemptive power of Christ's sacrifice as regularly re-enacted in the mass. Moreover the filling of the entire width of the east wall with saints' images will have greatly increased the capacity of the whole to bring home to all beholders the number and potency of the array of intercessors to whom they could address prayers for the dead in purgatory or on their own behalf. Supplications of the first kind are

---

54 P. Binski, *Medieval Death: Ritual and Representation* (London, 1996), 214. The view that the resurrected dead in the All Souls reredos represent those whose purgation is complete runs counter to the interpretation followed by the Victorian restorer, who showed the figures on Christ's sinister side anticipating their condemnation. In the well-known and unique miniature illustrating the Office of the Dead in the early fifteenth-century Rohan Book of Hours (Paris, Bibliothèque Nationale, MS latin 9471, f. 159r) a dying man addresses the Godhead (who is shown as both Father and Son) with the words of the *commendatio animae* based on Psalm 31 (32) and God responds: 'Pour tes pechiez penitence feras. Au jour du Jugement avecques moy seras.'; cf. Binski (as above), 42, 211. The wide divergence of view regarding the severity of the punishments in purgatory among late medieval Suffolk testators (for which see E. Duffy, 'Provision against Purgatory: Wingfield College, Suffolk', in idem, *Royal Books and Holy Bones: Essays in Medieval Christianity* (London, 2018), 239 – 53) is only one manifestation of the general lack of clarity prevailing in medieval Christendom about what would take place between death and the Last Judgement. Confusion between purgatory and hell is apparent in the work of some distinguished late medieval painters, for example the main artists of the Bedford Hours (London, British Library, MS Add 18850, f. 157r) and the Hours of Catherine of Cleves (New York, Morgan Library and Museum, MS M.945, ff. 105v, 107r). On the early fourteenth-century controversies regarding the Beatific Vision see C. W. Bynum, *The Resurrection of the Body in Western Christianity*, 200 – 1336 (New York, 1995), 283 – 9; Sheingorn (as n. 42), 287 – 8; Binski (as above), 212 – 14 and passim.

likely to have been foremost in the mind of Archbishop Chichele, who conceived of his College as a chantry for those who had died in England's wars with France. Chichele's main contribution to the religious life of England as a whole was his vigorous response to the threat which Lollardy posed to traditional religion, and an important component of that response was the fostering of an increase in the splendour and ceremoniousness of church services and processions. The prominence that was almost certainly accorded in Reredos I to St Thomas of Canterbury and St Edward the Confessor would have been fully in line with Chichele's desire to promote and enhance the cults of major national saints. But the main significance of this pairing will surely have been that it commemorated the extraordinary alliance between the English church and crown which Chichele and Henry VI's father had forged in order to wage war on the kingdom's spiritual and military enemies, the Lollards and the French. As befitted the chapel of an academic foundation, the saints populating the reredos were entirely male, except of course for St Mary, who will have been shown holding the Christ child and who in any case could not be left out of any large assembly of saints. The import of a complete apostolic college ranged above the principal source of revealed truth in scripture (the authors of the Gospels) and the main exponents of authoritative commentary and interpretation (the four Latin doctors) would not have been lost on anyone aware that part of the purpose behind the founding of new academic colleges was to boost the training of learned men to become parish priests charged with a mission to instruct the laity in their faith, and by implication to improve their resistance to heresy.[55] Reredoses I and II will both have presented a vision of the church triumphant that is likely to have been found compelling not only by academics but by those of the wider community who chose to enter the chapel through the street door provided specifically for their use.[56] As was still being

---

55 It has been suggested that the Latin doctors 'may have been included in the College's iconography as a self-conscious gesture against the memory of Oxford Wyclifism'; E. Duffy, 'The Four Latin Doctors in the Late Middle Ages', in idem (as n. 54), 275–88 at 278. To the examples of pairing of the Latin doctors with the evangelists noted ibid., 279, 285–6, may be added the roof corbels of the quasi-crossing at the east end of the nave of St Peter Hungate, Norwich, a setting which resembles the All Souls reredos to the extent that the central image here represents Christ in Judgement (fig. 4.31). For the chantry aspect of All Souls see E. F. Jacob, 'All Souls College', in VCH: Oxfordshire, iii (1954), 173–83 at 173. For Chichele's upgrading of the feasts of nationally important saints (St George, St David, St Chad, St Winifred and St John of Beverley) see E. F. Jacob and H. C. Johnson (eds), The Register of Henry Chichele, Archbishop of Canterbury, 1414–1443, 4 vols, Canterbury and York Society, 42, 435–47 (1937–47), iii, 8–10, 14–16 (1 April and 7 May 1416); J. Catto, 'Religious Change under Henry V', in G. L. Harriss (ed.), Henry V: The Practice of Kingship (Oxford, 1985), 97–115 at 107–8.

56 This door, which connected Catte Street to the west of the College with the vestibule south of the antechapel, was blocked only in 1784; Jones (as n. 4), 184.

acknowledged in the Ten Articles promulgated by the nascent Church of England in 1536, images of the saints had the capacity to serve as 'kindlers and stirrers of men's minds',[57] and the sight of an ensemble of sumptuously painted and gilded imagery such as that which adorned the successive reredoses at All Souls could hardly have failed to ignite religious fervour in the breasts of virtually all of its beholders.

The sources of the architecture of Reredos II

The architectural design of Reredos II owes much to the late fourteenth-century reredos at New College (figs 4.1, 22). The concept of bands of niches arranged in tiers occupying the full width of the east wall is the most obvious debt but there are a further two: the gradation in the heights of the central niches and the way in which that gradation is made to echo the curvature of the easternmost roof truss.[58] The other most important source drawn on in the overall design was the high altar reredos at St Albans Abbey (fig. 4.17), whence came the heavy stress placed on the vertical. But whereas at St Albans and its forerunner in Winchester Cathedral (fig. 4.16) the verticality was to a considerable extent a by-product of the decision to incorporate wide and shallow buttresses in order to stabilise what is essentially a tall and thin freestanding wall, at All Souls the emphasis on the vertical must have been purely a matter of aesthetic choice, because the reredos forms an integral part of a thick structural wall which had no need of buttressing. Not surprisingly, the planar complexity that was a corollary of the buttressing at St Albans and Winchester was not reproduced at All Souls. As has already been noted, Reredos II's retable in the form of a Crucifixion tableau was influenced by the central imagery at St Albans, although the size of the tableau was inevitably severely restricted by the need to combine it with the concept of tiered niches inherited from New College and Reredos I. That the designer of Reredos II was consciously drawing on Winchester and St Albans is evident from the canopies to the lowest tier of niches, for these imitate the two distinct types of tall canopy used over the doors in the two reredoses (figs 4.16, 17, 39, 40).

---

57   D. Wilkins (ed.), *Concilia Magnae Britanniae et Hiberniae*, 4 vols (London, 1737), iii, 821. Compare Thomas More's imagining of music in Utopia as something which 'animos auditorium mirum in modum afficiat, penetret, incendat'; E. L. Surtz and J. H. Hexter (eds), *Utopia* (New Haven and London, 1965), 236.

58   The elaborate and steeply pitched hammer-beam roof introduced into New College's chapel in the late nineteenth century differs radically from the original tie-beam roof and destroys the relationship established in the late fourteenth century between the profile of the easternmost roof truss enclosing the top of the reredos and the graduated heights of the upper tiers of niches in the reredos.

4.40 St Albans Abbey, high
altar reredos, canopy above
left-hand door

4.41 St Albans Abbey,
pedestal of image niche in
northern extension to high
altar reredos

A slight bias towards the more recent St Albans reredos is evident
from the blind tracery applied to the wall surface on either side of the
pedestals (figs 4.40, 41) and from the incorporation into some of the
pedestals to the right of the altar of heraldic shields borne by flying
angels (figs 4.39, 40).[59]

A striking feature of the image niches of Reredos II when viewed at
close quarters is the contrast between the wholeheartedly Perpendicular
character of the outwards-facing parts of their canopies, and the
strong admixture of curvilinear or flowing tracery forms used within
the canopies (fig. 4.6). Curvilinear tracery was apparently invented
in England shortly before 1300 and, although the English were
abandoning it in favour of Perpendicular tracery by the middle years of
the fourteenth century, it was taken up on the Continent around that
time and remained in use there well into the sixteenth century. From
around 1450 curvilinear tracery began to enjoy a limited revival in

---

59   The pedestals in the central section of the St Albans reredos now lack blind tracery, but clear indications
     remain that it was present originally. It is possible that the Winchester reredos also made use of this
     detail, but as it does not appear in photographs taken before the late nineteenth-century restoration
     there is also a possibility that the restorers copied it from St Albans.

4.39 All Souls College,
reredos, niches 7–10 of tier 3

England, both in architecture at full scale and in the 'micro-architecture' of major church fittings. An early and fairly closely dated example of the latter is some of the tracery decoration on the wooden vaulted canopy belonging to the monument of Archbishop John Kempe (died 1454) in Canterbury Cathedral, which can probably be assumed to have been made by London-based craftsmen (fig. 4.42).[60] There is no sign of curvilinear tracery in the Winchester reredos but it is discreetly present at St Albans (fig. 4.43). The total absence of curvilinear elements from Chichele's work at All Souls is no more than what one would expect to find in Perpendicular architecture of *c.* 1440. Chichele's master mason Richard Chevynton seems to have been concurrently master mason to Abingdon Abbey, but anything that he might have achieved there vanished with the near-total destruction of the abbey's buildings soon after its suppression in 1538. By far the most important monastic house in the vicinity of Oxford, Abingdon appears to have completely rebuilt its church starting in the late fourteenth century, when its master mason was William Wynford, the architect of all of William of Wykeham's buildings.[61] Chevynton's artistic formation in the mainstream south-western Perpendicular tradition is evident in the kinship between the All Souls sedilia and the approximately 80-year-old sedilia in the presbytery of St Peter's Abbey at Gloucester, the fountainhead of Perpendicular regionally and to some extent nationally. The rear walls of both sedilia are decorated with twice-repeated, two-light blind tracery units, a visually simple design but one that seems not to recur elsewhere in such a context (figs 4.25, 44, 45). The most attractive features of the All Souls sedilia are the miniature vaults of very varied design in the canopies over each of the three seats (fig. 4.44). The three stones needed for these

---

60   For the documentary evidence for Kempe's monument see Wilson (as n. 37), 481–2. There is no adequate general account either of fourteenth-century English curvilinear tracery or of its limited revival in the fifteenth and early sixteenth centuries. A key figure in the revival was Reginald Ely (fl. 1438–71), whose work on the earliest phase of King's College Chapel, Cambridge, and Burwell church, Cambridgeshire, reveals strong influence from the approximately 100-year-old non-Perpendicular works of William Ramsey, king's chief master mason 1336–49. The use of non-Perpendicular tracery in high-status decorative brickwork, exemplified by the vault of the vestibule at the top of the stair in the great tower of Tattersall Castle, in progress in 1446, is not surprising, given that the designers of ambitious brick buildings included men who were either Netherlandish or much influenced by Netherlandish work; J. Goodall, *The English Castle, 1066–1650* (New Haven and London, 2011), 348–50, 356. Curvilinear tracery occurs in some of the miniature vaults of the 'prayer niches' in the Teesdale marble base of the shrine of St William of York, installed in York Minster in the 1470s and now in the Yorkshire Museum, York (not currently displayed); C. Wilson, *The Shrines of St William of York* (York, 1977), 19–21. Unambiguously Perpendicular tracery occurs in only two of the image niches at All Souls (tier 2, niche 4 and tier 3, niche 9, fig. 4.47) but there are hints of it in other niches.

61   R. E. G. Kirk (ed.), *Accounts of the Obedientiars of Abingdon Abbey*, Camden Society, new series, 51 (1892), 28; M. Biddle, H. T. Lambrick and J. N. L. Myres, 'The Early History of Abingdon, Berkshire, and its Abbey', *Medieval Archaeology*, 12 (1968), 26–69 at 48–9.

4.42 Canterbury Cathedral, detail of canopy of monument to Archbishop John Kempe

4.43 St Albans Abbey, high altar reredos, vaults of small niches above dexter arm of crucifix

canopies were acquired from one of the Burford quarries in 1441.[62] By *c.* 1440 niches with canopies incorporating miniature vaults of complex and contrasting design had become a frequently occurring feature of high-quality micro-architectural ensembles in England (fig. 4.34), and

---

62   'Et solut' pro tribus magnis lapidibus emptis apud Wychslad' pro hovellis presbiterij fiendis precium pec' xviij d. iiij s. vj d.'; *Building Accounts*, 231. The use made of the stone is misconstrued here and in Jacob (as n. 4), 125 – 6. The English word 'hovel' and the Latinised version of it are both fairly frequently applied to the canopies of niches in medieval English texts; R. Willis, *On the Architectural Nomenclature of the Middle Ages* (Cambridge, 1844), 69; R. K. Ashdowne, D. R. Howlett and R. E. Latham, *Dictionary of Medieval Latin from British Sources* (Oxford, 1977 – 2013), 1181. 'Presbiterium' clearly means 'sedilia' rather than 'presbytery', a term usually applied to the sanctuaries of larger and more elaborate churches than the chapel at All Souls. The sedilia at Gloucester whose design influenced the All Souls sedilia must be the 'presbiterium' mentioned in the abbey's early 15th-century chronicle (W. H. Hart (ed.), *Historia et Cartularium Monasterii Sancti Petri Gloucestriae*, 3 vols, Rolls Series, 33 (1863 – 7), i, 50), although the reference has been misinterpreted as the eastern part of the choir in all the secondary literature. As well as a miniature vault, each of the three large stones for the All Souls sedilia encompassed a three-sided projecting canopy and sections of the rear parts of the niches.

4.44 All Souls College,
sedilia, rear wall tracery and
vaults

4.45 Gloucester Abbey
(now Gloucester Cathedral),
detail of high altar sedilia

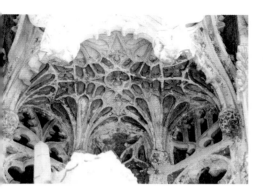
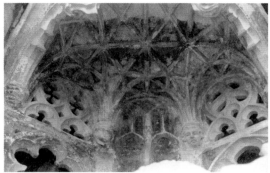

4.46 All Souls College, reredos, vault of niche 3 of tier 3

4.47 All Souls College, reredos, vault of niche 9 of tier 3

the relative inconspicuousness of such vaults, coupled with the fact that their designing must have been time-consuming, suggests that they were seen as the hallmark of a luxurious form of micro-architecture available only to particularly rich patrons. By the end of the fifteenth century the number of examples had multiplied, and it is therefore not surprising to find that in Reredos II each of the 33 partly original niche canopies incorporates a different design (figs 4.6, 46, 47). The more richly treated vaults are based on fan vaults and are concentrated in the lower tiers where they can be seen better. Four of the vaults incorporate curvilinear tracery motifs (fig. 4.6).[63]

Alongside the vaults, the main enrichment of the interior of the niches of Reredos II is small-scale tracery. This is confined to the upper parts of each of the three sides and serves as a kind of backdrop to the heads of the images (fig. 4.39). Tracery in this position, still a great rarity at the end of the fifteenth century, seems to have made its first appearance in England in the Beauchamp Chapel at Warwick, which was begun in 1443, although there exist a few earlier niches elsewhere in which the upper parts of the sides are treated as single lights. The tracery in the niches at All Souls consists of a central two-light unit of blind tracery flanked by pierced tracery units of similar design but with single lights below them. This combination of elements seems to have been anticipated in England only in the niches of the lowest tier of the high altar reredos at Winchester and in their close copies at St

---

63   The original total was 34 but niche 1 in tier 1 was destroyed in the 1660s (fig. 4.5). An early and potentially influential example of an ensemble of very varied miniature vaults is in the row of niches above the west entrance to Westminster Abbey. If, as seems likely, these date from the closing years of the fourteenth century, they will have been designed by Henry Yevele, master mason to Westminster Abbey and king's chief master mason.

Albans (fig. 4.48).[64] The unheralded appearance at Winchester of niches incorporating blind tracery units flanked by pierced tracery can be explained if one supposes that the designer had encountered the concept in the carved wooden retables that were being exported throughout much of Western Europe from the southern Low Countries, where specialist workshops had been established in several centres by c. 1400. It is easy to see how the concept of niches with blind tracery flanked by pierced tracery could have arisen from the process of making wooden retables whose micro-architectural components were inserted into box-like outer casings, for the solid backs of the latter would have been clearly visible through a centrally placed unit of pierced tracery. By a considerable margin the earliest surviving retable incorporating niches treated in this way is that on the high altar of the parish church of St Reinold in Dortmund, which has long been dated to the second decade of the century and attributed to the apparently Brussels-based workshop of the so-called Master of Hakendover. Although there appear to be no photographs in the public domain which show the architecture of the Dortmund niches clearly, enough can be glimpsed in those that are available to show that it is essentially similar in conception to the niches of Brussels- or Brabant-made retables dating from the late fifteenth and early sixteenth centuries (fig. 4.49). The next earliest examples of Dortmund-type niches to have survived belong to a retable of c. 1460 or slightly earlier in the parish church of the small village of Ternant on the western borders of Burgundy, but here the basic conception has been complicated by the substitution for the central tracery unit of a non-standard and distinctly secular-looking oriel window

64   The blind tracery-lined niches in the panel of rich architectural decoration above the door to the sacristy in the Beauchamp Chapel are likely to reflect the original appearance of the reredos of the immediately adjacent altar. The possibility that earlier fifteenth-century examples once existed is raised by the carefully detailed portrayals of image niches in the Sherborne Missal (British Library, MS Add. 74236), for example at pp. 218, 249, 276, 376. The niches with sides treated as blind foiled lights in the early fifteenth-century reredoses of the Lady Chapel at Christchurch Priory and in the north transept of St Cuthbert's at Wells are anticipated by the niches of the early 1390s on the Middle Gate of Winchester College. There is no reason to suppose continuity with the 'prayer niches' of English shrine bases or with the French and French-influenced examples of tracery-lined niches discussed in T. A. Heslop, 'The Episcopal Seals of Richard of Bury', in Coldstream and Draper (as n. 25), 154–62 at 157. For the Winchester and St Albans reredoses see G. W. Kitchin, The Great Screen of Winchester Cathedral (Winchester, 1891); H. H. Gibbs, An Account of the High Altar Screen in the Cathedral Church of Saint Albans (St Albans, 1890); P. Lindley, 'The "Great Screen" of Winchester Cathedral, Part II: Style and Date', Burlington Magazine, 135 (1993), 797–807 at 797–803; idem, 'The Great Screen and its Context', in M. Henig and P. Lindley (eds), Alban and St Albans: Roman and Medieval Architecture, Art and Archaeology, British Archaeological Association Conference Transactions, 24 (Leeds, 2001), 256–70.

4.48 St Albans Abbey, image niche in southern extension to high altar reredos

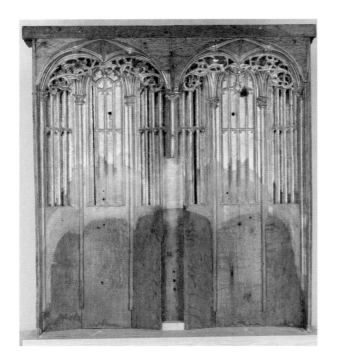

4.49 *Retable of Holy Kindred* from chapel of St Anne in Dominican nuns' convent of Hertoginnedal, Audeghem, Brussels, niches photographed after removal of figures during conservation work, 1968. (Brussels, Musées Royaux d'Art et d'Histoire, photo: KIK-IRPA, Brussels)

4.50 Ternant (Nièvre), church of Saint-Roch, *Retable of Passion*, left-hand niche

(fig. 4.50).[65] The evidence of Dortmund and Ternant suffices to show that niches with blind tracery flanked by pierced tracery were an established feature of Brabantine retable design well before the Winchester reredos was put in hand. Contrary to what its date of *c.* 1500 might lead one to expect, Reredos II at All Souls adheres more closely to the Dortmund-Ternant concept than do the lowest niches at Winchester and St Albans, since all the sides of the niches are treated as solid walls occupying the same planes as the tracery, whereas at Winchester and St Albans the sides occupy different planes from the pierced tracery

---

65 Evidence for the early fifteenth-century importation of works of art from the Low Countries into England, Scotland and Wales is assembled in K. Woods, *Imported Images: Netherlandish Late Gothic Sculpture in England c.* 1400–c. 1550 (Donington, 2007), 108–9, 112–3. For the Dortmund retable and the Passion retable at Ternant in the context of the origins of tracery-lined niches in Brabantine altarpieces see L. F. Jacobs, *Early Netherlandish Carved Altarpieces, 1380–1550: Medieval Tastes and Mass Marketing* (Cambridge, 1998), 118–9. For the Holy Family retable from Audeghem (fig. 4.49) see G. Derveaux-Van Ussel, 'Het retabel met de "Maagdschap van Sint-Anna" uit de Sint-Annakapel van Oudergem', *Bulletin des Musées Royaux d'Art et d'Histoire*, 47 (1975), 5–128 at 101. For Dortmund, Ternant and Audeghem see also R. de Boodt, 'Catalogue des retables bruxellois', in B. D'Hainaut-Zveny (ed.), *Miroirs du Sacré. Les Retables sculptés à Bruxelles XVᵉ–XVIᵉ siècles. Productions, Formes et Usages* (Brussels, 2005), 154–225 at 172–3, 192, 203–4.

in the upper parts (figs 4.39, 48).[66] This evidence that the designer of the All Souls reredos was influenced both by the St Albans reredos and by the kind of Netherlandish sources on which it and the Winchester reredos drew suggests a high degree of self-consciousness regarding the provenance of artistic ideas, something for which late medieval architects and craftsmen have rarely been given credit by art historians.

The tracery patterns employed in the backs and sides of the All Souls niches are mostly rather generic curvilinear designs but a few bespeak contact with the micro-architecture of Brabantine retables and possibly also with the region's architecture at full scale. At the centre of the two niches to the right of the Crucifixion tableau there is blind tracery incorporating a concave-sided polygon generated by adjacent circular forms, a motif much favoured in the late fifteenth- and sixteenth-century window tracery of Brabant, although hexagons are a great deal commoner there than pentagons (figs 4.51, 52). In the niche to the immediate right of the Crucifixion tableau the heads of the central lights in the pierced tracery units are of a closely related concave-sided form which occurs frequently in the openwork pendant foiling of Brabantine retables (fig. 4.53). There appear to be no other examples of either of these patterns in any English masonry structure dating from c.1500.

The most conspicuous non-standard feature of the architecture of Reredos II is the set of four uprights that enclose and separate the central niches of the upper tiers, the two outermost of which are continued down so as to enclose the Crucifixion tableau above the altar (figs 4.1, 10). The rectangular horizontal section of these features contrasts strikingly with the uprights in the outer parts of the reredos, which have the kind of compound section one would expect to find in an ambitious work of micro-architecture dating from c. 1500. It is possible that an influence on the designer had been the simply treated uprights in some much earlier reredos, such as that in the choir of Christchurch Priory (fig. 4.15), and if that was the case it would be further evidence that his commitment to the Perpendicular aesthetic was less than complete.[67] What label should be applied to these uprights is not obvious, but despite their considerable depth the term

---

66 At Winchester Cathedral the sides of these niches are at right angles to the front plane whereas at St Albans they are slightly angled. The curious concept of niches whose upper parts are half-hexagonal in plan and whose lower parts are rectangular in plan appears to derive from the late fourteenth-century niches on the Middle Gate of Winchester College, designed by William Wynford.

67 The possibility of influence from the mid-fourteenth-century high altar reredos at Christchurch Priory is reinforced by the partial parallel that its lowest central scene furnishes for the way in which the interruption of the two central strips caused by the Crucifixion tableau is mitigated by including similar strips at the edges of the cloth of honour.

4.51 All Souls reredos, detail of tracery in niche 6 of tier 3

4.52 Mechelen, Collegiate church of St Rombout, west face of west tower, tracery of clearstorey-level windows

'strip' seems appropriate as it conveys their rudimentary and barely architectural character and highlights their most eye-catching feature, the decoration of their front faces with small-scale blind tracery. It is clear that the designer was going out of his way to make this decoration as inconsequential looking as possible, for although most of it consists of simple curvilinear designs made up of single small and frequently repeated motifs, the lengths of the different patterns are conspicuously irregular and they give way here and there to vertical tracery lights. In the context of an exercise in Perpendicular micro-architecture the erratic and scrappy decoration of the strips is anomalous to a degree that can hardly be overstated, for the chief characteristics of Perpendicular, which distinguish it from all other national traditions of Late Gothic architecture, are its systemic rigour and its unwavering focus on overall effect rather than on variety of detail. The inconspicuousness of the varied miniature vaults within the image niches of the reredos ensured that they did not pose a significant threat to the Perpendicular aesthetic of consistency and regularity, but any properly trained fifteenth- or early sixteenth-century English architect would probably have looked askance at the randomised decoration of the strips. What then is the

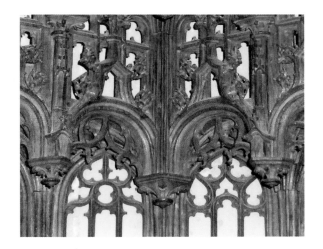

4.53 *Retable of St George* from Great Crossbowmen's Guild chapel of Notre-Dame-du-Dehors, Leuven (Brussels, Musées Royaux d'Art et d'Histoire), detail of canopy work in central section

explanation for its presence here? At least part of the answer would appear to be the same as that proposed earlier in connection with the question of the origin of the non-English features of the tracery within the niches: exposure to influence from the contemporary Netherlandish art.

During the late fifteenth and early sixteenth centuries Ghent- and Bruges-based workshops produced large numbers of high-quality books of hours which are notable for their generous allowances of large illuminations on textless pages and for their wide borders incorporating what were effectively still lifes showing assortments of non-sacred motifs. There appear to have been effectively no rules about what sorts of motifs could be included, and they were arranged in a conspicuously asymmetrical and casual-looking way calculated to display the painters' illusionistic skill. The only published book of hours in which the borders are predominantly made up of panels filled by Gothic tracery patterns is the late fifteenth-century Croy-Arenberg Hours, whose calendar indicates that it was made for the English market.[68] Unlike the borders in most comparable books of hours, asymmetry is not extended here to the widths of the inner and outer borders, but their content is highly asymmetrical. On the page showing a bust of Christ as Salvator Mundi, the rendering of three-dimensional architectural motifs in the left-hand border is notably inconsequential and completely

---

68   M. Smeyers and J. van der Stock (eds), *Flemish Illuminated Manuscripts 1475–1550* (Ghent, 1996), 130–4. The manuscript was sold in 2008 and the identity of the collector to whom it now belongs is not in the public domain.

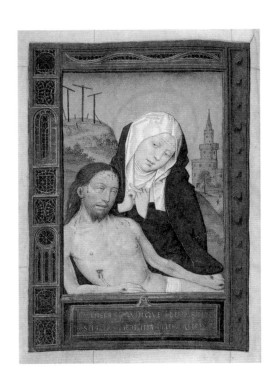

4.54a and b
Croy-Arenberg Hours,
f. 181v, *Pietà*, and detail
(European private collection)

unrelated to the simple repetitive tracery band that fills the right-hand border. On the page showing a close-up version of the Pietà, the tracery patterns in the left border are almost as disparate as those to be found on the strips at the centre of the All Souls reredos (figs. 4.54, 55). The most frequently occurring pattern here could be interpreted as paired segments of rose windows set tangentially but it looks more like the plan of Perpendicular fan vaulting. Perhaps it was included to please an English owner or perhaps the painter had travelled to England and seen fan vaults (fig. 4.56) for himself. The main interest of the Croy Hours in the present context is that its borders represent a viable source for the assorted tracery designs decorating the strips of the All Souls reredos. However, it is necessary to enter two caveats: further examples of manuscripts with this kind of border are not known to survive; and the different patterns in the borders of the Croy-Arenberg Hours are given their own frames, which prevent them from merging one into another as they do at All Souls.[69]

---

69   The concept of an ensemble of framed tracery designs of highly varied character was realised
     spectacularly in the wooden coving of *c.* 1500 from Durham Cathedral, which was preserved in
     Brancepeth church until its destruction by fire in 1998; Marks and Williamson (as n. 27), 352.

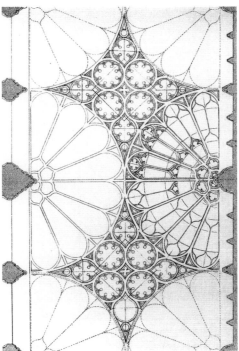

4.55 All Souls College, reredos, uprights in central section of tiers 1 and 2

4.56 Gloucester Abbey (now Gloucester Cathedral), fan-vault of north cloister walk (detail of plan drawn in 1891 by A. J. Dunn, *Architectural Association Sketchbook*, 3rd series, vol. 1, 1895, plate 21)

What appears to be the closest parallel to the tracery-decorated strips of the All Souls reredos is to be found far away from England and the Low Countries, in the great chamber of *c*. 1501 in the principal lodging of the archbishop of Salzburg's castle of Hohensalzburg (fig. 4.57).[70] The strips (whose role is taken over in some parts of the room by shafts) divide the walls into narrow rectangular compartments, but they resemble the All Souls strips in being entirely decorated with small curvilinear tracery motifs which are erratically varied. Salzburg might seem on the face of it a surprising place to find analogues for the All Souls strips, and unless the resemblance is a fluke, which seems unlikely, the most reasonable explanation for it, albeit not a very satisfying one, must be that both of those otherwise unrelated works were influenced by some kind of Netherlandish decorative ensemble that is not now represented by any survivals. By *c*. 1500 it seems that in London and its region a high proportion of joiners, the craftsmen

---

70   R. Schlegel, 'Die Baugeschichte der Festung Hohensalzburg', in E. Zwink (ed.), *900 Jahre Festung Hohensalzburg* (Salzburg, 1977), 11–79 at 25, 28. P. Schicht, *Die Festung Hohensalzburg. Der Führer zu Geschichte und Architektur* (Vienna, 2007), 105–9.

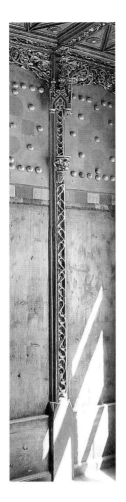

who produced the most important components of high-status domestic interior decoration, were immigrants from the southern Low Countries, and the possibility that the woodwork of the Hohensalzburg great chamber was in some measure influenced by Netherlandish joinery is not precluded by the clear indications that its workmanship is local or relatively so.[71] Nothing that has been said in this paragraph or the previous one diminishes the sheer oddness of the strips at the centre of the All Souls reredos, and the obvious explanation for their intrusion into a design which is otherwise of English Perpendicular character is that they were a somewhat unrefined way of providing visual interest to compensate for the unavoidable slenderness of the uprights in the more tightly packed central section of the reredos.

The brocaded cloth of honour hanging behind Christ in the Crucifixion tableau of Reredos II is edged with tracery-decorated strips of the same kind as those used to frame and separate the niches of the central section (figs 4.10, 55). Comparison with depictions of single standing saints on the wings of late fifteenth- and early sixteenth-century Netherlandish altarpieces shows that these strips have taken the place of the plain silk borders often shown on cloths of honour made from sumptuous textiles (fig. 4.58).[72] The possibility that the seemingly unique treatment of the cloth of honour in the Crucifixion tableau at All Souls had been anticipated in Netherlandish or Netherlandish-influenced paintings in England is raised by the images of single standing figures of saints and prophets painted on the dados of a group of East Anglian rood screens dating from shortly after 1500 (fig. 4.59). The lateral edges of the cloths of honour shown here cannot be seen but

4.57 Salzburg, Hohensalzburg Castle, detail of great chamber (*die goldene Stube*)

71 Some impression of the great extent of this immigration can be obtained by looking at the entries for joiners and carpenters in the nominal index to C. A. Stanford (ed.), *The Building Accounts of the Savoy Hospital, London, 1512–1520* (Woodbridge, 2015), 425–51. The stalls in Henry VII's Chapel in Westminster Abbey were undoubtedly designed and made by Netherlandish joiners and their obtaining of that commission is very likely to have caused resentment in the indigenous workforce. See also K. Woods, 'Immigrant Artists and Imports', in Marks and Williamson (as n. 27), 91–4. In common with decorated late medieval German wooden chests, Salzburg-made chests (for which see *Spätgotik in Salzburg – Skulptur und Kunstgewerbe, 1400–1530*, catalogue of exhibition, Museum Carolino Augusteum (Salzburg, 1976), 176–82) were heavily influenced by the chests very widely exported from the Low Countries from the late fourteenth-century onwards. Features of the woodwork of the Hohensalzburg great chamber indicative of local workmanship include the carved foliage and the seemingly pliable canopies of image niches.

72 For example, the painted panels which are all that remains of a Brussels-made altarpiece of *c.* 1490 at Queens' College, Cambridge; J. M. Massing, 'Three Panels by the Master of the View of Ste-Gudule in the Chapel of Queens' College, Cambridge', *Burlington Magazine*, 133 (1991), 690–93; N. Gliessmann, *Geschnitzte Kleinformatige Retabel aus Antwerpener, Brüsseler und Mechelener Produktion des 15. und 16. Jahrhunderts. Herstellung, Form, Function* (Petersberg, 2011), 94–5. For the Aylsham screen paintings see E. Duffy, 'The Parish, Piety, and Patronage in Late Medieval East Anglia: The Evidence of Rood Screens', in K. L. French, G. G. Gibbs and B. A. Kümin (eds), *The Parish in English Life, 1400–1600* (Manchester, 1997), 133–62 at 146–7.

4.58 Queens' College, Cambridge, chapel, St George on exterior face of panel from wing of dismembered altarpiece, by Master of the View of Ste-Gudule

4.59 Aylsham Church, Norfolk, rood screen, detail of painting of saints on dado

at their upper edges they incorporate very prominent strips of gilded tin relief made up of simple repeating tracery designs not too unlike those decorating the fronts of the All Souls strips. Whether or not the cloth of honour in the Crucifixion tableau was influenced by contemporary painting, the close resemblance of its marginal strips to the much longer strips framing and separating the niches of the central section of the reredos suggests strongly that these were primarily a site-specific device for generating some visual continuity between the Crucifixion tableau and the parts of the reredos above it.[73] That makes it all the more

73   For the possibility that this aspect of the strips was influenced by an earlier reredos see n. 67.

4.60 Windsor Castle,
St George's Chapel, choir
stalls, detail of screenwork
between north range of stalls
and return stalls

extraordinary that the right-hand strip on the cloth of honour is out of
alignment with the strip separating the central and right-hand niches
in the two tiers above. The cause of the misalignment is of course the
asymmetrical placing of the crucifix.

In highlighting the singularity of the strips in the central section of
the All Souls reredos, the assumption has been made that Perpendicular
ecclesiastical architecture was an all-embracing and more or less
closed system and one which was normally insulated from outside
influences. That is indeed what it was, and yet from around 1480
onwards it did successfully assimilate one element of Netherlandish

4.61 St Albans Abbey, high altar reredos, miniature onion dome at northern extremity, clearstorey level, seen from the east

4.62 *Crucifixion* by Rogier van der Weyden, detail of central panel of triptych (Vienna, Kunsthistorisches Museum)

origin: the miniature onion dome or 'domelet'. Among the earliest English examples are those on the screens between the lateral and western ranges of choir stalls in St George's Chapel, Windsor, and those which surmount the single spiral shafts flanking the topmost parts of the high altar reredos at St Albans (figs 4.60, 61).[74] By the late fifteenth century this motif was probably being realised in three dimensions quite frequently in the Low Countries, but it had probably occurred most often in painting, particularly in the context of imaginative visualisations of the Temple at Jerusalem (fig. 4.62).[75] There was no chance that the strange strips employed at All Souls would be assimilated in a way comparable to domelets, for they were both alien to and disruptive of the Perpendicular aesthetic. When the All Souls reredos was being reconstructed, England was importing Netherlandish wooden altarpieces in quantity, some of them specially commissioned but most

74   Perhaps not surprisingly, given the paucity of writing on late medieval English architecture, no account of the domelet has ever been attempted, but see C. Wilson, R. Gem, P. Tudor-Craig and J. Physick, *Westminster Abbey* (London, 1986), 51, 72; C. Wilson, *The Gothic Cathedral: The Architecture of the Great Church, 1130–1530* (London, 1990), 221. The miniature domes of the St Albans reredos were replaced during the late nineteenth-century restoration, but their authenticity is vouched for by their appearance in early views and by the existence of substantial parts of the originals in the cathedral lapidarium.

75   In Netherlandish painting the earliest important examples are probably those on the wings of the Passion retable painted in 1390–9 by Melchior Broederlam for the charterhouse of Champmol (Dijon, Musée des Beaux-Arts).

of them probably for sale on the open market.[76] The country was also host to considerable numbers of Netherlandish painters, glaziers, sculptors, carpenters and bricklayers, and a good deal of trouble would arise from their success at the expense of their indigenous rivals.[77] These men will usually have been self-employed craftsmen, and they were probably able without too much difficulty to assemble small teams of expert workers from among their countrymen. That was probably the situation with the brass-founder Thomas Dutchman, who in 1505–6 supplied for the tomb of Henry VII and Elizabeth of York in Westminster Abbey a bronze grille which parallels the juxtaposition in the All Souls reredos of conspicuously Netherlandish elements with others that are fully Perpendicular (fig. 4.63).[78] But the explanation for the hybrid character of the architecture of the All Souls reredos is most unlikely to have been authorship by a foreign-born master mason, for in late medieval England masonry was the major craft least penetrated by foreigners.[79] This is not surprising, as all the indications are that at this period there was a large pool of indigenous English masons available for recruitment. And notwithstanding the limited vogue for domelets, there is no sign that English patrons considered that the tradition of ecclesiastical architecture with which they were familiar stood in need of improvement by infusions of fresh ideas from abroad.

The authorship of the architectural design of Reredos II

The explanation for the prominent presence of non-standard forms in the architecture of Reredos II which probably has most to recommend it is that the work was directed by someone whose training was not that of a master mason and who was therefore less than fully versed in the grammar of Perpendicular. In modern terms, master masons were architects, for they drew up the designs for masonry structures and

---

76 Woods (as n. 65), 106–42.

77 Eadem (as n. 71), 91–2.

78 Howard Colvin considered that Thomas 'must have been working to a native design'; H. M. Colvin, D. R. Ransome and J. Summerson, *The History of the King's Works, Volume III, 1485–1660 (Part I)* (London, 1975), 219. This seems an unwarranted presumption given that Netherlandish craftsmen working abroad often showed themselves adept at adjusting to the artistic traditions of their adoptive countries.

79 There is no mention of master masons or carpenters in Sir Thomas Elyot's well-known comments lamenting the fact that in his day English patrons of arts and crafts seeking the best quality were obliged to recruit foreigners; C. Wilson, '"Excellent, New and Uniforme": Perpendicular Architecture c. 1400–1547', in Marks and Williamson (as n. 27), 98–119 at 118. A very few late fifteenth- and early sixteenth-century masonry buildings look as though they were designed by foreign or foreign-trained architects, among them the walls (but not the vault) of the chantry chapel of Bishop William Alcock in Ely Cathedral and the Christ Church gate at Canterbury Cathedral.

4.63 Westminster Abbey, Lady Chapel, detail of grille round monument of Henry VII and Elizabeth of York, by Thomas Dutchman

supervised their erection, and master carpenters did the same in relation to timber buildings and the timber components of predominantly masonry buildings. Master masons undoubtedly enjoyed the highest status of any artificers in the building and allied trades and it was their works which normally initiated and diffused innovations in architectural style. Yet it is important to stress that master masons had no monopoly in the production of architectural designs. From at least the early fourteenth century master carpenters were regularly being entrusted with the design of both large and small timber structures incorporating features derived from masonry architecture, and by the fifteenth century if not earlier comparatively small-scale timber structures such as church screens, particularly those incorporating substantial quantities of sculptural decoration, were being commissioned not from architects in the form of master carpenters but from carvers.[80] The occupational label 'kerver' was applied to a rather broad spectrum of artificers, including specialists in figure sculpture, specialist makers of decorative and architectural components and specialists of both kinds who worked in stone as well as wood, as John Massyngham did. Most documentary references to carvers relate to those whose work was predominantly or wholly decorative and carried out in wood. The exact nature of the craft formation of carvers eludes us, and although it seems inherently likely that their working lives began as apprentices to master masons or carpenters there is no hard evidence available for that. In the letter patent providing for the impressment of craftsmen to build St George's Chapel in Windsor Castle in 1475 the men who were to make the chapel's exceptionally splendid choir stalls, which included figural elements (fig. 4.60), were referred to as carpenters called 'kervers'.[81] The porousness of craft categories, as well as the likely indifference to them on the part of those who commissioned work from carvers, is evident in a contract of 1512 for work on the chancel of Tempsford church in Bedfordshire, which was to be carried out by an individual described as 'joyner, carver or carpinder'.[82] A lack of status, or at least of autonomy, is suggested by the dearth of examples of the title 'master carver' in late medieval England, and also by the fact that the crown never employed a carver equivalent to the king's chief master mason and master carpenter, both of whom were normally employed for life and given global responsibility for masonry and carpentry within the king's works organisation. That impression is reinforced by the absence of a carver from the portrayals in the late fourteenth-century stained glass of the east window of

---

80　A relatively early documented instance of a carver designing what will have been an ambitious piece of applied architecture executed in wood occurs in the record of the London carver William Hunt submitting drawings for a new rood screen at Winchester College in 1467–8; Harvey (as n. 31), 153.

81　W. H. St John Hope, *Windsor Castle*, 2 vols (London, 1913), ii, 375.

82　Harvey (as n. 31), 234. Examples of carvers who worked in both wood and stone: Robert Burwell, Robert Brown, Henry Corant, Richard Daw (a carver who also did building work in stone and timber), Laurence Emler, John Fustyng, John Massyngham, John Massyngham (son of the preceding), Edmund More, Thomas Johnson, Thomas Stockton; ibid., passim. The quite widely used term 'gravour' seems to denote what would be called a sculptor today, and there is at least one example of this term being used interchangeably with 'kerver'; ibid., 269.

the chapel of Winchester College of the individual master craftsmen responsible for the masonry, carpentry and glazing.[83] The lack of recognition of the carver's contribution here is all the more remarkable because the surviving sculpture of the College includes a superlatively fine sculpture of the Virgin over the main entrance gate. This image has sometimes been attributed to John Sampson, a mason who worked during the late
1380s and 1390s in an unspecified capacity, but almost certainly as a carver, at New College. The only reference to Sampson as a master craftsman occurs in the records of two unsuccessful attempts to prosecute him for receiving wages above the rates fixed by the Statute of Labourers, and it is significant that he is described there not as a master carver but as 'a master mason in freestone and capable and skilled in that art and in carving'.[84]

If the design of the All Souls reredos was indeed entrusted to a carver rather than a master mason that would probably be in itself sufficient explanation for the prominence of Netherlandish-derived elements not paralleled elsewhere in England in the late fifteenth and early sixteenth centuries. During that period many English-born carvers of all types will have found themselves obliged to get to grips with some aspects of the Netherlandish idioms which were increasingly favoured by élite patrons, particularly in the figural arts. Likely examples are the joint creators of an altarpiece for the Lady Chapel of Syon Abbey in the 1490s, the London-based decorative carver Robert Fille and the figural carver James Hales, the latter of whom worked for Henry VII and probably also for his mother, Lady Margaret Beaufort. Hales, who had spent time working in the southern Low Countries and France, is spoken of in the documentation for the Syon altarpiece as the carver who was more

---

83   Apparently the only example of a master carver ranking alongside a master mason and a master carpenter is William Berkeley, who supervised the making of (and no doubt also designed) of fifteenth-century England's most splendid choir-stalls, those in St George's Chapel, Windsor; Hope (as n. 81), ii, 402. For the imagery of master craftsmen in the glass of the east window of Winchester College and for some reflections on the relative status of sculpture and architecture in late medieval England see C. Wilson, 'Rulers, Artificers and Shoppers: Richard II's Remodelling of Westminster Hall, 1393–99', in D. Gordon, L. Monnas and C. Elam (eds), The Regal Image of Richard II and the Wilton Diptych (London, 1977), 33–59 at 46–9.

84   The sculpture of the Virgin on the outer gate at Winchester College is hailed as 'the high-point of fourteenth-century sculpture in England' and the attribution of it to John Sampson is dismissed, on good grounds, in J. Alexander and P. Binski (eds), Age of Chivalry, catalogue of exhibition, Royal Academy of Arts (London, 1987), 470. If the justices who gave their verdict in the case against Sampson were using the term 'master mason' in the same sense as it was routinely being used in other contemporary documentation Sampson must have been in charge of buildings on his own account that we do not know about. That is quite possible, as his appearances at New College seem to have been very intermittent.

skilled in the carving of narrative scenes than anyone else in England. Evidently it was Fille who had the architectural expertise, and while he contracted with the patron of the altarpiece Hales was employed by him as a sub-contractor.[85] Another London-based craftsmen who successfully adapted to the new fashions was William Berkeley, the chief carver and therefore presumably the designer of the most heavily Netherlandish-influenced church woodwork to have survived from late fifteenth-century England, the already-mentioned choir stalls of St George's Chapel, Windsor (fig. 4.60).[86]

To postulate that the All Souls reredos was designed by a carver helps to account not only for its exotic traits but also for its shortcomings as a work of Perpendicular architecture. The clumsily detailed canopies of the right-hand image niches in the uppermost tier, the bizarre and un-idiomatic strips at the centre of the reredos and the strange amalgam of shields and encircled quatrefoils in the blind tracery above the crucifix are by no means the sum total of the solecisms in the design.[87] Yet there is arguably nothing here that can be deemed more inept than the scrambled architecture to be found on the tomb-chests of two major late medieval English monuments. The earlier of these is the monument in Canterbury Cathedral of Archbishop William Courtenay (died 1396), where the alabasterer responsible for the design imitated the tomb-chest of the very recently completed monument to William of Wykeham in Winchester Cathedral but included shields obscuring most of the blind tracery lights that decorate the spandrels above the arches enclosing

---

85   Harvey (as n. 31), 108, 128; C. Barron and M. Erler, 'The Making of Syon Abbey's Altar Table of Our Lady, c. 1490–96', in J. Mitchell and M. Moran (eds), *England and the Continent in the Middle Ages: Studies in Memory of Andrew Martindale*, Proceedings of the 1996 Harlaxton Symposium (Stamford, 2000), 318–35; Woods (as n. 65), 118. That Hales was English or naturalised is the clear implication of the comments on his expertise made by the patron of the altarpiece in his petition to the Lord Chancellor: that he was the 'most expert in ymagery of eny oder in that land [i.e. England]' and that there was 'no werkeman yn this land so well as the seid James'.

86   Hope (as n. 81), ii, 400–6; Tracy (as n. 2), 48–58.

87   Among other aspects of the design at odds with Perpendicular aesthetics the most fundamental is the inconsistency of detailing, which encompasses the external treatment of the niche canopies in all three tiers but particularly tier 3, the blind tracery flanking the niche pedestals in tier 3, the placing of figures on top of only two of the uprights between the niches and the exceptionally erratic blind tracery on one of the niche vaults (fig. 4.6). The application of animal motifs to the central compartment of the niche vaults is unusual but less challenging to the Perpendicular aesthetic than the quasi-Romanesque semi-domes covering the small niches at the edges of tier 1. The integrity of the individual plinths to the pedestals of the eight niches in the side sections of tier 3 is compromised by the painting of the whole plinth level with a green and white chequerboard pattern (fig. 4.39) and by the fact that the colours are differently disposed in the two groups of niches. This treatment, which seems not to be paralleled elsewhere, could well have been nothing more than a fancy of the painter who devised the colour scheme but it is not impossible that it was meant to allude to the Tudor livery colours. Woodstock Manor, one of the largest and most frequented of English royal residences in the Middle Ages, lay only about 12 km to the north-north-west of central Oxford.

4.64 Canterbury Cathedral, monument of Archbishop William Courtenay, detail of south side of tomb-chest

4.65 Warwick, St Mary's church, Beauchamp Chapel, monument of Richard Beauchamp, earl of Warwick, south side of tomb-chest

4.66 Westminster Abbey, south side of tomb-chest of King Edward III

images of 'weepers'. The result is that the shields appear as if carried on short sticks, lollipop-fashion (fig. 4.64).[88] Scarcely less absurd is a prominent detail of the tomb-chest supporting the effigy of Richard Beauchamp, earl of Warwick (died 1439) in the Lady Chapel of St Mary's, Warwick. Beauchamp's monument was the centrepiece of a project on which only the best craftsmen were employed and where a great effort was clearly being made to ensure an outstandingly fine result (fig. 4.65). Yet nobody seems to have spotted how crude and inept was the London marbler John Essex's adaptation of the design used in the previous century for the tomb-chests of two royal monuments in Westminster Abbey, that of Edward III (fig. 4.66) and that of Richard II and Anne of Bohemia, both of which will have been designed by the long-serving royal master mason Henry Yevele. The angels in the smaller niches at

---

88   Wilson (as n. 37), 473–4.

Warwick ought to stand on the pedestals below but they cannot, because there are interpolated between their feet and the pedestals blind tracery units borrowed from the equivalent compartments on the royal tombs, where there are no figures.[89] We can be fairly sure that the *bêtises* evident in the Courtenay and Beauchamp tomb-chests and the All Souls reredos would have attracted the disapproval of any architect who happened to see them, but we can probably be even more confident that most viewers of those works will have been untroubled by what they saw. For them, the main focus will quite inevitably have been on the imagery which the architecture served to frame and to present.

In the first section of this paper reference was made to an entry in the All Souls Computus and Expense rolls for 1502–3, a part payment for the canopy of one of the niches of Reredos II. The recipient is said to be the person named in the preceding entry, which is a payment for a basket of lime to Robert Fustyng.[90] There must be a very good chance that we have here the name of the chief carver of the reredos and the man who will have drawn up the design. Fustyng's activities are documented in only two other contexts: payments to him for working a small number of days carving stones for the bell-tower of Magdalen College in 1506–7 and 1507–8, and an inventory of his goods taken after his death in 1508. Although not explicitly described as such in the inventory, he was clearly a mason and a carpenter and a carver working in stone and wood. He rented one of the largest properties owned by St John's Hospital in the parish of St Mary, which directly adjoined All Souls to the west. That he was in a considerable way of business on his own account is evident from the fact that he had in his possession £30 worth of wrought and unwrought timber pertaining to a piece of work he was carrying out for Godstow Abbey, a house of Benedictine nuns to the north of Oxford, and also from the itemising of payments that were due to him in respect of three separate works in St Mary's church: the stone pulpit in the nave, the tie-beam roof and ceiling of the library over the Congregation House on the north side of the chancel (fig. 4.67), and the tomb-chest of a monument to Edmund Croston, a former principal of Brasenose College (died 1507).[91] Fustyng's

---

89 There appears to be no mention of this anomaly in the literature on the monument.

90 CTM, 416, Computus and Expense roll, 1502–3.

91 Jackson (as n. 24), 179–80, 215; E. A. Gee, 'Oxford Masons, 1370–1530', *Archaeological Journal*, 109 (1953) 54–131 at 90; idem, 'Oxford Carpenters, 1370–1530, *Oxoniensia*, 17–8 (1954), 112–84 at 156; entry by R. H. C. Davis in Harvey (as n. 31), 113. In 1507 Fustyng's annual rent was 33s. 8d.; H. E. Salter (ed.), *A Cartulary of the Hospital of St John the Baptist*, 3 vols, Oxford Historical Society, 46, 48, 49 (1914–17), iii, 290. The fact that Fustyng's rent was the second highest of any paid to St John's for a property in the central parish of St Mary suggests that he needed considerable space for workshops and storage.

4.67 Oxford, St Mary's church, ceiling of library over Congregation House

profile as it emerges from documents originating from beyond All Souls tallies perfectly with the All Souls evidence: a craftsman who was capable of drawing up designs, who was in a position to undertake works involving hiring other carvers and who was able and willing to participate personally in the execution of his designs.

Conclusion

The reredos installed when the chapel at All Souls was being built in the late 1430s and 1440s (Reredos I) can readily be linked to well-documented concerns of Archbishop Chichele both in his role as Primate of all England – the reinforcement of orthodox piety by means of visual splendour – and in his role as founder of the College – the training of learned clergy and the incitement of the faithful to pray for the souls of those who had died in the French wars. The tympanum's singular portrayal of purged souls on the point of being judged worthy to enter the heavenly kingdom, when seen in conjunction with the array of potential intercessor saints in the niches below, suggests that the reredos as a whole was conceived as an affirmation of the efficacy of prayer for souls in purgatory. The extensive reworking of Chichele's reredos around 1500 (Reredos II) was almost certainly carried out under the direction of the Oxford-based carver John Fustyng, and his work may well be the most ambitious masonry structure still extant for the design of which a carver rather than a master mason was responsible. Its substitution for Reredos I after the lapse of only sixty years is a notable instance of the exuberant production of church architecture and fittings in the decades to either side of the year 1500.[92] During that period the English economy was much more buoyant than when Chichele founded All Souls, and though a high proportion of what was created then has been destroyed it is still clear from physical survivals and from documentary evidence that great numbers of reredoses, rood screens and other fittings were being introduced into new and pre-existing church buildings. We can safely assume that Bishop Goldwell's renewal of the rood screen in the chapel at All Souls during his lifetime had produced a more impressive structure than the screen given by Chichele, and his posthumous funding of the completion of Reredos II will surely have seemed to contemporaries both inside and outside the College an even more notable enhancement of the chapel's capacity to excite devotion to God and the saints.

92 Alongside economic factors, the main cause of the greater richness of Reredos II by comparison with Reredos I must have been a decline in the view that decorum required academic buildings to be restrained in treatment, a view exemplified by the University of Oxford's condemnation of the richness of the Divinity School in 1440 and Henry VI's statement in 1448 that rich decoration should be eschewed in the buildings provided by him for King's College, Cambridge. For a necessarily brief rebuttal of John Harvey's assertion that those statements were symptoms of a general shift in English architectural taste and that they amounted to 'a clearly enunciated programme of artistic reform' see C. Wilson (as n. 79), 117. The single most important instance of the abandoning of restraint in academic buildings in the early Tudor period is Henry VII's completion of the chapel of King's College, Cambridge.

Acknowledgements

I am grateful to the following people for invaluable and varied forms of assistance during the preparation of this paper: Eric Cambridge, Lorne Campbell, Jill Channer (who took photographs at Wells Cathedral specially for this paper), John Crook, Nick Doggett, Eamon Duffy, John Goodall, Sandy Heslop, the late Bronac Holden (whose transcriptions of Computus and Expense rolls are cited in notes 4 and 7), Emily Howe, Jacqui Julier, Julia Low, Gaye Morgan (whose many clarifications of archival arcana at All Souls were indispensable), John Steyaert and Dominique Vanwijnsberghe. Particular thanks are due to John Drury, who invited me to research the reredos at All Souls and helped make the process of doing so pleasurable, and to Peregrine Horden, who has fulfilled the roles of editor and general facilitator with skill, generosity and tact.

PART 3
BREAKING

CHAPTER 5
ICONOPHOBIA
AND ICONOCLASM

DIARMAID
MACCULLOCH

The two words in my title are different in their implications: iconophobia means the hatred of sacred images, while iconoclasm is the active product of iconophobia: doing something about that hatred. Both have been neglected by historians of the English Reformation, which says more about their squeamishness on a distasteful topic than about the subject's lack of importance. When I began taking an interest in iconophobia in the early 1980s, one of the few significant discussions of it was by the great Free Church historian Geoffrey Nuttall in the *Transactions of the Congregational Historical Society* from the 1930s: a worthy journal indeed, but not necessarily the first place that one would turn to for cutting-edge treatments of the Reformation.[1]

That illustrated the way in which the iconoclastic impulse in the Tudor Reformation had been marginalised by the dominant Anglo-Catholic tradition in English ecclesiastical history. In fact it was one of the English Reformation's most distinctive features, ranging the transformation of the Church of England firmly alongside churches in the Reformed Protestant tradition rather than those of the Lutheran camp. Hence the importance of the large body of work by the late Margaret Aston published over the last thirty years, beginning with her hugely important study, *England's Iconoclasts*.[2] Yet we need a longer perspective than merely the sixteenth century to understand what happened in the sixteenth century. That may help us to see how venerable was the hostility to Christian sacred images that led to the destruction at All Souls: a hostility that, in view of the transformation of attitudes represented by the nineteenth-century recovery and restoration of the reredos, now seems such a bizarre and baffling feature of the English Reformation.

---

1 G. F. Nuttall, 'Was [Oliver] Cromwell an Iconoclast?', *Transactions of the Congregational Historical Society*, 12 (1933–6), 51–66.

2 M. Aston, *England's Iconoclasts: 1. Laws against Images* (Oxford, 1988).

One of the reasons why the Church of England forgot its iconoclastic roots is that Anglicanism has come to value tradition, continuity. Iconoclasm represents hatred of the past and the wish to destroy it, to root it out from people's memories. For the more radical Protestant reformers, destruction of the past represented one of the best ways to extirpate the way of life which centred on the Mass. Anything might lead to seduction by the past. On a large scale, the bones of the recently dead were disturbed, first when the monastery churches were for the most part rifled and wrecked, later when the parish churches became fair game. One minor growth area of research has been to take up post-Reformation monumental brasses from their stone indents and examine the backs. It has become clear that a large proportion are palimpsest, that is, engraved on the reverse side of older brasses which were the loot first of English monasteries at the end of the 1530s and, second, of the churches of Flanders in the 1560s. Many of these brasses were only a decade or two old. Protestant English people seem to have had no scruples in conniving with the destruction of tombs which were sometimes very recent, and were not squeamish about cannibalising them for their own use.[3]

Even although many of those in charge of the English Reformation did not go as far as this, it was very difficult to know where to draw a line in destroying the popish past. Most notably, Queen Elizabeth disapproved of excessive destruction, and tried in a proclamation in 1560 to save funeral monuments being wrecked alongside images which might attract superstitious worship, but her efforts were largely futile and missed the point. Medieval tombs also spoke of the old devotional world which was the enemy of all godly Reformation, so their funerary portraits of clergy in eucharistic vestments and laypeople with rosaries, their inscriptions summoning up the ghost of purgatory with an insistent cry of 'Pray for the soul', simply had to be disposed of along with the statues and altars. Sometimes the destruction was discriminating, and the soul-prayer was neatly removed – examples from one English county, Suffolk, all of which are clearly the product of direct interest from descendants of the person creating the inscription, are the treatment of a monumental brass at Metfield, a Catholic recusant's tomb at Wetherden and the south chancel aisle parapet at Lavenham – but more often destruction was root and branch.

---

3   R. Rex, 'Monumental Brasses and the Reformation', *Transactions of the Monumental Brass Society*, 14 (1990), 376–94; the *Transactions* regularly itemise and illustrate discoveries of brass palimpsests, generally in their notes on the conservation activities of the Society.

In fact controversy over images and the place of tangible things in religion was probably more acute in England than in mainland Europe. There is a strange English inability to get excited about questions of abstract doctrine, contrasting with the way in which Puritanism was defined in its opening years by rows over ceremony and clerical dress. Externals seem to play a large part in the English perception of religion. Also it may be important that although the level of violence against people in the English Reformation was fairly horrific by modern standards, by comparison with the rest of Europe it was mild. In view of this, images might act as surrogates for violence on people – objects on which fury at human enemies could be discharged.

There was a long Christian history to discussion of the place of images in the Church's life, reflecting the unstable foundations of Christianity itself in two very different previous cultures, Judaism and Hellenism. The legacy of the Greeks was ambiguous: on the one hand, a compulsion to depict divine figures as beautiful versions of humans, and to make such depictions central to Greek religious observance, and on the other an austere ascetic impulse as exhibited in the philosophy of Plato, in which all that is physical is inferior to the world of the spirit. Judaism, by contrast, has rarely deviated from disapproval of visual representations of the divine, particularly sculpted, carved or 'graven images'. That is the subject of prohibition in the Ten Commandments – of which more below.

Christianity, in its melding of the two cultural streams, has never decided quite where it stands on the issue of depicting the divine, and in fact its attitudes have oscillated violently over time. At least from the 2nd century CE there had been figure-paintings in Christian churches, but even then there was a heritage of mistrust and prohibition. The greatest row before the Reformation had been in the Church of Constantinople during the eighth and ninth centuries, perhaps in reaction to the rise of Islam, a religion which had no hesitation in condemning all sacred images; this was the Iconoclastic controversy, pitching haters of images – 'iconoclasts' – against their supporters – 'iconodules'. The 'iconoclasts' sought to destroy all figural images in the Church. It was a major ideological confrontation that much weakened the Eastern Empire at a time of steady Muslim territorial encroachment.

The iconodules eventually won. At a second general Council of Bishops held in the city of Nicaea (787), the iconodulic leaders, emboldened by the support of the then Emperor, tried to classify attitudes to images and decide which attitudes were acceptable and which were not: the eventual distinction that was made there and subsequently refined was between *latria*, *dulia* and *hyperdulia*. *Latria* was the worship due to God alone, *dulia* the respect due to his creatures (and that could be very considerable respect in gesture and word, as in the case of the *dulia* offered to the Emperor). *Hyperdulia* was the particular and unique respect owed to the creature who was also the Mother of God, the Virgin Mary. Making this distinction meant that the Church could give its seal of approval to *dulia* and *hyperdulia* towards images, but ban *latria* to anyone else except God, thus leaving Christians free to proliferate representations of the sacred.

This careful set of definitions cut little ice in popular devotion, but it satisfied theologians of Eastern Christianity. Sixteenth-century Protestants naturally found these distinctions false, and were driven to condemn the decisions of Nicaea II. In this, they made a useful scholarly rediscovery from the remote past of Western Christianity: a text known as the *Libri Carolini*, a text prepared by the Westerner Charlemagne's Latin theologians in 794, which condemned both the iconoclasts and the definitions of Nicaea II. Charlemagne had his own reasons for condemning any theological decision made with the consent of the Eastern Emperor whose title he was emulating within a few years, and it was a mark of his self-confidence that he could give his backing to such a direct challenge to the still mighty ruler and Church in Constantinople.

Charlemagne's encouragement of an iconophobic mood in his dominions might have suggested an iconophobic future for the Western Latin Church, but it proved to be a passing phase. Instead, for the next seven centuries, all Western churches became a riot of statuary and sacred images of all sorts in stone, wood and glass. Yet always lurking alongside that development was the counter-theme of image destruction, embodied in particular by the legend of the supposedly late third-century Roman soldier Sebastian. Iconographically, St Sebastian himself is generally remembered as standing with a soulful expression in the manner of a holy pin-cushion, pierced with multiple arrows, but in fact this was not his death scene, and the rest of his developed legend explains why he incurred the displeasure of the Roman authorities: he destroyed images of gods who were not the Christian God. The Philadelphia Museum of Art preserves a striking and paradoxical work of art embodying this theme, a late fifteenth-century French reredos from a side-altar of St Sebastian, depicting his life in strip-cartoon fashion. One of its panels shows the saint in the process of destroying non-Christian sacred images – of course, amid all the iconodulic splendour of Western Christian art in gilding, carving and figural art (fig. 5.1).

That subterranean iconophobia was to emerge with a vengeance in the sixteenth century, but its first manifestation was not in the Protestant Reformation, but in the encounter of Western Christianity with non-Christian religions in what was for Europeans the New World – central and south America. There, for the first time in centuries, Christians encountered cultures with abundant sacred imagery, unlike the long-standing foe on their southern and eastern frontiers, Islam. They went about destroying the art of the Incas and Aztecs with pious fanaticism; and the Portuguese did the same in the small coastal enclaves of Asia which they could dominate militarily, principally in Goa (the art and literature of non-Western Christians suffered the same fate there). The resulting paradox is that Spanish and Portuguese Catholics destroyed far more sacred art than Protestants during the sixteenth century.

Finally, the Protestants. The first European image-smashing took place in January and February 1522 in Wittenberg, but it was not the work of Martin Luther. Under the influence of the preaching of Andreas Karlstadt, while Luther was away in his hideout at the Wartburg, crowds began wrecking images in the Town Church. Luther was furious and put a stop to it on his return; this was the first sign of his consistent sympathy for images as a help for popular devotion and his reluctance to attack them. For Luther, images remained 'things indifferent' (*adiaphora*); in fact, to attack or destroy them was a form of idolatry, since it suggested that the perpetrator thought that they had power of their own. Luther made sure that those who listened to him, and the Churches that they created – the 'Lutherans' – did not yield to iconophobia. Consequently the Lutheran churches of northern Europe shelter a treasury of medieval sacred art that sailed through the Reformation upheavals with relative serenity.

Matters went differently in the parallel Reformation of Switzerland. Again, there was popular violence inspired by preaching but, in contrast to Wittenberg, the authorities in Church and Commonwealth usually co-operated, and took matters further. So, in the Swiss Reformation, popular direct action had more profound consequences. At Zurich in 1523 one of Zwingli's fellow-preachers, Leo Jud, gave an inflammatory sermon which led to bouts of image-smashing. Zwingli and the authorities considered the matter and in summer 1524 they ordered a systematic and orderly clearing of the churches. Various Swiss cities imitated Zurich, though few of them took up the city's parallel ban on sacred music that reflected Zwingli's worries about its power to distract from the worship of God.

The most violent change was at Basel in 1529, where a mob forced the hand of the city council; while the council was deciding what to do, the radical clique in the city smashed images in the city churches on a huge scale. The council then gave orders for the destruction to be extended officially throughout its territory. It prompted Erasmus to leave the city for Freiburg-im-Breisgau, even though his own writings had often made fun of images and pilgrimages, and were held responsible by many traditionalists for all the trouble.

The dominant reformer in a belated Reformation emerging during the 1530s on the fringes of Switzerland, in Geneva, took up the earlier Swiss mood. John Calvin saw two permissible images in worship: the two scriptural sacraments, baptism and eucharist, which, in the *Institutes*, he described as images of Christ. Their completeness removed the need for any other representation, and therefore necessitated blanket destruction of such idolatry. It was in Calvin's Geneva that the iconophobic message of the ancient *Libri Carolini* was first put into print. The contrast between the patterns of Lutheran Wittenberg and of the Reformed Swiss became permanent, and gave rise to a fundamental Protestant split on an important aspect of Christian life, the use of images. Central to the Protestant upheaval was the interpretation of the Bible, and here Holy Scripture spoke with an ambiguous voice.

Through all discussion of images, there was one central debate: how to arrange the Ten Commandments, which gave the key text against graven images for Protestants in its opening precepts. Here is one version, from Exodus, of two simiar versions of the ten, the other being in Deuteronomy 5:

> [Exod. 20] [a 1] 'I am the LORD your God, who brought you out of the land of Egypt, out of the house of bondage. You shall have no other gods before me.
>
> [a 1] [b 2] 'You shall not make for yourself a graven image, or any likeness of anything that is in heaven above, or that is in the earth beneath, or that is in the water under the earth; you shall not bow down to them or serve them; for I the LORD your God am a jealous God, visiting the iniquity of the fathers upon the children to the third and the fourth generation of those who hate me, but showing steadfast love to thousands of those who love me and keep my commandments.

How do we number this textual material, given that it is a textual fragment of ten commandments? There have always been two alternative ways of numbering the commandments in Christian interpretation of them, and this apparently trivial issue is related directly to Christian attitudes to images. One use (*method a*) was to make the command against graven images part of the first commandment, not a second on its own, thus reducing its relative importance. Obviously there still need to be ten, so the number of commandments is made up by splitting material at the end, and thus having two commandments against different aspects of covetousness. There is a certain logic to this. Scriptural commentators had noticed how long the graven image clause was in comparison with the other commandments, and therefore decided that it was marginal comment, and even omitted much of the text of it. This appealed to the early Church as images became more and more part of its ordinary devotion; Augustine of Hippo, himself a great lover and promoter of pilgrimages and miraculous places, leant his great authority to this interpretation. It became normal in the medieval Western Church, and significantly, Martin Luther stuck with it.

There was, however, an alternative tradition (method b), which made the graven image command no. 2 in the list, and ran together the last two commandments on covetousness to restore the tenfold numbering. It had impressive credentials; it had its roots with the Jewish commentators Philo and Josephus, and was also to be found in Origen. This ordering had been kept by the Eastern Orthodox churches, which was the reason that, even after the victory of the 'iconodules' at the second Council of Nicaea, their images were not graven, but paintings on flat wooden surfaces or flat walls – what we now think of as 'icons'. In the West, John Wycliffe pointed out the historic pedigree of this interpretation, and all Protestant Reformed commentators outside the Lutheran world took it up as being ideal for their condemnation of images. The first appearance of this rediscovered tradition was predictably in Zurich, with the publication of Zwingli's commentary on Exodus by the active iconoclast Leo Jud in 1527.

In this as in so much else, English Protestantism turned out to be on the side of the Swiss. For English admirers of Luther, his tolerance of images became a great embarrassment to equal his affirmation of eucharistic real presence, and these problems contributed to the rapid decline of Lutheranism's reputation in this country. As in mainland Europe, at certain crucial stages in the English Reformation people took direct action. Under Edward VI, at the very beginning of Elizabeth's reign and in 1640–41, popular violence by a minority played a decisive role in changing events, and pushing the politicians and church leaders into measures against images. There was, after all, a pre-existing iconophobic tradition in England, from the Lollards. Wycliffe himself considered the issue as part of a contemporary academic debate about images, but he was comparatively moderate about images, in the manner of Luther. Nevertheless, as is often the case with inspirational founders, what caught the imagination of later Lollards was not what Wycliffe primarily taught.

Medieval Lollards took up the hatred of images as one of their main themes; Margaret Aston suggested that it was the commonest of their beliefs.[4] Most recorded Lollard activity indicates only verbal abuse, refusal to take their part in the image culture, or minor pranks, like the Devon man who in 1441 drew a beard on a Madonna with the smoke of a candle.[5] However, there were one or two more serious incidents, the most dramatic of which was actually in the decade of the first European Reformation iconoclasm, probably in 1522: the burning of Rickmansworth church (Hertfordshire). This took place in the heart of an area where Lollardy had survived in relative strength, and in a parish where the chief landlord was that symbol of the old Church Cardinal Thomas Wolsey. Here the culprits, who were never found, set fire to the rood with oily rags at dead of night, and that spread to burn the whole church down.

It was probably significant that the chosen means of destruction was fire. That has other parallels in other iconoclastic Lollard acts, and also in several acts of destruction of the early 1530s. The motivation was partly from the Old Testament (e.g. Deuteronomy 7, Isaiah 44), which emphasised that burning was a good way of showing the futility and lack of power of the image. But it was also a riposte to the penalty for heresy, burning, which became common in England after the passing of the Parliamentary statute *De haeretico comburendo* in 1401. Almost certainly an East Anglian campaign of burning images in 1531–2 was a reply to the burning at Norwich in 1531 of the popular local preacher Thomas Bilney, who had made attacks on pilgrimages and images the central theme of his sermons.

Bilney was put to death for preaching against images, but only four years later the first English printed book wholly devoted to encouraging thoroughgoing destruction of images was published with official licence (1535): a Strassburg pamphlet translated into English by William Marshall, a client printer of the King's current chief minister Thomas Cromwell. Strassburg was in the vanguard of radical reform in the Swiss manner, and its spiritual leader, Martin Bucer, had already become a friend by correspondence of Archbishop Thomas Cranmer; their relationship

---

4   Aston, *England's Iconoclasts*, 105.
5   Ibid., 109.

strengthened over the years. Marshall's text had both the 'old' (a) and the 'new' (b) numberings of the Ten Commandments – the first time that the latter had appeared in England. It was actually Bucer who had produced the German original of this text in 1530; so indirectly it was Bucer who introduced the new (a) ordering of the Ten Commandments to English theology. A year after Marshall's book, Archbishop Cranmer was openly preaching the same message and Hugh Latimer, Bishop of Worcester, was echoing it in a sermon to no less an audience than the Convocation of Canterbury. At much the same time (1536), Latimer was mounting a campaign against images and shrines in his own diocese of Worcester.

The first general official campaign came in 1538, on the orders of the layman for whom Henry VIII had created the unprecedented office of Vice-Gerent in Spirituals, Thomas Cromwell. All the major monastic shrines were destroyed and the main images gathered and burnt, but this time by the government, unlike the vandalism of 1530-31. In one case in 1538 the government itself made the linkage between the burning of images and the burning of religious deviants in the most gruesome way; they used a wonderworking Welsh image, Derfel Gardarn, to burn a staunchly Catholic preacher and confessor, Friar John Forest. There had been an old prophecy that the image would one day set a whole forest on fire, and this execution looks like Henry VIII's idea of a joke. One of the spectators was Bishop Latimer, who preached a sermon at the event.[6]

It was at that moment, with typical inconsistency, that the king drew back. Forest was burnt in May 1538; Cromwell issued his injunctions with their orders against images in October. A royal proclamation only a month later (November) was as much concerned to stop the contentions and seditions which resulted from the ending of old ceremonies, though it was confused in tone, with some final clauses against idolatry and very aggressive orders against the cult of the 'political' saint Thomas Becket. Henry was beginning to move into his own new conservative phase, in which Cromwell's own individual policies were sidelined.

Henry was never consistent in his reshaping of England's now insular Church between Protestant possibilities and persistent traditionalism. Although even after Cromwell's death in 1540 the government pressed on with the destruction of shrines, the doctrinal statement called the King's Book (1543) was aimed more to condemn those who wanted to get rid of all images than to condemn the dangers

6   D. MacCulloch, *Thomas Cromwell: A Life* (London, 2018), 459.

of the images – a change from the earlier Bishops' Book (1537). We know that the King himself was responsible for the most significant changes, most changes being towards traditionalism. Yet still the King's Book kept the new numbering (♭) of the Commandments.

The next phase would have to wait on the king's death, but then it came very quickly. Action followed swiftly; royal injunctions of that summer ordered the official removal of all abused images throughout the parishes, and, for the first time, there was a requirement that superstitious stained glass should be removed. This was highly significant, because, throughout debate on idolatry, it was a moot point whether glass should be included, because it was not a graven image like a statue and therefore did not seem to come inside the Ten Commandments prohibition. Zwingli had allowed the glass to remain in Zürich, as did John Knox in Scotland (in theory). The problem was that it was not possible to maintain the difference between superstitious and non-superstitious images; an activist minority took the law into their own hands, especially in London and East Anglia. In a series of rows over these acts of destruction, the Duke of Somerset's regime nearly always took the side of the iconoclasts, rather than the outraged conservatives who sought to use the law against them. The definitive order to remove all images came on 21 February 1548. After that, destruction both official and unofficial went on until the king's death, although Northumberland did insert a clause against the destruction of tombs in an act of Parliament confirming all the destruction in 1550. All through his brief reign, there is no doubt that the young king approved of all the moves against images.

The reaction of Mary's reign only increased Protestant fury against images, and the activist minority were determined on her death that they should be purged. Once more the celebrations round Elizabeth's coronation gave a chance for some Protestant pageantry to set the agenda for destroying superstition and idolatry. The same pattern followed as in 1547: agitation followed in London and in East Anglia, with the government doing its best to contain but little to punish; and, in the summer of 1559, royal visitors toured the country encouraging the rounding up of popish trash. There are signs of uncertainty in their brief: there were two sets of documents available to them. As far as the subject of images went, the injunctions which they carried were based on the half-way house of 1547, but the model of the articles of enquiry for their visitation was not 1547, but the thoroughgoing orders for destruction in 1548; and it was the articles rather than the injunctions which the commissioners enforced.

Much of the ambiguity must come from the queen. She was prepared to let the rood figures stand on the screens until her senior clergy threatened mutiny; in 1561 she did secure the survival of the screens which had supported the rood, and we have already noted her 1560 proclamation against the destruction of tombs. Above all, she was the cause of one of the first rows of her reign over Church matters, when she kept a silver crucifix on the altar of her private chapel against the protests of most of her leading clergy. When Dean Nowell tried to preach to her on the subject of idolatry in 1565 in the presence of this crucifix, she shouted him down, to his great terror. Yet the queen only got her way to a limited extent; all other crosses were put down. It is not often remembered that popular iconoclasm even extended to repeated direct action against the queen's crucifix in her own chapel, four times in 1562, in 1567 and in 1570: an extraordinary act of *lèse-majesté* whose perpetrators were nevertheless treated with significant leniency.

The first decade of Elizabeth's reign shows bishops and lower church officials all over the country settling down to systematic vandalism even on the crucifixes which the queen wanted to keep. Only one bishop (Edmund Guest of Rochester) echoed the queen's order to preserve funeral monuments. Destruction was gradual, but almost always orderly. I have even found an instance of an Essex man, John Baker of Fordham, who in 1582 left money in his will to take down the stained glass window over the pew where he had sat in his lifetime, 'in token that I do utterly disallow all manner of idolatry as well in glass windows as in all other places'.[7] Now there was rare calculation in iconoclasm: murder, not manslaughter.

Part of the new drive to establish Protestantism was to get everyone to learn the Creed, Lord's Prayer and Commandments; probably every church in the end acquired boards with these texts, many of which remain. In the new Protestant arrangement of the Commandments, the second was of course the long order not to worship graven images. The positioning of the boards was usually at the east end over the site of the high altar, the place where the memory of idolatry might be most seductive. The official collection of sermons, the Homilies, contained two 'against peril of idolatry and superfluous decking of churches', and they were the longest in the book; they also owed much to an earlier work by the Swiss reformer Heinrich Bullinger. The queen took modest steps to modify their violent language in 1563 — a pre-corrected copy

---

7   F. G. Emmison, *Essex Wills: The Archdeaconry Courts 1577–84*, 12 vols (Chelmsford, 1983–2000), iv, no. 669.

survives – and delayed their issue, but she did not radically change the message. In this, as in so much else, she was the prisoner of her own image: the Protestant Deborah leading her people away from popery.

Even when the Elizabethan church settled down and the campaign against images had achieved most of its goals, there remained a profound suspicion of images and pictures of any sort in church, way beyond any logical commentary on the 'graven image' specified in the Ten Commandments clause. Just at the time when portraits were becoming common in the home, figure-painting was banned from church. The only lasting pictorial images were the inspired and dramatic illustrations of that phenomenal publishing success, John Foxe's *Acts and Monuments* ('Foxe's Book of Martyrs'). In domestic decoration, there was a certain time lag in eliminating the old iconography; it was presumably deemed less dangerous in homes than in places of public worship, and there was a shakier legal foundation for dealing with it. After about 1570, however, such items as pictures of the Virgin and the saints took refuge in the houses of Catholic recusants. Elsewhere they gave way to secular subjects and themes from the Old Testament which could not be accused of directly inviting superstitious traditional devotion and obstructing the worship of God. Images of Death survived and multiplied, for the same reason.

A change only began with the new or rediscovered theology of the proto-Arminians and Laudians. An early and surprising convert to lavish decoration was the statesman Robert Cecil, who paid for a most richly decorated private chapel for himself at Hatfield House in 1607-12.[8] This was exceptionally early; it was only in the late 1620s that the ascendancy of William Laud and his circle produced the first widespread restorations of images since the Reformation.

In the Civil War, this new move produced an equally violent reaction; it tarred the entire traditional structure of the Church of England with the same brush, and led to indiscriminate destruction. One of the most ironical illustrations of this was at Chichester, when, in 1642, one of the soldiers in the Cathedral is said to have 'picked out the eyes' of King Edward VI's picture, saying 'that all this mischief came from him, when he established the Book of Common Prayer'.[9] So even the regime which had caused the most previous destruction was now tainted. The Civil War launched the biggest official national initiative against images since 1559. As early as 1641 there were proposals in

8 P. Croft, 'The Religion of Robert Cecil', *The Historical Journal*, 34 (1991), 773–9.
9 Aston, *England's Iconoclasts*, 94.

the Long Parliament to destroy images, which the Commons sent out despite Lords opposition; when the Civil War actually broke out, Parliament passed legislation on 28 August 1643, which was extended with a further list of objects for destruction in 1644.

From December 1643 for the next year, the most famous agent of the campaign toured East Anglia – William Dowsing. Dowsing represents an interesting continuity with the earlier iconoclastic traditions of the English Reformation, because, although always called Dowsing of Laxfield by hostile Victorian antiquaries, since that was the village where he was born, he lived most of his life in Stratford St Mary in the Stour Valley, an area of militant popular iconoclasm since the 1530s.[10] There is an interesting parallel with the witch craze of the same period: the self-styled 'Witchfinder General' in East Anglia was Matthew Hopkins, a man of the same social level as Dowsing among the yeomanry, and he came from Manningtree, a mile away from Stratford. Both were making their own contribution to the Parliamentarian war effort, fighting Satan and purifying England in their own way.

Dowsing gloried in what he was doing, and kept a detailed diary, which partly survives. Even in Puritan-dominated East Anglia, he faced varying reactions to his work. In some places he records that destruction had gone before him; in others he was obstructed, for instance at Ufford, where the parishioners were exceptionally proud of their church and refused him the key. All over England the destruction went on; the cathedrals suffered the most, because they were the flagships of Laudian change, where the revival of ceremony had been most thoroughgoing. However, Lichfield was the only cathedral so thoroughly wrecked as to need rebuilding from ruins, and that was thanks to the siege of the city.

Like so much in the Church of England, the trauma of the Interregnum had a lasting effect in modifying the iconoclastic impulse. After the Restoration, the impulse to active destruction seems finally to have disappeared in the established Church; it was associated with fanaticism, sectarianism and all the ills which the Civil War had brought. Even so, though, the suspicion of providing images was strong down to the nineteenth century even within Anglicanism, and still persists in some evangelical circles. Such a major theme in Anglican history cannot be treated as trivial, even if it has little appeal to the age of the National Trust and English Heritage.

---

10 T. Cooper (ed.), *The Journal of William Dowsing: Iconoclasm in East Anglia during the English Civil War* (Woodbridge, 2001).

CHAPTER 6
ICONOCLASM
IN THE CHAPEL

**PEREGRINE
HORDEN**

Thirty shillings. That was what it cost to begin the next chapter in the history of the reredos – its disfigurement. At some point in 1548 a man called Plummer was called upon. Very likely he was the William Plummer who had previously done odd repair jobs and cleaning in the chapel, including work specifically on the high altar, since 1533 if not earlier.[1] Plummer was paid now for undoing some of his labour. His thirty shillings were much more than he was used to being paid by the College. (Did anyone think of thirty pieces of silver?) They were for *detrudenti imagines super altari summo*: tearing down, dislodging – the Latin is ambiguous between destruction and removal – the images, meaning sculptures, above the high altar, i.e. the reredos. Plummer was also paid 6s. 8d. to take (or throw) down the figures of the Saviour, Mary and John the Baptist. These must have stood on the rood screen provided by Bishop James Goldwell at the end of the fifteenth century.[2] It is hard to envisage one man doing all this unaided, even though only Plummer is mentioned in the list of payments authorised by the bursars. He must have been left to redistribute some of the 30s. to assistants. In New College it was the 'servants' of 'Master Plummer', presumably the same man, who were paid 10s. 8d. for taking down and breaking images.[3] Plummer might have hoped to corner the local market in collegiate iconoclasm, but at Magdalen College it was one Dole who earned only 3s. 4d. for 'deforming' ancient images.[4]

---

1   What follows is drawn primarily from the Computus and Expense rolls and early inventories for the years in question in the ASC archives. For assistance with this material, over many years, I am indebted throughout to the late Bronac Holden.

2   See Wilson, this volume, 115–17, for Goldwell's architectural patronage.

3   A. H. Smith, *New College, Oxford, and its Buildings* (London, 1952), 79.

4   J. R. Bloxham, *A Register of the Presidents, Fellows, Demies… of Saint Mary Magdalen College*, ii (Oxford, 1857), 272. For Merton, see J. M. Fletcher and C. A. Upton, 'Destruction, Repair and Removal: An Oxford College Chapel during the Reformation', *Oxoniensia*, 48 (1983), 123. For Cambridge parallels see C. Law, *Contested Reformations in the University of Cambridge, 1535–84* (Woodbridge, 2018), 59.

6.1 Photograph of *c.* 1907 showing sculptural fragments presumably from the Winchester Cathedral 'great screen' (and three nineteenth-century plaster casts in the foreground) previously housed in the feretory

Plummer's task in All Souls cannot have been simply to climb a ladder and bash away until pieces of statuary crashed to the ground. For one thing, the chapel is so high, nearly forty feet from the ground in the sanctuary, that he must have needed scaffolding. For another, the College was not in fact parting with its statues, despite the implication of the entries in the accounts just quoted. Someone, probably Plummer yet again, earned 2s. for taking the sculptures and a shrine to a little hut in the garden and then 4d. for repairing and cleaning the choir after their *deportatio*. A further 4d. went on a new key and a repair to the lock of the hut in which the statues were laid down. They were almost certainly not in one piece, but they had not been pulverised. For a possible analogy, if on a larger scale, note the collection of heads and torsos squirreled away after an earlier act of destruction (probably in the reign of Henry VIII, around 1538) wrought on the 'great screen' at Winchester Cathedral (fig. 6.1).[5] The All Souls chapel was still left in a mess. The College

---

5   P. Lindley, 'The Great Screen of Winchester Cathedral I', *Burlington Magazine*, 131 (1989), 604–15 at 605-6. For the dating, see also M. Aston, *Broken Idols of the English Reformation* (Cambridge, 2016), 131, 148-9.

disbursed 8d. for a shovel and a pair of scoops to collect the dust and rubble. Not all was loss, however. At some point before demolition the gold was removed from reredos figures or other 'images' and 8s. was made from selling it off.

The statuary was not the only casualty of these mid-century years. In 1550 the six side altars of the chapel and the one in the vestry were destroyed. The following year, £27 3s. 4d. were realised from the sale of copes and other vestments and 'ancient and superfluous' church ornaments. One Henry Bolton (who also worked for Magdalen) provided a communion table to be placed in the choir area along with two benches; some sort of hanging was bought to cover an area where an altar had stood; new psalters were procured; for 6s. Jeffrey Whyte lived up to his name by whitewashing the choir walls.

In this period, we must envisage further acts of destruction. Service books had to go (51 are listed in an early inventory and that must be reckoned a minimum estimate). A fragment of the true cross held within a free-standing crucifix would have been another casualty of reform. So, too, reliquaries — those of the tooth of John the Baptist and the bone of St Jerome that the College held inter alia — and also images of the Virgin and Thomas Becket, the latter having already been the target of a campaign by Henry VIII and Thomas Cromwell in 1538. (The Virgin and Becket were two of the College's dedicatees alongside Edward the Confessor.)

And yet amid the destruction of the middle years of the sixteenth century there were survivals. The chapel stained glass was seemingly unaffected by iconoclasm in All Souls, as it was in many other colleges (although in New College the glass was reportedly spared only because the fellows pleaded that they were too poor to replace it with plain windows[6]). Perhaps the organ probably given by Chichele, though frequently needing repair from 1447 onwards, was still there in the reign of Elizabeth I; if not the original then a direct successor certainly was. Along with the rood loft, another surprising survivor, the organ was not taken down until 1562. (There was then no organ in chapel again until 2014.) Even so, like the statuary, the organ was stored; it would not be taken to pieces and sold until 1573.

The final great survivors, remarkably, were the statue-less reredos niches. No attempt is documented to restore any figures to them in the reign of the Catholic Mary. Nor is there any reference in the College archives to their being plastered over or otherwise covered until the

---

6   Smith, New College, 47.

1660s, when, as we shall see, they disappeared behind Isaac Fuller's *Last Judgement*.[7]

That is distinctive. At New College, unlike All Souls, a few stone fragments of the dossal of the altar survive (showing the five Joys of the Virgin) but the whole was plastered over in 1566–7 and the organ disappeared at the same time as the statues.[8] In Magdalen, the other college with a reredos, even under the foot-dragging President Oglethorpe the empty niches were eventually, in 1551, bricked up and plastered over. The organ had already been removed with speed, in 1549, and seems, rather impetuously, to have been burned in situ under the wooden roof. Luckily the chapel did not catch fire, but frankincense was promptly required to fumigate the interior.[9]

Among Oxford colleges, then, only at All Souls, did the 'reformed' reredos stay in the worshippers' view for any length of time; and at All Souls it stayed, I believe, for over a century. There was no more iconoclasm, so far as we can tell from the archives, not even at the hands of Parliamentary troops in the Civil War. Their damage was limited to the High Street. The glass, which might have been their obvious target, instead decayed, and was replaced piecemeal until the eighteenth century.[10]

Two further points deserve emphasis, both arising from the recent work represented in this volume. First, the reredos may have been completed far more recently than has been supposed. If Wilson is right, then in 1547 the fellows had to observe the removal of reredos figures that were nearly all less than half a century, not a whole century old. It was the work of their fathers' generation, not their distant predecessors. Second, arising from the examination of the polychromy, as Howe shows, the coloration of the niches was added only once the sculpted figures were in position. The removal of these figures therefore left behind their ghostly silhouettes. Though of course much damaged and faded, the polychromy endured until it was thoroughly recorded only a few years ago, so the silhouettes must have been quite noticeable in the sixteenth and seventeenth centuries.

---

7   J. Gutch (ed.), *The History and Antiquities of the Colleges and Halls in the University of Oxford by Antony Wood*, M.A., 2 vols (Oxford, 1786–90), i, 289: 'the niches remained until an. 1664'; Liversidge, this volume, 213–14, reasonably conjectures covering and whitewashing of the All Souls reredos, as happened at New College and Magdalen. My point is simply that there is no evidence of that. We agree to differ.

8   See Wilson, this volume, 138 nn. 39, 40; G. Jackson-Stops, 'The Architecture of the College', in J. Buxton and P. Williams (eds), *New College Oxford 1379–1979* (Oxford, 1979).

9   L. W. B. Brockliss (ed.), *Magdalen College Oxford: A History* (Oxford, 2008), 58, 126.

10 See Darwall-Smith, this volume, 243.

How had this all come about? After the vacillating and ambiguous religious policies of the late years of Henry VIII,[11] the Protestant government of the boy-king Edward VI, under Protector Somerset, embarked rapidly and decisively on a programme of radical change. That programme was probably more momentous for Tudor society than the dissolution of the monasteries. The aim was purification – from popishness and from what in the eyes of reformers amounted to the same thing, paganism. The target was idolatry: first the idolatry of the Mass with its worship of the supposed real presence of Christ in the consecrated host; then the idolatry of all images before which priests and laity might bow and scrape and, worse, which they might kiss; finally the idolatry of superfluous decoration – in practice, almost all decoration. If this programme were carried through, the early Edwardian government believed, the result would be a return to the primitive purity of the apostolic Church. Most at risk were *imagines*, images, meaning primarily statues. The third dimension was adjudged a greater incitement to idolatry than the other two. Stained glass figures might escape vandalism on those grounds, as they did at All Souls. The regime of Cromwell and Cranmer in the 1530s had begun the governmental attack on image worship, but the zeal of the evangelicals could be fully unleashed only after the ailing and erratic king's death in January 1547. Thus, to quote two contributors to this volume, there emerged the 'Tudor Church Militant' (MacCulloch); under which 'iconoclasm was the central sacrament of the reform' (Duffy).[12]

There was no delay. The nine-year old Edward VI was hailed as the new Josiah. He was a reincarnation of the Old Testament king who acceded to the throne of Judah, conveniently at the age of eight, and won divine favour by purifying religion and especially by smashing altars and idols (2 Chronicles 34: 1–3). Archbishop Cranmer's chaplain Nicholas Ridley preached iconoclasm to the king within days of his coronation in February 1547.[13] A set of injunctions were soon published, a copy of which All Souls would have purchased, to be followed by royal visitations of the entire realm and, in 1549, specific visitations of the two universities. Injunction no. 28 articulated the goal of the first, general,

11 MacCulloch, this volume.

12 D. MacCulloch, *Tudor Church Militant: Edward VI and the Protestant Reformation* (London, 1999); E. Duffy, *The Stripping of the Altars: Traditional Religion in England 1400–1580*, 2nd edn (New Haven, 2005), 480.

13 M. Aston, *England's Iconoclasts: I. Laws against Images* (Oxford, 1988), 247; but see now D. MacCulloch, *Thomas Cranmer: A Life*, rev. edn (New Haven, 2016), 364–5. *The Works of Nicholas Ridley* (Cambridge, 1843), 83–96.

visitation: the clergy were 'to take away, utterly extinct and destroy all shrines … candlesticks … pictures, paintings and all other monuments of feigned miracles, pilgrimages, idolatry, and superstition: so that there remain no memory of the same in walls, glass-windows [sic], or elsewhere'.[14] Later the same year, in December 1547, the Chantries Act removed All Souls' core function of praying for the souls of deceased founders and benefactors so as to ease their passage through Purgatory. Chantries were now 'phantasising vain opinions of purgatory and masses satisfactory, to be done for them which be departed'.[15] Purgatory and Masses satisfactory were pronounced 'papisticall supersticions and abuses' by Cranmer in his Homilies (also 1547), of which every parish was to obtain a copy.[16] The commemoration of All Souls was in effect abrogated in the Book of Common Prayer of 1549. The destruction of images was accompanied by the destruction of the College's primary spiritual purpose.

This was to say the least unwelcome. In religious affairs, as in political, All Souls was a predominantly conservative college. But the fellows were also pragmatic. They endured — by doing what they were told but no more than they were told. Whether by design or inertia, they left the empty reredos as a lasting reminder of what had transpired at the east end of the chapel in 1548.

14 W. H. Frere (ed.), *Visitation Articles and Injunctions of the Period of the Reformation*, 3 vols (London, 1910), ii, 126; Aston, *England's Iconoclasts*, 253–6. For the later articles specifically redacted for All Souls, see Frere, ii, 197–203.

15 Quoted Duffy, *Stripping*, 454.

16 R. B. Bond (ed.), *Certain Sermons or Homilies (1547) and, a Homily against Disobedience and Wilful Rebellion (1570): A Critical Edition* (Toronto, 1987), 112. See also Duffy, *Stripping*, 449.

All Souls
Coll:

PART 4
COVERING

CHAPTER 7

'TOO FULL OF NAKEDS FOR A CHAPELL': ISAAC FULLER'S LAST JUDGEMENT

MICHAEL
LIVERSIDGE

A French visitor to Oxford in the summer of 1663 supplies the earliest reference to the restored and transformed interior of the chapel at All Souls. In a journal entry for June Balthasar de Monconys records seeing the new work that had recently been carried out. The original medieval stone reredos and altar, comprehensively desecrated and mutilated between 1547 and 1551, were replaced by a communion table and whitewash, leaving the niches empty and uncovered. A hundred years later there may have been more damage to repair after Royalist Oxford had surrendered at the end of the English Civil War. Although Monconys actually records very little of what he saw, what he describes signals an extraordinary departure from the reformist austerity it had replaced:

> I went to the College of All-Souls where I noticed at the end of the Chapel and against the wall a painting of the Resurrection. The painter had depicted a Saint Francis in a niche as we do, with a cross in his hand.[1]

A little more information is given by John Evelyn in a diary entry for 24 October 1664 in which he records visiting All Souls and Magdalen colleges to see the recently completed renovations of their chapels and describes their newly painted altar walls:

> Thence to see the Picture on the Wall over the Altar at All-Soules, being the largest piece of Fresco painting (or rather in Imitation of it, for tis in oyle of Terpentine) in England, & not ill design'd by the hand of one Fuller: yet I feare it will not hold long, & seemes too full of nakeds for a Chapell: Thence to … the painting of Magdalen's Chapell … a … Judgement on the Wall by Fuller, as is the other, somewhat varied.[2]

---

1   Balthasar de Monconys, *Journal des Voyages de Monsieur de Monconys, Conseiller du Roy en ses Conseils d'Estat et Privé*… 2 vols (Lyon, 1665–6), ii, 53, my translation.
2   *The Diary of John Evelyn*, ed. E. S. de Beer, 6 vols (Oxford, 1955), iii, 385–6. Was Evelyn alluding to the anecdote in Vasari's *Lives* about how the papal master of ceremonies found disgraceful the shameless nudity in Michelangelo's *Last Judgement*?

Very little now remains of what Monconys and Evelyn saw, and almost no visual records of the new work exist. Gothic Revivalists removed everything they considered out of place, aesthetically as well as liturgically. At All Souls a few painted fragments have survived; of Magdalen there is an engraving which shows the altar wall as it was when the new work was completed, and a later drawing which records the interior after it had been remodelled in the eighteenth century. Reconstructing what the painter Isaac Fuller carried out requires some imagination.

The artist himself remains a relatively shadowy figure. Bainbrigge Buckeridge supplies a brief life of him in *An Essay towards an English School of Painters* published thirty-four years after he died. Isaac Fuller, he says,

> Was an English history painter of good note. He had a great genius of drawing and designing history, which yet he did not always execute with due decency ... there being sometimes a rawness of colouring in them ... but notwithstanding all that a critic may find fault with in his works, there are many perfections in them, as may be seen by his Resurrection at All Souls College Chapel at Oxford, to which that at Magdalen College ... cannot in the least compare. There is also at Wadham College ... a history picture of his, in two colours only, admirably well performed .... He studied ... in France under Perrier, and understood the anatomical part of Painting, perhaps equal to Michael Angelo, following it so close was very apt to make the muscelling too strong and prominent.[3]

Francois Perrier spent the last three years of his working life in Paris, dying there in 1649; before 1646 he had been in Rome for ten years, producing while he was there a series of influential books of etchings reproducing antiquities, mainly sculpture. These, and similar works by Italian artists, inspired a *Libro da Designiare* by Fuller which was published in London in 1654 (fig. 7.1).[4] It is a manual in which he shows how to draw face and body details, together with a few figures

---

3   Bainbrigge Buckeridge, *An Essay towards an English-School* (London, 1706), 420 (modernised). The *Essay* was first published as an addendum to the first English edition (1706) of Roger de Piles, *The Art of Painting*, translated from French by Richard Graham. The only published reference to Fuller in his own lifetime occurred when he was praised 'for story' (painting historical subjects) by William Sanderson, *Graphice: the Use of Pen and Pencil, or, The Most excellent Art of Painting* (London, 1658), 20.

4   Isaac Fuller, *Vn LIBRO da designiare. J.c Fuller Fecit* (London, 1654), 14 pages (illustrated title and 13 pages engraved with figures, heads, limbs, feet, faces and facial details of eyes, ears, mouths) with no text. The only recorded copy is held by the British Museum, Department of Prints and Drawings, BM 1973.0224. 1-14. The title-page is captioned below the printed image: 'Londom. Printed & sld by P. Stent at the white horse in Guiltespur Strete betwixt Newgate & Py Corner 1654'. Anthony Griffiths, *The Print in Stuart Britain* (London, 1998), catalogue no. 112.

7.1 Isaac Fuller, *Un Libro da Designiare*, 1654, etching, 9.6 × 15.4cm, title page for drawing book (British Museum, London, Department of Prints and Drawings, 1973.0224.1)

exhibiting his knowledge of baroque and classical models which he later put to use in his compositions at Magdalen and All Souls. Other than those very large and elaborate projects, he painted some portraits, and also a set of paintings now in the National Portrait Gallery of *The Escape of Charles II*;[5] his most memorable pictures are the four versions of a strikingly flamboyant self-portrait, two of which are in Oxford, one of them dated 1670 (fig. 7.2).[6]

With the exception of Buckeridge in 1706 Fuller was seldom much noticed, except occasionally in Oxford guides and histories: Horace Walpole dismissively remarked in his *Anecdotes of Painting in England* that 'in his historic composition Fuller is a wretched painter: his colouring was raw and unnatural, and not compensated by disposition or invention.... His altar-pieces at Magdalen and All Souls ... are despicable.'[7] Magdalen he would have seen; All Souls he could not –

5 D. H. Solkin, 'Isaac Fuller's Escape of Charles I: A Restoration Tragicomedy', *Journal of the Warburg and Courtauld Institutes*, 62 (1999), 199–240.

6 The four painted self-portraits are: Oxford, Bodleian Libraries (no. LP142), dated 1670; Oxford, The Queen's College; London, National Portrait Gallery (no. 2104); private collection, France (formerly Georges de Lastic 1927–1988; exhibited Paris, Musée de la chasse et de la nature, 2009–10, *Le cabinet d'un amateur*, catalogue no. 16). There is also a self-portrait drawing in pen and ink in the Victoria and Albert Museum, London, Prints and Drawings Collections (no. DYCE 615). The French private collection version (reproduced at: https://www.wikiart.org/en/isaac-fuller/self-portrait, accessed 16 Aug. 2020) is a head and shoulders painted in a fictive stone oval whereas the others are seated half-lengths with different accessory details referring to Fuller's artistic interests, the Bodleian example showing him holding a drawing of *putti* playing which is similar to some of the designs in in his *Libro da Designiare* (n. 4 above). The Victoria and Albert Museum drawing is a head and shoulders study only, but very highly finished, possibly intended for an engraving: S. Owens, *The Art of Drawing: British Masters and Methods since 1600* (London, 2013), 42 (fig. 23).

7 Horace Walpole, *Anecdotes of Painting in England* (Twickenham [Strawberry Hill], 1761), ed. R. N. Wornum, 3 vols (London, 1888), ii, 80.

since in 1716 it had been replaced by James Thornhill's far superior wall-painting in full-blown baroque style.[8] Walpole was, however, relatively complimentary about Fuller's *grisaille* painting 'in two colours only' at Wadham College. This was a cloth hanging carried out in an encaustic wax process, with *The Last Supper* across the whole width of the chapel's east end over the altar, and *Abraham and Melchisedek* and *The Israelites gathering Manna* on the north and south walls. Walpole described it as 'an altar-cloth in a singular manner, and of merit; it is just brushed over for the lights and shades, and the colours melted in with a hot iron'. Since there are no visual records, however, its character can only be guessed at.

The Magdalen *Last Judgement*, with the College founder William of Waynflete rising from his grave immediately beneath Christ in majesty, is known from the engraving by Michael Burghers which illustrated an English version of a wildly eulogistic Latin poem originally composed in 1698 by Joseph Addison, *Resurrectio delineate, ad Altare col[legium]*.

---

8   On which see Johns, this volume. For an overview of sources relating to Fuller and Oxford, see M. J. H. Liversidge, 'Prelude to the Baroque: Isaac Fuller at Oxford', *Oxoniensia*, 57 (1992), 311–29.

Magdal[enae] Oxon[*oniensis*] (fig. 7.3). The print was used again as an illustration for a collection of *Poems on Several Occasions* by Addison published in 1719 together with an extravagantly florid English translation which has been attributed to Nicholas Amherst and was first printed in 1718.[9] Without once mentioning the painter's name, Addison indulges in plenty of 'ekphrastic fantastic' hyperbole about the vivid palette, radiant light, boldly modelled figures and what the translator renders as 'thick Daubings all the Wall o'erspread':

> The hallow'd Field, a bare white Wall of late,
> Now cloath'd in gaudy Colours, shines in State;
> ...

---

9   Joseph Addison, *Resurrectio delineate, ad Altare Col. Magdal Oxon*, first published 1698 in *Examen Poeticus Duplex*, 38–43; English translation (attributed to Nicholas Amherst), *The Resurrection. A poem: written by Mr Addison* (London, 1718); reprinted in *Poems on Several Occasions. With a Dissertation upon the Roman Poets. By Mr Addison* (London, 1719), 80–108 (Latin original and English translation), with Michael Burghers's engraving inserted (p. 93). E. Haan, *Virgilius Redivivus: Studies in Joseph Addison's Latin Poetry* (Philadelphia, 2005), 104–124.

7.4 Ink and sepia drawing by G. Cooper of east end of Magdalen College chapel showing Fuller's mural (decoration added in eighteenth century) and altarpiece of Christ carrying the Cross, 1817

O! may the Painter's Labours never fade,
Nor wastful Time their shining Charms invade,
'Till the first Dawn of that Eternal Light,
Which by his fruitful Pencil shines so Bright.

The anonymous author of *The New Oxford Guide* writing in 1759 observed that Fuller's Magdalen work 'wants grace and composition, and has too much of the Flemish colouring and expression'.[10] As well as the Burghers engraving there is a drawing of the Magdalen interior as it was in 1817, after changes had been made to accommodate an altarpiece acquired in the eighteenth century (fig. 7.4). The *Last Judgement* by Fuller remained in place, but by mid-century it had been swept away when the present Victorian stone reredos was installed to restore dignity and ecclesiological decency to the chapel.

10 Anon., *The New Oxford Guide, or, Companion through the University* (Oxford, 1759), 21.

There are no visual records at all to show what the 'somewhat varied' *Last Judgement* on the altar wall in All Souls looked like. Its general iconography was probably similar to that at Magdalen, with at its centre the College founder Archbishop Chichele resurrected to receive his salvation. From near the end of the seventeenth century, we have Thomas Baskerville's observation that among all the other figures was 'old Chichly rising out of his Tombe'.[11] Although the surgeon James Yonge still noted obsequiously on a visit in 1681 that the chapel was 'delicately painted', Evelyn was quite right that Fuller's work would 'not hold long'.[12] Already in 1677 Robert Plot reported in his *Natural History of Oxfordshire* that its condition was 'somewhat defaced'; and in 1714, just fifty years after Evelyn had seen it, the architect Nicholas Hawksmoor drew up a detailed estimate totalling £49 for scaffolding, boards, plastering and priming to make ready for painting the surface on which a replacement for Fuller's *Last Judgement* had been commissioned from James Thornhill.[13]

The new work over the altar was finished by 1716; it remained in place until it was taken down in 1872, revealing the original medieval stone reredos in its mutilated state. Its uncovering was reported to the Chapel Committee on 2 April 1872:

> All members of the College may not be aware of the existence of the original reredos of stone on the Eastern wall of the Chapel behind a fresco supposed to have been painted by [Robert] Streater, Court painter to Charles II, which in its turn had been hidden by Thornhill's fresco ....[14]

The reference to Robert Streater, who had completed painting the Sheldonian Theatre ceiling in 1669, is a confusion which was already current when Thornhill's replacement of Fuller's work was in hand: George Vertue recalled that, 'When at Oxford An. 1715 I was told then ... All Souls Chappel [was] painted by ... Streeter .... Thornhill painted the resurrection.' It was not until an article by Kerry Downes appeared in the *Burlington Magazine* that the All Souls *Last Judgement* seen by John Evelyn in 1664 was definitively restored to Fuller's name when Downes correctly identified him as the painter of a few related seventeenth-century fragments that had been discovered in 1872,

---

11 'Thomas Baskerville's Account of Oxford', *Collectanea Fourth Series*, Oxford Historical Society 47 (1905), 200.

12 F. N. L. Poynter (ed.), *The Journal of James Yonge (1647–1721)* (Hamden, CT, 1963), 178.

13 Robert Plot, *The Natural History of Oxford-shire* (Oxford, 1677), 276; K. Downes, 'Fuller's "Last Judgement"', *Burlington Magazine*, 102 (1960), 451–52; Johns, this volume.

14 H. Clutton, *A Narrative and Correspondence Relating to the Restoration of All Souls College Chapel, Oxford* (privately printed, 1872), 21–2.

when Thornhill's work was taken down, broken up and some of it discarded.

Exactly what Evelyn saw in 1664 can be at least partially reconstructed by working back from the nineteenth-century restoration to the eighteenth-century reconfiguration of the chapel interior, and from thence back to the seventeenth century. For this, there are two key visual documents: a coloured lithograph in Rudolph Ackermann's *History of Oxford* showing the Chapel looking towards the altar (fig. 8.8), and a painting from about 1760 which shows the altar and Thornhill's grand baroque replacement for Fuller's *Last Judgement* (fig. 8.3). Ackermann's print is especially informative as it clearly shows that Thornhill's painting was part of a larger scheme which extended to figures in fictive classical niches between the windows, and a 'classicised' ceiling painted with coffering set into and between the medieval components of the hammer beam construction of the roof. This features importantly in an account of what was found when work began to remove the eighteenth-century intrusions included in a report written in 1872 by the architect initially entrusted with restoring the chapel, Henry Clutton, who was summarily dismissed when the College Fellows 'discovered' they were inadvertently employing a Roman Catholic. In his own privately printed account of the affair he describes what he found:

> I proceeded to take down the canvas ceilings of Thornhill, when instead of coming on the remainder of the original fifteenth-century roof as I had expected, the work of the seventeenth-century restorer presented itself, and I found that the whole series of Streater's paintings were in existence, and had been merely covered by the canvas of Thornhill. These were, however, at once removed, and then it was that Chichele's roof stood out in all its integrity and beauty.[15]

As the rediscovered paintings from 'Streater's' ceiling were on sturdy oak boards they were cut up into shorter planks and kept to be reused around the College. Much later some remnants were by chance rescued from a timber store, recognised for what they were by the then Warden John Sparrow, cleaned up and restored (figs 7.5–7; also above, p. 16). In a few cases they could be joined together to make up whole or nearly complete figures. It was Kerry Downes who rightly concluded that they had originally been a continuation on the ceiling of the *Last Judgement*

---

15   Clutton, *Narrative and Correspondence*, 10–11. See also Green and Hall, this volume.

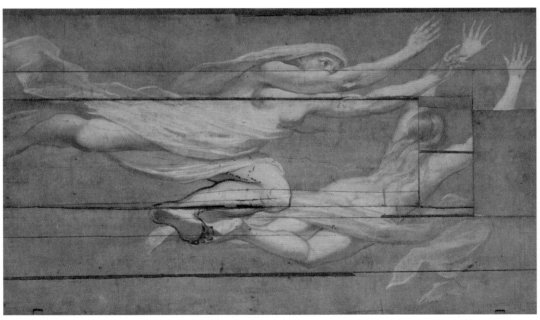

7.5–7.7 Isaac Fuller, resurrected figures from All Souls College chapel ceiling, 1660 – 63, oil on wood, each 90 × 150 cm

which Evelyn had seen over the altar in 1664.[16] Together, the altar wall along with the ceiling covered with energetically resurrected and flying figures would have made up an extraordinary baroque spectacle on a scale no English painter had attempted before. By carrying the subject from the altar wall across the ceiling Fuller was trying to create a visually and iconographically unified effect – one of the first examples in England of treating a whole interior decoratively in the baroque idiom as a single spatial and thematic entity.[17]

The ceiling paintings are painted in oils on thinly primed wooden boards. They must have been specially put in place at the time – there would have been no need to cover up Chichele's roof for religious reasons as there was nothing awkward in the way of imagery to hide for the sake of theological decency. That leaves the altar wall: what did Fuller paint his *Last Judgement* on? It is very unlikely that the mutilated remains of the stone reredos would have been left visible after the dilapidations wrought by fervent iconoclasts when they took

16 Downes, 'Fuller's "Last Judgement"'.

17 Note the total absence of Fuller from the 2020 Tate Britain exhibition and catalogue, *British Baroque: Power and Illusion*, a strange omission as he was the pioneer, even if overtaken by others.

7.8 Isaac Fuller, resurrected figure from All Souls College chapel ceiling, 1660 – 63, oil on wood, 190 × 150 cm.

control of Oxford after the Royalists left.[18] More likely a screen wall made of wood was erected, probably then plastered and whitewashed to keep the chapel plain and without any distracting decoration, in conformity with purist Protestant propriety. Joseph Addison's strange 1698 encomium to the Magdalen Resurrection, quoted above, offers a clue: there had been, he says, 'a bare white Wall of late'. He was writing long after it was painted, but probably he had heard about its prior blank state from some elderly decaying don or ancient retainer who still remembered it. As at Magdalen, Fuller most likely had either a similar pre-existing blank surface to paint on in All Souls which he refreshed with new plaster and priming before painting, or he took whatever was already there down to start again. That presumably was what Nicholas Hawksmoor estimated the cost of replacing, or reworking, in 1714. At the very least Thornhill would have required Fuller's already 'somewhat defaced' surface to be scraped down, freshly plastered and newly primed. No more can be deduced from the rather forlorn survivals of his own painting which the College carefully preserved after it was taken down in sections for the Victorian restoration.

As well as the surviving painted boards from the ceiling there is one other autograph visual record of the baroque style Fuller deployed for All Souls. It is a red-chalk drawing in the National Gallery of Ireland collection which shows a muscular angel of the Resurrection flying energetically through the heavens (fig. 7.9). From the viewpoint the artist has chosen the figure must have been intended for a place on a ceiling. Although it has been inscribed in a later hand as 'one of Fullers mad figures in Mag. Coll: Ox' it must in fact be a study for All Souls. Its style evidently recollects the baroque idiom he had acquired when he was abroad in the 1650s, and as the only known drawing for a decorative scheme by Fuller it offers a valuable insight into the sources he absorbed from contemporary Continental artistic currents.

Lastly, what can be said about the subject the College chose for Fuller to paint? Circumstances following the Restoration were completely different from those which had caused the fine earlier figured reredos to be desecrated. As Clare Haynes has shown, the modest Restoration revival of religious painting which came with regime change was driven by politics as much as it was by doctrine, but in the early years it was still wise to be circumspect.[19] The Resurrection and Last Judgement were ideologically acceptable subjects for Protestant eyes, provided nothing

---

18   But see Horden, this volume, 199. Note also Wilson's comment (pp. 108 – 9 above) on the two horizontal channels cut into the niches at some point.

19   C. Haynes, *Pictures and Popery: Art and Religion in England 1660 – 1760* (Aldershot, 2006).

7.9 Isaac Fuller, *Angel of the Resurrection*, 1660 – 63, red chalk heightened with white on wove paper, 26 × 17 cm. A study for a figure on the ceiling of All Souls College chapel, incorrectly inscribed in ink by a later hand, 'One of Fullers mad figures in Mag. Coll: Ox' (National Gallery of Ireland, Dublin, NGI.2114)

overtly idolatrous or indecorous was included. Evelyn's comment, 'too full of nakeds for a Chapell', registers the shock of the nude, but it was appropriate to the subject, though presumably not for Archbishop Chichele. Politics may have played a part: in the context of the moment, the Restoration was a kind of national Resurrection, and the Last Judgement could be perceived as a potent metaphor for retributive justice in the post-Rebellion world. In Oxford circles, the Magdalen and All Souls iconographies would presumably have been all the more acceptable because they were images which venerated the memory of their founders. Their presence validated the subject, as Joseph Addison clearly conveyed in his encomium to the Magdalen painting:

> But whence this sudden Blaze of dazzling Light!
> What Mitred Brow is that, which greets my Sight?
> Forth from a stately Tomb he lifts his Head,
> And to the Skies on Angels Wings is sped.
> I know the Form – alike the Look and Mien,
> Another WAINFLET in his Face is seen:
> When will, alas! Such spotless Worth be found?
> When will a Mind with equal Virtues crown'd?
> Fearless he sees almighty Vengeance rise,
> And fixes on his GOD his guiltless Eyes.

As with Waynflete at Magdalen, Chichele must have featured prominently at All Souls among the resurrected. In that respect James Thornhill's replacement followed the precedent set by Isaac Fuller.

CHAPTER 8

RE-COVERING THE EARLY EIGHTEENTH-CENTURY CHAPEL: JAMES THORNHILL'S RESURRECTIO VESTITA

RICHARD JOHNS

It is unusual for the destruction of a work of art to be remembered as an act of restoration. When the skeleton of the fifteenth-century reredos of All Souls was discovered behind an eighteenth-century mural in 1872, at the height of Gothic revivalism, there was no question over the removal of the painting, by then partially obscured by more than a century of candle soot. Nevertheless, several fragments of the monumental mural were carefully cut from the wall and preserved, like archaeological finds, and today hang unobtrusively on a staircase in the north-west corner of the Hawksmoor quadrangle. These heavy tablets (see, for example, figs 8.1 and 2) give a good indication of the visual and material qualities of the work, initiated by George Clarke and painted by the renowned artist James Thornhill in 1715–16.[1] The chronology and accounts of Thornhill's intervention at All Souls are reasonably well documented. However, as a result of the nineteenth-century destruction/restoration, relatively little attention has been given to the appearance of the early eighteenth-century redecoration and its significance in the chapel's longer history. This chapter pieces the fragments together to bring the early eighteenth-century chapel back into view, suggesting new ways of understanding the work that was undertaken and its importance for

---

1   Among the Warden's Manuscripts in the College archive is a retrospective summary of Thornhill's work in the chapel (Warden's MS 3, ff. 83r–84v), kindly supplied by Robin Darwall-Smith:

     1715: In this year was begun (and finishd before Easter 1716) the Painting att the East End of the Chappell over the Marble, done by Mr. Thornhill. For this work Henry Seymur-Portman Esq. (Heir to Sr Wm Portman Bart a former Benefactour to our College) gave 200 LL; Mr. John Webb late Fellow 20 LL

     1716: This year in the Spring the Roof of the Inner Chappell was richly adorn'd with Gilded Roses and network, being Done upon Canvass sett in Frames: and also the sides Painted and adorned with Figures, all by the Hand of Mr. James Thornhill aforesaid, att the Expence of the Honourable Dodington Grevile Esqr (Uncle to the present Lord Brooke) now a Fellow of the College. Itt cost him 262 Ll 10s.

     See also Warden's MS 17, item 31. For a modern summary, see Colvin and Simmons, 58 (with 83).

8.1 James Thornhill, *Henry Chichele*, from the east wall of All Souls College chapel, 1715–16 (removed 1872), oil on plaster, 320 × 220 cm

the dramatic transformation of the College in the decades that followed. The reconstruction is helped by other visual remnants of the eighteenth-century scheme, including a handful of works on paper, an oil sketch and, crucially, an early painting of the chapel's east end commissioned

8.2 James Thornhill, *St Peter with St Paul and St John*, from the east wall of All Souls College chapel, 1715–16 (removed 1872), oil on plaster, 246 × 185 cm

OVERLEAF

8.3a Attrib. 'Green', study
of the east end of All Souls
College chapel, between 1716
and 1773, oil on wood,
100 × 63.2 cm (All Souls
College, Oxford)

8.3b Surviving fragments of
Thornhill original overlaid
on Green's painting

by Clarke from a long-forgotten artist named Green (fig. 8.3a; fig. 8.3b
shows the surviving mural fragments superimposed).[2]

Thornhill was an obvious choice for a new decorative scheme at All
Souls. Over the previous decade he had established a successful career
as a painter of grand-scale allegorical and mythological decoration,
in a manner introduced to the English court by the Italian painter
Antonio Verrio in the 1670s.[3] One decisive early commission in 1707,
for a staircase and saloon for the Duke of Devonshire at Chatsworth,
confirmed Thornhill's reputation as the only English-born painter
capable of competing alongside the most prominent foreign artists for
the most prestigious projects. It led to his most visible and celebrated
scheme, an all-encompassing fantasy of Protestant succession, naval
power and imperial ambition in the great hall of the Royal Naval
Hospital at Greenwich, the first stage of which was completed in spring
1714. Clarke was among the hospital's commissioners, and the hospital's
then surveyor, Nicholas Hawksmoor, had already begun drawing up
plans with Clarke for rebuilding the College. Thornhill's arrival at All
Souls in 1715 coincided with another career-defining commission, to
decorate the inner dome of St Paul's Cathedral with a series of eight New
Testament scenes from the life of Paul. Thornhill thus had a claim to be
the most successful British painter ever to have lived, and the All Souls
commission brought him into close company with a new and lucrative
circle of patrons whose High Tory politics set them apart from the
artist's predominantly Whiggish clientele.[4]

Green's painting of the east end of the chapel shows the
extraordinary apotheosis scene that Thornhill devised for this wall.

---

2   The provenance and likely attribution of the painting were outlined by John Sparrow shortly after it was
    acquired by the College in 1959. See 'An Oxford Altar-Piece: A Further Note', *Burlington Magazine*, 102
    (October 1960), 452–3.

3   For an overview of Thornhill's work see E. Croft-Murray, *Decorative Painting in England 1537–1837*, 2
    vols (London, 1962–70), esp. i, 69–78; also, R. Johns, '"Those Wilder Sorts of Painting": The Painted
    Interior in the Age of Antonio Verrio', in D. Arnold and D. Peters Corbett (eds), *A Companion to British
    Art: 1600 to the Present* (Oxford, 2013), 79–104.

4   The art historian Matthew Craske identifies the renewal of devotional art in early 18th-century Oxford,
    of which Thornhill's work at All Souls was the most fulsome expression, with a revived 'Anglican
    nationalism', directed by George Clarke and rooted in the politics of Restoration, and in the formal
    innovations of an English baroque that Christopher Wren introduced to the city in the 1660s. M. Craske,
    'George Clarke's Oxford: The Patriotic Creation of a Monumental City', in R. Darwall-Smith and P.
    Horden (eds), *The Unloved Century: Georgian Oxford Reassessed*, forthcoming. Immediately after All Souls,
    Thornhill went on to paint an *Ascension* for the chapel of Queen's College. He later painted a staircase
    for Henry Seymour Portman at Sherborne House in Dorset. Thornhill's ability to navigate between the
    stiffening party lines of early 18th-century politics (exemplified by his enduring friendship with Clarke)
    was a significant factor in his professional success. His proclivity towards the College was also personal:
    the physician, Thomas Sydenham, a distant cousin who had brought Thornhill to London as a teenager
    and set him on a path to becoming a painter, was a former fellow.

8.4 James Thornhill, design
for the east wall of
All Souls College chapel,
c. 1715, pen and wash,
32.3 × 20.2 cm (Art Institute
of Chicago. Leonora Hall
Gurley Memorial Collection)

Henry Chichele kneels at the right of the picture, attracting the viewer's
eye with his blue cope edged with a heavy band of gold decorated
with pearls and gemstones (fig. 8.1). He looks towards the light with
open arms, a gesture that reveals a simple white cassock beneath the
rich materials of his vestments. Two winged angels guard his staff and
mitre. Seated at the centre of the scene is St Peter (fig. 8.2). Holding
the keys to heaven in one hand, Peter gestures with the other in
confirmation of Chichele's ascent. Either side of Peter, we see Paul with
his sword and John with the poisoned chalice. Other apostles survive
among the fragments of Thornhill's painting, each identifiable by the
tools of their martyrdom and other saintly attributes. Green's closely
observed painting, as well as providing a contemporary impression
of the composition and colour of Thornhill's design, offers the most
complete visual record of the classical marble altar frame that Clarke
had presented to the College in 1713. The painter devoted as much

8.5 James Thornhill,
*Apotheosis of Archbishop
Chichele*, c. 1715, oil on canvas,
38 × 51 cm (Museum of Fine
Arts, Budapest, 85.3)

attention to the rich textures of the different marbles, and the gilt
candlesticks and velvet communion cloth also gifted by Clarke, as to the
details of the painting above.[5] The predominance of the architectural
setting in Green's painting underlines the transformative intent of
Clarke's intervention in the chapel and its importance for Thornhill's
design. By introducing the 'Roman Order' into the Gothic interior,
partially obscuring (and in the process condemning) Isaac Fuller's
decayed *Last Judgement*, Clarke established a scale and a centre of gravity
for all that followed. Its effect can be traced across a succession of
drawings (figs 8.4, 7) and the oil sketch (fig. 8.5).[6] These preparatory
designs, characteristic of Thornhill's working practice, provide us with

5   J. Gutch (ed.), *The History and Antiquities of the Colleges and Halls in the University of Oxford by Antony Wood*,
    M.A., 2 vols (Oxford, 1786–90), i, 289.
6   Five known drawings relate to the scheme. As well as the two drawings illustrated here, two others are
    in the collection of the Ashmolean Museum, Oxford. Another was formerly in the collection of George
    Oprescu (now coll. Institutal de Istoria Artei 'G. Oprescu', Bucharest). See J. Sparrow, 'An Oxford Altar-
    Piece: A Further Note', *Burlington Magazine*, 102 (January 1960), 4–9; and K. Garas, 'Two Unknown
    Works by James Thornhill', *Burlington Magazine*, 129 (November 1987), 722–3.

8.6 James Thornhill, *Apotheosis of Romulus*, sketch for a ceiling, possibly for Hewell Grange, Worcestershire, *c.* 1710, oil on canvas, 48 × 52 cm (Tate, London, N06200)

a vivid sense of the evolution of the east wall – of the creative work and compromise of painting on a grand architectural scale – as the artist rearranges Chichele and an extended cast of apostles on a billowing mass of cloud between the outlines of Clarke's pedimented structure and the medieval roof.

Thornhill's scheme indeed occupied the space between the present and the past. If the composition and manner of the painting followed Clarke's formal 'Roman' lead, its protagonists maintained a purposeful continuity with the medieval iconography of the College. Images of Christ's apostles are among the most prominent survivals (then as now) of the original fifteenth-century chapel, occupying the upper tier of the four stained-glass windows on the east side of the antechapel. An attentive observer in the eighteenth century would have been struck by the dramatic shift in style as the same characters moved from window

8.7 James Thornhill, design for the east wall of All Souls College chapel, c. 1715, pen and wash, 45.5 × 32.5 cm (All Souls College, Oxford). The reverse includes Nicholas Hawksmoor's estimate for the cost of scaffolding in the chapel and for boarding, plastering and priming the east wall ready for painting.

to wall. Released from the perpendicular symmetry of the fifteenth-century glass, Thornhill's apostles reconvened on the east wall with an animated informality, seemingly competing for each other's – and the viewer's – attention. In another context they might be mistaken for an assembly of pagan gods contesting the posthumous fate of a military hero, as envisaged, for example, in Thornhill's sketch for a now-lost ceiling showing the apotheosis of Romulus (fig. 8.6). In one early design for the east end of All Souls (fig. 8.7), Thornhill introduced Christ and the Virgin seated on top of a cloud as if they were Jupiter and Juno presiding over an Olympian feast on the ceiling of a country-house dining room. In the final design they are lifted from view, their presence implied by the haloed light that Thornhill conjured from beyond the medieval rafters. Contemporary commentators could not agree on a precise interpretation of what they encountered in the chapel. Early Oxford guidebooks described Thornhill's scheme alternatively as an 'Assumption-piece' and a 'Resurrectio vestita' — the latter, by referencing Chichele's archiepiscopal robes, distracting the reader from the fact that he was not a saint or a martyr.[7] Neither description conveys the unorthodox fusion of medieval ecclesiology and baroque fantasy in which a fifteenth-century archbishop takes his place among the saints as if he were Romulus or Caesar being welcomed by the gods.

Thornhill's work on the east wall was completed before Easter 1716, by which time plans had been agreed to extend the scheme into the main body of the chapel. In February and March that year, the fellows agreed to repair and remodel the rest of the chapel following new ideas and designs proposed by Thornhill. The artist's expanded scheme, undertaken at the expense of the long-standing fellow Dodington Greville, covered the ceiling with feigned coffering and rosettes 'heigten'd with Gold'.[8] This additional decoration was painted on canvas panels inserted between the rafters, as recorded in Frederick Mackenzie's early nineteenth-century view in Rudolph Ackermann's History of the University of Oxford (fig. 8.8).[9] The piers between the windows on the north and south walls were painted with feigned niches filled with statues of the four doctors of the Church (the chapel's dedicatees) and other historical figures, including Chichele and Henry VI. Cartouches above the niches were reserved for the arms of more recent benefactors and college worthies.[10] None of this survives, although something of its general effect may be gleaned from the painted coffering and trompe l'oeil niches that Thornhill went on to design for the chapel

---

7   See, for example, A Pocket Companion for Oxford (Oxford, [1753]), 55; Wood ed. Gutch, 290; and Rudolph Ackermann, A History of the University of Oxford, its Colleges, Halls, and Public Buildings (London, 1814), as in caption 8.8. Thornhill's painting is described by Stephen Niblett (Warden 1726 – 66) as 'ad Resurrectionem quem dicunt Vestitam' (Warden's MS 17, item 31). In most eighteenth-century accounts of Thornhill's career, where the chapel typically receives a brief but prominent mention, 'Altar Piece' is used to describe the whole east wall.

8   ASC archives, Acta in capitulis, 22 [February] and 16 March 1715/16.

9   The relevant entry in the Acta implies that the ceiling was already panelled, in part at least, as part of Fuller's earlier decoration (see Liversidge's chapter, this volume).

10 Several of these are visible in Mackenzie's print. For a full list see Wood ed. Gutch, 290 – 91.

8.8 Joseph Constantine Stadler after Frederick Mackenzie, *Chapel of All Souls College*, aquatint coloured by hand, 270 × 205 mm (All Souls College, Oxford), illustration for *Rudolph Ackermann, A History of the University of Oxford, Its Colleges, Halls and Public Buildings*, 2 vols (London, 1814), i, between 218 and 219. The print shows James Thornhill's replacement for Fuller's *Last Judgement* over the altar, together with the later, classically framed, eighteenth-century altar-piece by Anton Raphael Mengs; above, the painted coffering on the sloping sides and flat centre of the ceiling conceal the areas also painted by Fuller but covered over by Thornhill.

at Wimpole in Cambridgeshire.[11] In the most substantial alteration to the fabric of the chapel, the door leading to the old vestry on the north side, between the choir stalls and the altar frame, was blocked, plastered over and painted with a large trompe-l'oeil vase, heightened with more gold and decorated with the Baptism of Christ; another vase on the

---

11 Croft-Murray notes that details of Thornhill's work at All Souls, including his prices, were sent to Lord Harley at Wimpole by William Stratford, Canon of Christ Church, in 1721. *Decorative Painting in England*, i, 273.

corresponding wall featured a depiction of the Lord's Supper.[12] The vestry itself was demolished without ceremony soon after, clearing the way for the new north quadrangle designed by Hawksmoor. Thornhill also recommended that the wainscoting and seating in the chapel be painted 'a clean Stone Colour', and the same extended to the walls and ceiling of the antechapel.[13] Other work, including new gilding and bell-glasses for the sconces, and the replacement of the great west window with painted white glass, was designed to channel more diffused light into the main body of the chapel. As work progressed, Thornhill suggested further alterations to improve the symmetry of the building, reshaping one of the great pillars and blocking the two north windows in the antechapel. He also proposed that the existing screen separating chapel and antechapel be modified according to his own design, an elaborate Corinthian structure more in tune with Clarke's altar frame, topped with a broken pediment and decorated with the arms of Chichele and William Portman (whose heir, Henry Seymour Portman, contributed £200 towards the east wall).[14]

The overall impact of so much new paint and gold leaf was a substantial brightening and partial flattening of the chapel interior, as suggested in Mackenzie's view. Fifteenth-century beams and braces protruded through the canvas ceiling, and the carved wood and stone of the original choir stalls and windows skirted the two-dimensional illusionism of Thornhill's brush. The resulting intersection of medieval and classical forms throughout the scheme is key to understanding the desired effect, and eventual fate, of the eighteenth-century chapel. What Victorian tastes eventually rejected as an imposition on the Gothic purity of the building had been intended as a necessary 'beautifying' of a place of worship that still bore the scars of iconoclasm, which the raw English mannerism of Fuller's *Last Judgement* had only partially and impractically hidden. In the eyes of Thornhill's contemporaries, both were in need of covering. Clarke's purpose was never fully to obscure the Gothic styling of the chapel, but to fold the pre-Reformation iconography of All Souls into the here and now, aligning the fabric and

12 *Acta in capitulis*, 16 March 1715/16. The vase on the north wall is visible in a rare etching from George Cooper's *Oxford Portfolio* (1817), here fig. 9.2a. Both vases are singled out for attention in early college guides. See, for example, *A Pocket Companion for Oxford* [1753], 55.

13 *Acta in capitulis*, 22 [February] 1715/6.

14 *Acta in capitulis*, 17 April 1716; Warden's MS 17, 31. For glass in the eighteenth-century chapel see further Darwall-Smith, this volume 237–8.

early history of the College with the interests and aspirations of a new generation of benefactors.[15]

Such an alignment is also at work in two full-length portraits given by the fellow Nathaniel Lloyd for display in the hall in the late 1720s or early 1730s (figs 8.9 and 10). These posthumous portraits of Chichele and Christopher Codrington, who left a fortune to All Souls in his will, have been attributed to Thornhill, although it seems likely they were completed (if not painted entirely) by his contemporary and sometime collaborator Thomas Gibson.[16] In the context of Clarke's extended vision for All Souls, which included the building work then under way to Hawksmoor's designs, the two paintings converse in ways that echo

---

15 Over time, monuments to Greville and Clarke were added to the antechapel and the painted cartouches above the figures on the north and south sides of the chapel were filled with the arms of a new generation of benefactors who transformed the fabric and fortunes of the College.

16 Both portraits were the gift of Nathaniel Lloyd, whose own likeness by Gibson was painted for the hall in 1733. See J. Guinness, 'Portraits of Sir Nathaniel Lloyd', *Oxoniensia*, 25 (1960), 96–101. The firm attribution of Lloyd's likeness to Gibson adds to speculation over the authorship of the other two. The most detailed and often-cited eighteenth-century history suggests that all three were 'painted by the same hand' (Wood ed. Gutch, 280), a claim that has been interpreted subsequently as 'painted by Thornhill'.

the play of Gothic and classical forms initiated in the refurbishment of the chapel. As Matthew Craske has suggested, by pairing the College's founder with its most prodigious modern benefactor, the portraits identified Codrington as its 'second founder'.[17] Codrington's huge wealth derived from slave plantations in the Caribbean. He died and was buried in Bridgetown, Barbados, in 1710, but six years later his remains were exhumed and returned to England to be interred at All Souls. In accordance with the terms of his will, his new grave in the antechapel was marked by a £20 black marble slab.[18] His credentials as a colonial pioneer are made visible in the portrait by his Romanising fancy dress and a standing globe, while the telescope refocuses the profits of his Caribbean estates on to a pile of books and a copy of his will, with its bequest that included his own library and £4,000 to buy books. As part of the broader remodelling of the College, Codrington's portrait performed a pictorial sleight of hand that subsumed the riches generated through the violence of the Atlantic slave trade into a virtuous narrative of spiritual wellbeing and intellectual freedom. It seems strangely fitting that another important painting produced by Thornhill for the College (fig. 8.11), a large Old Testament subject commissioned by Thomas Palmer for the new hall (the rebuilding of which began in 1729), represents Josiah tearing his clothes after recognising the ungodly behaviour of his forbears.[19]

Thornhill's painting in the chapel survived for more than 150 years, longer than any other scheme for its east end (so far). Its appearance and eventual erasure marked one episode in the long-running battle of styles that has shaped Oxford over the centuries. Its ultimate fate also fits a pattern of destruction of baroque decoration that began earlier in the nineteenth century with the wholesale removal of Verrio's painted ceilings at Windsor Castle, as part of Jeffry Wyatville's plans to remodel the royal palace. In the 1870s Thornhill's painting in the inner dome of

17 Craske, forthcoming.

18 Wood ed. Gutch, 298. For Codrington see S. Mandelbrote, 'The Vision of Christopher Codrington', in S. J. D. Green and P. Horden (eds), *All Souls under the Ancien Régime* (Oxford, 2007), 132–74.

19 2 Kings 22:11–13. Signed and dated 1733, the canvas is among the most ambitious of a series of late easel paintings by Thornhill. It is also the last painting he is known to have completed before his death the following year. Among a rich and strange cluster of other early eighteenth-century paintings at All Souls is a grisaille overmantel in hall, representing Chichele directing the building of the College. The restricted palette, and the curious inclusion of two figures in eighteenth-century dress, put this canvas in the company of four other grisaille paintings, all Old Testament or mythological subjects, which Marco Riccòmini has identified as translations of seventeenth-century prints after paintings by Raphael and Annibale Carracci (correspondence with Riccòmini kindly shared by Noel Malcolm). Whether this group of grisailles were made by Thornhill or (as seems more likely) by one or more unidentified contemporaries, they made a significant contribution to the iconography of the eighteenth-century College.

St Paul's Cathedral narrowly avoided destruction as part of the Gothic resurfacing of the building's interior. In the same decade, in country houses across England, numerous painted staircases and ceilings were lost without visual trace, torn down or overpainted to make way for the tastes and aspirations of another century. Calls to replace the artist's work at All Souls had gathered pace for a generation[20] – and, after much debate, as Green shows below, the discovery of what was believed to be the original fifteenth-century reredos provided the catalyst to make it happen. For the same reasons, a proposal by the art dealer and picture restorer Raffaele Pinti to reassemble Thornhill's painting at the new South Kensington Museum, a monument to high Victorian tastes, never

---

20 See Darwall-Smith, this volume, 254 – 5.

8.12 James Thornhill, *Putti and curtain*, from the east wall of All Souls College chapel, 1715–16 (removed 1872), oil on plaster, 222 × 193 cm (All Souls College, Oxford)

had a realistic chance of success. Clarke's marble altar frame was sold for £113.[21]

To focus on significant moments of change – of covering and uncovering – draws attention to the chapel as a site of continual negotiation (slow moving, sometimes violent) between the actions and aspirations of the living and the entangled legacy of those who came before. It also prompts us to question, if only momentarily, the presumption of permanence that prevails in our own time. Among the surviving fragments of Thornhill's painting is a section, now barely legible through the bloom of old varnish, in which two putti cling playfully to a swag of bright red fabric – part of a curtain that has just dropped to reveal the apotheosis scene behind (fig. 8.12). Such details were part of the stock-in-trade of the eighteenth-century decorative painter. The fabric and limbs that tumble out of the picture space mediate between the timeless, fictive realm of the painting and the three-dimensional present of the chapel. They dramatise the reveal, and revel in the potential of art to conjure a fantastical, gravity-defying display. Together, the surviving pieces of Thornhill's painting reveal how the complex interplay between the main fabric and its decoration – between the solidity of carved wood and stone and two-dimensional illusionism – once brought the founding mythology of the College into closer communion with the eighteenth-century fellowship. But it always was an illusion performed for the moment, anticipating the next act.

21 See Sparrow, 'An Oxford Altar-Piece: A Further Note', 6. Pinti estimated the cost of transporting and reassembling the painting at around £100, 'if a room can be obtained for the purpose'.

CHAPTER 9

MORE THAN MENGS: THE CHAPEL BETWEEN THORNHILL AND SCOTT

ROBIN
DARWALL-
SMITH

The late eighteenth century is perhaps the obscurest and remotest period in the history of All Souls chapel, as seen from the perspective of the reredos: the obscurest, because by then next to nothing was known about a structure which had by now been hidden from view for a century; and the remotest, because the aesthetic which inspired the decoration of the chapel at this time was so comprehensively rejected in the following century that even in the early twenty-first century it has few defenders. This period is best known for the commissioning of a major painting, Noli me tangere, by Anton Raphael Mengs (fig. 9.1), but we should see the Mengs as the centrepiece of a dramatic redecoration of the chapel which at the time won the College many admirers. In this chapter, then, I will discuss this redecoration, but also consider what people of the late eighteenth century knew — or thought they knew — about the long-lost reredos. I will also show how a redecoration which at the time was so highly esteemed gradually fell completely from favour.

After James Thornhill had completed his work in the chapel, as described by Richard Johns in the previous chapter, very little was done there for the next half-century, save for the addition of some monuments in the antechapel, most notably those to George Clarke and Dodington Greville. Perhaps the most significant thing to bear in mind during this period is the chapel's glass, and activity in the antechapel provides useful evidence for this. By now there remained no pieces of medieval glass in the chapel proper. The east windows of the antechapel still held (and still do hold) almost all of their original glass, but the north windows were blocked up in 1716, and the other windows, especially the great west window, appeared to have no coloured glass, or at best fragments of them.[1] Indeed, in 1717, the College agreed to

9.1 Anton Raphael Mengs,
Noli me tangere, 1771,
oil on wood, 300 × 180 cm
(All Souls College, Oxford)

---

1   These are the conclusions drawn from F. E. Hutchinson, *Medieval Glass at All Souls College* (London, 1949), especially pp. 14–37.

remove such painted glass as there was in the west window, to recycle in the other windows in the antechapel, and to replace it with 'that white painted glass of the same sort with that in the Windows in the inner Chapel'.[2] This detail is important: the mid-century visitor to the chapel would have seen Thornhill's great painting lit not by clear glass, but glass painted white – and presumably with Thornhill's approval. With George Clarke at hand, the College was unlikely to do anything to the lighting of Thornhill's paintings which would have dissatisfied the artist.

The next chapter of the story of the east end of the chapel only begins in earnest in 1766, when Archbishop Thomas Secker appointed John Tracy as warden. Tracy was one of the best Wardens of All Souls in *ancien régime* Oxford. If not a great scholar, he was certainly a good man of business, and the College was the better for his appointment. In the early years of his wardenship, there are the sounds of a new broom being swept as the College commissioned fresh maps of some of its properties, created a new store for its archives, and exercised renewed rigour over the cases of candidates claiming Founder's Kin.[3] Not for nothing was Tracy a friend of William Blackstone. The redecoration of the chapel took place on Tracy's watch, and even if there were fellows ready to advise him, he must take the ultimate responsibility – and credit – for what follows.

By now Tracy and his colleagues would have known little for certain of the decoration of the chapel before Thornhill's time. As Liversidge has shown above, even Isaac Fuller's painting was sufficiently forgotten that his work was regularly misattributed to Robert Streater, and the awareness – or lack of it – of earlier work can best be seen in a manuscript history of All Souls compiled by Thomas Wenman (fellow 1765–96) in the last third of the eighteenth century. Wenman became Keeper of the University Archives in 1781, and his work on All Souls shows that he combed his own College's archives carefully. When it came to describing the chapel in its original state, he wrote 'the Roof was ornamented with Angels carv'd in wood; the high altar was adorned with the Image of the Holy Trinity gilt and painted & over it were plac'd two great Images of Stone; and the Windows were all glaz'd'.[4] In his accompanying notes, Wenman shows that he was using data from the

---

2   ASC archives, *Acta in capitulis*, 24 May 1717.

3   These details are taken from the *Acta in capitulis* for 1766–68. In 1777 Tracy and the College even persuaded Archbishop Frederick Cornwallis to restrict the proportion of fellows selected as Founder's Kin (CTM, 324 no. 267).

4   ASC Warden's MS 22(4), f. 397r.

College's building accounts for the year 1440, the week beginning 1 October 1440, and the week beginning 21 January 1442.[5] Thus the full magnificence of the reredos remained quite forgotten by the College's late Georgian fellows. On the other hand, those same late Georgian fellows would have urged us to admire the magnificence which they wished to create in that same chapel, and it is to this that we must turn.

The first hint of something afoot is a series of benefactions made towards the chapel, starting in 1767, with a donation of £100 from Sir Banks Jenkinson, who had resigned his fellowship that year. In the following year, another £100 came in from William Blackstone, £90 5s. 6d. from William Craven (fellow 1759 – 68), and gifts of £25 each from two young Fellows, Brownlow North (fellow 1763 – 69) and William Neville (fellow 1765 – 68).[6]

These donations amounted to almost £350 – a tidy sum – and Tracy and the fellows decided that its best use would be to commission a major new work of art to add fresh splendour to the chapel, and their eyes were attracted to the conveniently picture-shaped blank space in the marble-clad tabernacle-like structure installed by George Clarke immediately above the altar.[7] The College minutes of 7 April 1769 show that they were nothing if not ambitious in their plans, for it was agreed 'that a Picture representing the appearance of our Savior to Mary in the Garden after his resurrection be procured from the Hands of Mengs, a celebrated Painter now at Madrid, to be put up over the altar in the Chapel; and that the Warden be requested to write to Mr. Skipp for his further direction'.[8] John Skippe (1741 – 1812), alumnus of Merton, was an amateur artist and collector, who regularly travelled on the Continent.

Anton Raphael Mengs (1728 – 1779) was in 1769 one of the most highly regarded painters of his age, patronised by aristocracy and royalty – indeed, he was at this time in Spain at the express invitation of King Carlos III. Thus the College's next step seems to have been that on 9 May 1769 Thomas Bever (fellow 1749 – 91) wrote, not to Skippe, but to James Harris, the British chargé d'affaires at Madrid.[9] Bever explained that the College has received a 'handsome legacy' for improving the

---

5   Building Accounts, 167, 239, and 264.

6   MS 424, pp. 42 – 43.

7   Fuller accounts of this remarkable commission are given in P. Horden, 'All Souls and Mengs', in S. J. D. Green and P. Horden (eds), All Souls under the Ancien Régime: Politics, Learning and the Arts, c. 1600 – 1850 (Oxford, 2007), 299 – 323, and idem, 'The Oxford Colleges as Patrons of Religious Art in the Eighteenth Century', in R. Darwall-Smith and P. Horden (eds), The Unloved Century: Georgian Oxford Reassessed (forthcoming).

8   Acta in capitulis, 7 April 1769.

9   Hampshire Record Office, Malmesbury Family Papers, 9M73/144/201. Lengthy extracts from this letter are quoted in Horden, 'All Souls and Mengs', 311 – 12.

chapel, and wished to commission a picture for the altarpiece. As Bever put it, advice from 'our Freinds [sic] of taste about the best means of procuring something very elegant' had led them to wonder whether Mengs might be approached. Harris evidently did put in a good word in the right place, because the College minutes of 3 November 1769 ordered 'thanks of the College be presented to Mr. Harris for his assistance & his Letter concerning the Picture for the Chappel'.[10]

There was another tale, though, about the commissioning of the Mengs. An anonymous translator's preface to an English translation of Mengs's collected writings, published in 1796, concludes with a claim that Mengs's All Souls painting 'was ordered by a gentleman of that College whilst on his travels through Spain; but being limited to the price, he was obliged to choose a subject of few figures'.[11] That 'gentleman' can be identified from College records. On 31 March 1764, the College granted William Vyse (fellow 1763–74) leave of absence for a year, as he was 'desirous of making a Tour into Foreign Parts for the sake of improving himself", leave which was renewed on 17 December 1765.[12] The College's minutes for 8 July 1769 then report that 'Mr. Vise be empower'd to offer Mr. Mengs a Sum not exceeding three hundred guineas for a Picture for the Altar in the Chappel'.[13] This suggests that it was Vyse whose travels had taken him to Madrid, where he could meet Harris, and negotiate directly with Mengs himself.

The decision of the fellows of All Souls to go to the top like this was a very audacious one: there are very few instances of colleges at either Oxford or Cambridge having the ambition to go to one of the leading artists of their day to commission a major work of art. Bever's letter is rather modest about this: as he put it to Harris, 'On consulting our Freinds of taste about the best means of procuring something very elegant, we have been advised to apply to *Mengs*, now at Madrid, and said to be the greatest Painter in Europe'.[14] In fact Bever was writing with a certain careless affectation here, because the fellowship in the late 1760s included several men who were well aware of the latest trends in art and were purchasing major texts on classical antiquities for the College Library. Several of them, too, had links to the influential Society

10 *Acta in capitulis*, 3 November 1769.
11 Anon., *The Works of Anthony Raphael Mengs, First Painter to his Catholic Majesty Charles III. Translated from the Italian Published by the Chevalier Don Joseph Nicholas D'Azara Spanish Minister at Rome*, 2 vols (London, 1796), i, 4.
12 Warden's MS 36: minutes of 26 June 1761 and 31 March 1764 (unpaginated).
13 *Acta in capitulis*, 8 July 1769.
14 Quoted in Horden, 'All Souls and Mengs', 311–12.

of Dilettanti.[15] These men will have known Mengs's importance very well indeed, and one must admire their self-confidence in presuming that so respected a painter might respond to their request.

Nevertheless, one can find similarly audacious international commissions elsewhere in the late eighteenth century. In 1785, for example, a confraternity based in Cadiz, the Hermandad de le Santa Cueva, contacted Joseph Haydn, then resident in Eszterhaza in Hungary at the other end of Europe, to ask him to compose music for the special Good Friday services held in their underground chapel. The result was *The Seven Last Words*, one of Haydn's greatest works. Rather like the fellows of All Souls, the Hermandad included well-born and wealthy members, ambitious to seek out the very best.[16]

Undoubtedly the fellows hoped that such a commission would bring lustre to All Souls, not least among tourists visiting Oxford, and proclaim the College to the world as a community of connoisseurs. One might ask, though, what was in it for Mengs. Although Mengs did enjoy royal patronage, he could not live entirely on royal commissions. In addition, during the periods when he was resident in Rome, he did much work for English gentlemen on the Grand Tour, and was considered a rival to the great portraitist Pompeo Batoni. In their meetings, William Vyse could reasonably point out to Mengs that a commission for an Oxford College chapel might serve as a fine advertisement of his skills for young Oxonians who might be travelling to Italy.

Bever and his colleagues were ambitious, but they were also professional. His letter to Harris of May 1769 included detailed advice for the painter about the size of the picture required, where it would hang, and how it would be lit. They now had to wait for Mengs to fulfil his commission, which, it seems to have become clear, he would only do once he was back in Rome. In the meantime, the College was thinking more generally about how it might redecorate the chapel to house its potential acquisition to best effect. The minutes of a meeting of the warden and officers of 3 November 1770 show that the College had some worries about the low levels of its cash reserves, owing to several unpaid property entry fines, but also 'the great Sums that will be necessary for the repairs of the Chapel the ensuing year'.[17]

---

15 See further Horden, 'All Souls and Mengs', 313–16.
16 See, for example, the sleeve note by Jaume Tortella to the recording of the *Seven Last Words* performed by Jordi Savall (Alia Vox AVSA 9854). Savall recorded the music in the very chapel where it was first heard.
17 Warden's MS 35 (unpaginated).

When Mengs was back in Rome, the College had arranged an intermediary in the shape of James Byres (1734–1817), a resident Scottish antiquary and art dealer, who had even taken painting lessons from Mengs.[18] On 21 September 1771, Byres wrote to an unnamed addressee at All Souls with important news.[19] He had now paid Mengs the £315 commission fee, and the picture was finished. He excitedly declared that it was 'among the very best that I ever saw of his painting'. A few weeks later, on 30 November 1771, Byres was in touch once more.[20] Now he reported that the picture had been displayed for a fortnight at the Villa Medici, where 'it gave very general satisfaction'. Any criticisms made of it, he thought, 'were more the Effect of Envy and Ignorance than founded on Knowledge or Reason'. So Byres now devoted himself to settling the complexities of packing a very large painting safely and finding a ship big enough to transport it, and to advising his correspondent on the best ways to clean the painting when it reached Oxford.

There were certainly criticisms of Byres's esteemed master's new work. One observer, a Jesuit priest called John Thorpe (who happened to be an agent for Mengs's rival Pompeo Batoni) wrote to Lord Arundell of Wardour on 25 December 1771 with his own impressions. He thought that the image of Jesus looked too much like the Apollo Belvedere, and showed 'too much of dancing master in the position of the feet'. He was also unimpressed with the control of the drapery both on Jesus and Mary Magdalen. Interestingly, Thorpe also wrote that Mengs acknowledged at least some criticisms of his work, but defended himself with the explanation that 'he conformed himself to the taste of the nation, where his painting was to be placed'. Experience with all those Grand Tourists had clearly left Mengs with ideas on what would be well received back in England.[21]

Various documents at All Souls bear witness to the preparations made in Rome to send the painting from Civitavecchia in October and November 1771, but also to the cost of the whole process. A bill recording the total costs of the refurbishment of the chapel suggests that the College had to spend over £110 – over a third of the cost of the painting – in paying commission to James Byres and transportation

---

18 See Byres's entry in ODNB.
19 CTM, 297 no. 103b.
20 CTM, 297 no. 103a.
21 Quoted in J. Sparrow, 'Mengs's All Souls Altar-piece: A Further Note', *Burlington Magazine*, 107 (December 1965), 631–32. See too Horden, 'All Souls and Mengs', 320–21.

costs.[22] But in May 1772 the painting finally travelled from London to Oxford.[23]

Even before their new treasure had arrived, Tracy and the fellows were planning how to display it to best effect. At a College meeting of 4 November 1771, it was agreed that the warden and officers form a committee 'for improving & ornamenting the Chapel'.[24] The committee seems to have taken most interest first in what to do about the windows in the chapel, which presumably were still painted white, as they had been in Thornhill's time. On 22 February 1772, William Vyse (now back from his travels) was asked to treat with a Mr Pearson and pay him 35 guineas for 'his trouble concerning the Chapel Windows'. A month later the College agreed that 'any Gentlemen of the College, who know any Glass-Stainers, be impowered, to desire to send in proposals for the Chapel Windows'.[25]

Fortunately, one Gentleman of the College did know such people. This was Salusbury Price (fellow 1749 – 76), vicar of Little Marlow, Bucks.[26] In his parish was one Henry Lovegrove (1705 – 1774), who certainly knew about glass painting. He had two sons, John (1735 – 1798) and James (1740 – 1808), who followed him in this profession. Thus a meeting of the warden and officers of 3 April 1773 agreed that 'Mr. Lovegrove of Marlow be order'd to execute another compartment in the Chappel according to the Design already given in, but of a tint and colour similar to the windows of Magdalen College Chappel'. Once again, William Vyse was deputed to treat with Lovegrove on this matter. However, other plans for the chapel were being considered that day, for it was also agreed that 'a stuff damask Curtain of a deep crimson Colour be purchas'd to hang over the large West Window of the Chappel'.[27]

The Lovegroves' suggestions clearly found favour. On 3 November 1773 the warden and officers had more plans for the chapel. Not only should the roof be repaired, Thornhill's painting be cleaned and repaired, and the chapel be painted and gilded, but also it was agreed 'that the Windows in the Chaple be executed according to the plan deliver'd by Mr. Vyse to Mr. Lovegrove, provided that the Necessities of

22 CTM, 297 nos. 103c–f and 106a.
23 The date of arrival is based on the 'Benefactors' section in CTM 415, 'New Titling Book', 1771. This New Titling Book, like the others, starts its financial year in November or December, and, although it has '1771' written on its cover, the greater part of its entries come from 1772. None of the New Titling Books are paginated, and so references here and elsewhere are to sections in each book.
24 Acta in capitulis, 4 November 1771.
25 Acta in capitulis, 22 February and 27 March 1772.
26 The story of Price and the Lovegroves is told in G. D. Lovegrove, 'Without a Suggestion of Vanity', Oxford Magazine no. 109 (0th Week, Michaelmas Term 1994), 5 – 8.
27 Warden's MS 35, 3 April 1773.

the Bursary will admit thereof', and that Lovegrove should execute one window as a sample of his work.[28]

John Lovegrove was the member of the family most involved in the All Souls project, for an undated bill and a letter (the latter written deferentially in the third person) from John shows what he could offer. In his bill, he offers 'To Paint, anneal and Glaze each Window in Chiara Oscura [sic]'. In his letter Lovegrove admits that the job may be tricky, as 'it is a new species of Glass Painting'. On the other hand, he proudly writes that 'without a suggestion of Vanity he is firm in believing no Person in the Kingdom can execute a work of this kind with equal expedition, his original business of Coach Painting having taught him a quickness and facility in Working (Ornament particularly) which no Glass Painter has or can easily obtain, consequently cannot afford to work so cheap'.[29]

What at Magdalen College had so inspired Warden Tracy and his colleagues — and John Lovegrove? In the 1740s the president and fellows there had their altar substantially redecorated so as to install a newly presented Spanish painting of Christ carrying the Cross. At the same time, a set of black and white windows (Lovegrove's 'Chiara Oscura') commissioned a century earlier for the antechapel from Richard Greenbury were moved into the chapel proper, from where, just as at All Souls, the original medieval glass had long disappeared.[30] People at Magdalen evidently thought that the subtle light which the Greenbury windows would shed on the chapel in general and their painting in particular would be a great improvement on plain glass, and Tracy and the fellows of All Souls liked what they saw. They had already gone one better than Magdalen by commissioning a brand-new piece, and they might hope that the brighter colours of the Mengs (as opposed to the austerity of the Magdalen painting) would be shown off to better effect.

Evidently John Lovegrove found the All Souls contract harder than expected: an anonymous account of the College's chapel from 1835, evidently based on some first-hand memories, claims that he was 'obliged to destroy many of the panes of glass which were discoloured

---

28 Warden's MS 35, 3 November 1773.

29 CTM, 297 nos. 105 and 106b. Note that Lovegrove talks of glass *painting*. The art of stained glass making was not revived until the nineteenth century, and Lovegrove, and later Francis Eginton, painted, rather than stained, the glass they produced for All Souls and elsewhere.

30 R. Darwall-Smith, 'The Monks of Magdalen 1688–1854', in L. W. B. Brockliss (ed.), *Magdalen College Oxford: A History* (Oxford, 2008), 352–53. The Greenbury windows were re-installed in the antechapel in 1857, where they remain; see M. D'Ancona, L. W. B. Brockliss, R. Darwall-Smith and A. Hegarty, '"Everyone of us is a Magdalen Man": The College 1854–1928', in Brockliss, *Magdalen College*, 496–97.

9.2a and b East end of
All Souls chapel with the
Mengs altar painting,
Thornhill fresco and larger
decorative scheme, lithograph
(and detail showing
windows) from G. Cooper,
The Oxford Portfolio (1817)
(Bodleian Library G.A. Oxon
b.82 no.9)

in the furnace during the progress of burning in'.[31] To judge from
payments made to him, he finally got to work in 1775, and the work
was finished in 1776, by which time he had been paid £500.[32] Lovegrove
did better financially out of the College than the great Anton Raphael
Mengs, but then he had had to produce ten new windows, as opposed to
one altarpiece.

Unfortunately, no trace of Lovegrove's work at All Souls has
survived, and attempts to find windows created by him elsewhere have
proved unavailing.[33] The 1835 observer calls them brown in colour, 'a
sober and sedate colour, grave and solemn'.[34] More information comes
from a lithograph of the chapel from 1817 produced by G. Cooper
(fig. 9.2a). This appears to show in the windows a succession of circles
one on top of the other, suggesting designs which were abstract rather
than pictorial (fig. 9.2b). Fortunately, Cooper is a reliable witness:

31 Anon., *Advice to Proprietors, of the Care of Valuable Pictures Paintd in Oil ... By an Artist* (London, 1835), 73.
32 He was paid £350 in 1775 and £150 on 28 March 1776. See CTM, 415, New Titling Book, 1774 and 1775
    (under 'Benefactors').
33 A search through the indexes of the complete set of the Pevsner *Buildings of England* series, including the
    revised editions, failed to reveal a single mention of him, and W. J. Drake, *A Dictionary of Glasspainters and
    'Glasyers' of the Tenth to Eighteenth Centuries* (New York, 1955), 90, only knows Lovegrove's All Souls work.
34 Anon., *Advice to Proprietor*, 73.

also in 1817 he drew Magdalen's chapel, and in it some of Greenbury's windows are clearly visible (fig. 7.4).[35] If, therefore, one conceives of Lovegrove's windows more as examples of high-class decorative art than of figurative art, like Greenbury's windows, then one may understand why his somewhat utilitarian claims both that his experiences as a coach painter were to his advantage, and that he could do the work quickly and cheaply, carried weight with Tracy and the fellows. As it was, Lovegrove's work at All Souls was well enough regarded that in 1775 New College asked him to advise on the windows in their chapel.[36]

The rest of the chapel was now ready for attention. Back in November 1773, the College had received a detailed estimate for painting the woodwork in the chapel. Attention, of course, was paid to redecorating the screen, not least all the gilt paint on it, but in addition it was proposed to paint 'all the Carved and Plain Wainscot in the Chapel twice over in Oyl of a bright green Olive Colour'. The estimate was accepted, and Green the painter was paid £67 18s. for his work in the College in 1773/4.[37] Three years later, however, the College was ready for a final major campaign on the chapel. A meeting of the warden and officers on 27 June 1777 agreed to selling old chapel furniture, including the eagle, and purchasing new replacements, that new benches 'to kneel on' be bought. More dramatically they agreed 'the large West Window be cover'd with a Venetian Blind, and – significantly – that 'a proper person be employ'd to take off the Varnish from Mengs's Picture'.[38] Evidently the varnish was starting to darken the painting too greatly, and its removal was no easy matter: 25 guineas was spent for this purpose in December that year.[39] It also appears that the crimson damask curtain bought for the west window in 1773 was now thought surplus to requirements.

At some point in the late 1770s someone in the College sat down to draw up an itemised account of the costs of all the work carried out in the chapel in the previous decade, and calculated that it had cost the

---

35 Cooper's drawing of Magdalen is also reproduced in R. White and R. Darwall-Smith, The Architectural Drawings of Magdalen College Oxford: A Catalogue (Oxford, 2001), 20.

36 G. Jackson-Stops, 'Restoration and Expansion: The Buildings since 1750', in J. Buxton and P. Williams (eds), New College Oxford 1379 – 1979 (Oxford, 1979), 235, and Lovegrove, 'Without a Suggestion of Vanity', 7 – 8. Lovegrove also points out that coach painting could involve such complex and detailed work as armorial bearings.

37 Estimate: CTM, 297 no. 104; payment: CTM, 415, New Titling Book, 1773 (under 'Benefactors').

38 Warden's MS 35, 27 June 1777.

39 Warden's MS 35, 22 December 1777. Mengs's painting has created many conservation problems since its arrival in England, mainly because he created it on wooden panels rather than canvas, for all Thomas Bever's warnings that, because of the English climate, canvas would be better. For the sad consequences of this decision, see further Horden, 'All Souls and Mengs', 322 – 23.

College £1508 4s. 9d. in all.[40] One can get an idea of the scale of these costs from the fact that the College's income from its estates in 1780 was just over £4000.[41]

Now one should imagine walking around the chapel in the late 1770s, using Cooper's lithograph, and the coloured engraving prepared by Auguste Pugin for Ackermann in 1814 as guides. On entering the antechapel, with, first a crimson curtain, and then a great Venetian blind covering the west window, one would find this space significantly darker than it is now. The screen into the chapel proper had been freshly gilded. Inside the chapel proper all the woodwork was now painted olive green, much like the woodwork in the College Library today. The lighting in the chapel, coming in through Lovegrove's grisaille windows, would have been suffused, with no bright sunlight. Some idea of the effect of an interior lit only by black and white coloured glass can be seen today by visiting the antechapel at Magdalen College. It is true that the interior can appear murky on a dark winter's day, but in summer sunshine the light comes through more subtly to considerable effect. This was clearly what Tracy and the fellows were intending for All Souls.

At the far end of the chapel was the Mengs painting, surrounded by Thornhill's great mural, and it is time to look at it again.[42] It is a large painting, three metres high, its height emphasised by the large tree in the centre and the upright figure of Christ. Reproductions do not do full justice to the vibrant colours of his and the Magdalen's clothes, which would have stood out all the more in the subtle lighting of the chapel, as one's eyes were drawn towards the east end. It feels as if the chapel had been redesigned as a great jewel box to show the Mengs off to best effect. But the Mengs is not an easy painting to love today. The artist's delicate neoclassicism (for example, the very understated depiction of Christ's wounds (figs 9.4, 5)) is in danger of seeming anaemic: Father Thorpe's criticisms of the figure of Christ and his dancing master's feet are not so wide of the mark. It has also been observed that his legs do not quite fit with his torso. Meanwhile the sentimentalising depiction of the Magdalen, tears welling up in her eyes, has not survived well (fig. 9.6).

We need, however, to remember the comment made by Mengs in response to criticisms about the work that 'he conformed himself to the taste of the nation, where his painting was to be placed'. What did he mean by that? One should compare here the Noli me tangere created by

40 CTM, 297 no. 106a.
41 Information from the College's expense rolls for 1780 (CTM, 406).
42 For another judgement on the Mengs, see Horden, 'All Souls and Mengs', 320–22. I am very grateful to Dr Lucy Chiswell of the National Gallery for letting me inspect the Mengs in February 2020.

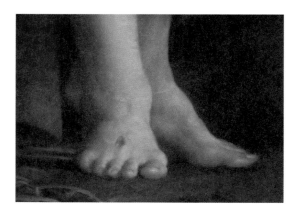

9.4, 5 and 6 Mengs, Noli *me tangere*, details from fig. 9.1

Mengs for All Souls with a very different version of this same episode painted in 1763 and now in Madrid. This work has the advantage of not having had to be made for a rather tall and narrow space, and is perhaps rather better composed. But the lighting on this painting is darker, and the colours of the clothing more muted, than the All Souls image. Furthermore, the face of the Magdalen is almost turned away from the viewer, whereas the expression on the face the Oxford Magdalen is very clear. The landscape on the All Souls painting also has a very Italianate appearance, with luminous Mediterranean light. Was Mengs deliberately 'lightening up' his Oxford picture for his English clients? And was the intense emotion given to the Oxford Magdalen intended to appeal to an audience brought up on the poetry of Edward Young or the novels of Samuel Richardson to appreciate the depiction of affecting sentiment?[43]

Certainly the painting's immediate audience, Tracy and his colleagues, was delighted with it. As if to show its almost totemic status, in official documents, especially accounts, it is always just called 'the Picture', as if no other artwork in the College was worthy of note. Warden and Fellows had a chance to show their personal appreciation of the Mengs in another way. In 1778 an engraving of the painting was produced (not, it seems, commissioned by the College), and Tracy and 23 of the 40 Fellows between them bought 88 copies of the print. Most bought at least a couple of copies, but Tracy bought ten, and Thomas Bever showed his enthusiasm by buying twenty.[44]

Others were interested in All Souls's new acquisition. Since 1768, the College had arranged for one of its servants, Thomas White, to show the Chapel to visitors, receiving in turn a quarter of the fees paid. Normally, the total fees from visitors were added up in April or May. In April 1771 and 1772, the takings amounted to just over £6, but in April 1773, the year when the Mengs was installed, they were £9 13s. We do not know how much each visitor had to pay, but if the fee was 6d, then that would amount to almost 400 visitors that year. Income remained above £7 for the rest of the decade, but in the late 1780s and 1790s, there were some bumper years, such as 1789 (£10 14s.) and 1793 (£19 8s.). No doubt as travel on the continent became more difficult, so British travellers were more inclined to explore local places of interest.[45]

Other Colleges felt inspired to acquire their own Italian works. Jesus College in 1773 was given a copy, possibly by George Romney, of a Guido Reni painting of St Michael and the Dragon; Queen's College was given a copy of Correggio's *Notte*; New College received a Carracci school canvas depicting the Adoration of the Shepherds; Merton was given in 1779 a *Crucifixion* based on Tintoretto; and Corpus Christi acquired a copy, possibly by Pompeo Batoni, of Reni's *Annunciation*. Some Cambridge Colleges followed the fashion: in 1783, Sidney Sussex College acquired a Nativity scene by the recently deceased Giambattista Pittoni in Venice in 1783.[46] These, however, were all existing paintings or new copies of old

---

43 On Edward Young, see now C. Bucknell, 'Edward Young in England', and C. Seth, 'Cross-Channel Memorialisation: Edward Young in France', in Darwall-Smith and Horden, *Unloved Century* (forthcoming).

44 CTM, 415, New Titling Book, 1777 (in the 'Borrowing' section, under the names of individual Fellows). Curiously, although a print of the Mengs dating from 1784 is known, none from the late 1770s has so far turned up.

45 Warden's MS 70, pp. 8–19 and 41–44.

46 For a detailed discussion of these paintings, see Horden, 'Oxford Colleges as Patrons', passim.

work. All Souls still stood out in its commissioning of a brand-new work of art, and eyebrows were raised at the College's choice of a foreign (and Catholic) artist.[47]

Nevertheless, concern about the Mengs lay more with the choice of artist than with the decision to commission a painting for the altar. The default image of an Anglican eighteenth-century church is one of a preaching box, devoid of any decoration, but the truth is more complex.[48] Parish churches might have images of Moses and Aaron, as creators of the Hebrew Law, on their altarpieces, and wealthy churches commissioned grander artworks. Furthermore, a more elaborate degree of decoration was thought acceptable in the private chapels of stately homes or Oxbridge colleges, where it was felt that a discerning congregation could appreciate these works of art without falling into the trap of idolatry. The one art form which remained proscribed was sculpture, except for funerary monuments, because it could be argued that three-dimensional forms were condemned as 'graven images' under the First Commandment.

Meanwhile, some contemporaries were unimpressed by the Mengs on stylistic grounds. Sir Joshua Reynolds, the high priest of English academicism, paid Thomas White his entry fee to see the Mengs for himself in July 1773, and in a letter to a patron, Lord Grantham, he said of this and another Mengs which he had seen that they both had what he called 'a plausible appearance', but he feared that they 'discover no vigour of mind, on the contrary I think great feebleness both in the conception of the picture, which is commonplace, and in the execution'. In a lecture delivered to the Royal Academy in 1788 he considered Mengs once again, this time in comparison with his recently deceased rival Pompeo Batoni. He placed them among those painters 'whose names, though equally renowned in their lifetime, are now fallen into what is little short of total oblivion', and with striking percipience compared their work unfavourably with the landscapes of Thomas Gainsborough, declaring that 'we have the sanction of all mankind in preferring genius in the lower rank of art to feebleness and insipidity in the highest'.[49]

---

47 Horden, 'Oxford Colleges as Patrons', discusses these reactions.

48 The themes in this paragraph are discussed fully in T. Friedman, *The Eighteenth-Century Church in Britain* (New Haven, 2011), 105–26, and C. Haynes, 'Anglicanism and Art', in J. Gregory (ed.), *The Oxford History of Anglicanism. Volume II, Establishment and Empire 1662–1829* (Oxford, 2017), 371–91.

49 Reynolds's letter is quoted in J. Black and N. Penny, 'Letters from Reynolds to Lord Grantham', *Burlington Magazine*, 129 (Nov. 1987), 732, and his lecture in T. Petzel, 'Anton Raphael Mengs and His British Critics', *Studies in Romanticism*, 15 (1976), 421.

In the 1770s and 1780s, however, Reynolds was still in the minority. This can be seen from an examination of some contemporary guide-books to Oxford. One such is *The New Oxford Guide*, first published in 1759. That first edition examines the chapel when it had changed little since the 1710s. Thus the writer praises the 'fine Assumption-piece of the Founder, by Sir James Thornhill', and the 'two inimitable Urns by the same hand', and declares that 'The whole has an air of much splendour and dignity'.[50] The next editions reproduce the above text unchanged, but an edition of the later 1770s, produced after the installation of the Mengs, has something else to report. Thornhill's work is still fine, but our writer's eye is drawn inexorably and ecstatically to the new arrival:

> The Compartment immediately over the Communion Table is filled with a Picture painted at Rome, in the year 1771, by the celebrated Mr Mengs. The subject of this Piece is our Saviour's first Appearance to Mary Magdalene after his Resurrection; which is generally called, by the Painters, a Noli me tangere, in Allusion to the first Words of Christ's Speech to her, 'Touch me not.' This Picture is reckoned, by all good Judges, to have a great Merit. The Colouring is exquisite; especially in the Body of our Saviour. There is something very amiable, mixed with great dignity, in the Countenance and Character of this Figure; while the mild composure of it is finely contrasted by that extasy of Joy and Astonishment which appears on the Face of Mary.[51]

Mengs would have smiled that he had very clearly 'conformed himself to the taste of the nation'. The later editions of this book up to about 1800 preserve this rave review largely unchanged.[52]

While Tracy and the fellows continued to enjoy their 'new' chapel, New College became the next centre of interest within Oxford for religious art. Fresh glass had been introduced from the 1760s to the 1780s, culminating in a great west window executed by Thomas Jervais, and designed by Joshua Reynolds, which, sadly, has ever after been considered something of an artistic miscalculation. New College had had a medieval reredos too, which had been revealed as early as 1695, but then plastered over once more, and covered with what must have been a

50 Anon., *The New Oxford Guide: Or, Companion through the University, Exhibiting Every Particular Worthy the Observation of the Curious in each of the Public Buildings, Colleges, Halls, &c.*, 1st edition (Oxford, 1759), 28–29.

51 Anon., *The New Oxford Guide: Or, Companion through the University, Exhibiting Every Particular Worthy the Observation of the Curious in each of the Public Buildings, Colleges, Halls, &c.* (unnumbered edition, but dated by Eighteenth-Century Collections Online to c. 1778), 39.

52 I have examined the editions of *The New Oxford Guide* published between 1785 and c. 1800.

striking trompe l'oeil painting of an altar in a landscape by Henry Cook. The reredos was rediscovered in 1779, but this time the fellows decided to keep it uncovered, and its restoration became the centrepiece of a refurbishment of the whole Chapel in the Gothic style from 1789 – 94 by James Wyatt.[53]

Meanwhile back at All Souls, the next few decades were a great deal quieter, although some money continued to be given for the use of the chapel, and various repairs were carried out there.[54] One of the largest items of expenditure dates from 1794, when £201 17s. 10d. was spent on a 'Grate for Chapel', presumably installed in the antechapel screen to keep viewers at a distance from the painting.[55] Instead the main concern of the warden and fellows became the great west window in the antechapel: evidently something better than a curtain or Venetian blind was sought. This is not the place to discuss in detail the long debates about that west window, but something should be said here about the climax to the Georgian recreation of the chapel.[56]

In November 1785, Warden Tracy, with his eventual successor, Edmund Isham, and Thomas Wenman were invited to offer the College ideas for the west window, and in the following August they suggested that it be 'glazed with ground glass plain'.[57] However, the College began to consider something more ambitious, and in March 1792 began to treat with Francis Eginton from Birmingham, one of the leading glass painters of the age.[58] Once again, Tracy and his colleagues were taking a leaf out of Magdalen College's book, for in 1791 Eginton had completely reworked the black and white west window in the chapel by Richard Greenbury to dramatic effect. Martin Routh, president of Magdalen, and the fellows were sufficiently impressed with his work to

53   A. H. Smith, New College Oxford and its Buildings (Oxford, 1952), 101–02 and 110–14, and G. Jackson-Stops, 'Gains and Losses: the College Buildings, 1404–1750', and 'Restoration and Expansion: The Buildings since 1750', both in Buxton and Williams, New College Oxford, 219–20 and 233–44 respectively. Cook's painting is completely lost, and no depictions of it appear to survive. Wyatt also worked at Magdalen College (Darwall-Smith, 'The Monks of Magdalen', 355–56, and White and Darwall-Smith, Architectural Drawings of Magdalen, 21–25). See further Hall, this volume.

54   In August 1786 a former fellow, Daniel Lysons (fellow 1751–69), gave £100 'for the use of the Chapel' and in October 1797, John Shaw Brooke (fellow 1780–97), on succeeding to an estate, gave £200 'towards improvements in Chapell' (CTM, 415, New Titling Books, 1785 and 1796 (both under 'Benefactors')). Various chapel repairs were recorded in the Acta in capitulis for 25 November and 26 December 1791, and 19 February 14 March and 9 April 1792.

55   CTM, 415, New Titling Book, 1793 (under 'Benefactors').

56   It is intended that a fuller account of Francis Eginton's great west window for All Souls will be given in the planned history of All Souls by P. Horden, R. Darwall-Smith and S. J. D. Green.

57   Acta in capitulis, 3 November 1785 and 9 August 1786.

58   Acta in capitulis, 14 March 1792.

commission Eginton in 1795 to design windows for the rest of the antechapel.[59]

Eginton's dealings with All Souls were interrupted by the death of Warden Tracy in 1793, and the appointment of Edmund Isham as his successor, but eventually, in July 1801, the College asked Warden Isham to 'apply to Mr. Egginton of Birmingham to send in to the College plans for a new West Window for the Chappel (to be executed by him) together with an Estimate of the expence of putting up the same'. Eginton obliged with a design and an estimate, which was approved in November of that year.[60] The College's accounts show that Eginton was paid £500 in 1802/3, when, presumably his window was installed.[61] Unfortunately, no depictions of Eginton's west window for All Souls survive; one of the few descriptions of it, from an Oxford guidebook published in 1817, says that it was 'painted in compartments, each of which represents an empty niche'.[62] Interestingly, some of Eginton's earlier designs for the smaller windows in the antechapel of Magdalen consist in large part of empty niches, and these designs may give some idea of what the All Souls window could have looked like.[63]

Now the Georgian makeover of the chapel of All Souls was complete, with Eginton's window an additional attraction. Rudolph Ackermann in his history of Oxford now made sure to praise 'the fine west window by Eggington [sic]', but still gave pride of place to the Mengs, claiming that the artist himself 'may justly be ranked among the first painters of the age in which he lived', and calling the All Souls painting 'this fine specimen of his talents'.[64] Ackermann's description was accompanied by an almost luscious engraving of the east end of chapel (fig. 8.8) as imagined during a service of Holy Communion, the white-surpliced fellows meekly kneeling to receive the sacrament. It shows better than any words the full mystery and beauty for which Tracy and his colleagues must have been aiming.

59 Darwall-Smith, 'The Monks of Magdalen', 352 and 356–57, and White and Darwall-Smith, *Architectural Drawings of Magdalen*, 27–9. Eginton's 1795 windows were removed in 1857, and they are now lost. On the later vicissitudes of Eginton's west window, see D'Ancona *et al.*, 'Everyone of us is a Magdalen Man', and L. B. Brockliss, 'Fit for Purpose: Magdalen, 1968–c. 2000', both from Brockliss, *Magdalen College Oxford*, respectively 496–97 and 847.

60 *Acta in capitulis*, 9 July and 11 November 1801.

61 CTM, 415, New Titling Book, 1802 (under 'Benefactors').

62 W. M. Wade, *Walks in Oxford: Comprising an Original, Historical and Descriptive Account of the Colleges, Halls and Public Buildings of the University*, 2 vols (Oxford, 1817), i, 59.

63 White and Darwall-Smith, *Architectural Drawings of Magdalen*, plate 3, reproduces one of Eginton's designs for these smaller windows.

64 Ackermann, *History of the University of Oxford* (1820). i. 221.

Even in the 1810s, however, some did not find the art and the décor of All Souls chapel to their taste. In a guidebook published in 1817, W. M. Wade was certainly struck by the lighting of the Chapel, observing that 'even in the brightest day, a peculiarly solemn and grateful light is diffused through the interior of this fine chapel'. So far so good, but when Wade turned to the Mengs, he observed:

> This piece has undoubtedly merit; but it has we think been praised too highly, and with too little discrimination. The attitudes of the Saviour and of Mary are certainly fine; the colouring of both figures approach to excellence; and the Redeemer's countenance beams forth a union of mild benevolence and dignified composure; but we confess ourselves to have been unable to discover that exquisitely fine expression of joy, mingled with astonishment, and chastened by reverential awe, by which the face of Mary has so often been said to be distinguished. It may almost seem invidious to remark, that a tree in the background is an absolute deformity.[65]

On the other hand almost the reverse judgement was made in 1833 by a German traveller, Johann David Passavant. He thought the Mengs 'a good work of this Master' (ein gutes Werk dieses Meisters), but then thought the windows 'meagre' (mager), for all that the light made 'a good effect' (eine gute Wirkung).[66] Posterity has preferred Wade's opinion on Mengs: the National Gallery has never been presented with a work by him, let alone purchased one.[67]

By 1847, however, J. H. Parker was deeply unimpressed by almost everything he found at All Souls. Although he thought Eginton's west window worthy of note, as far as he was concerned he yearned to see the chapel restored 'to its primitive lovely condition'. 'Take away', he urged, 'the screen, the canvassed ceiling, hiding the old chestnut roof, the Grecian cornice over the stalls, the Grecian altar-piece enclosing the "noli me tangere" of Mengs, Sir J. Thornhill's assumption of the founder, and above all well wash the chapel throughout, and let the genuine oak or chestnut, as it may be, speak for itself, and we have more than enough left to make it one of the most interesting things amongst us'.[68] Another visitor from 1845, Charlotte Elizabeth White, thought that everything in the Chapel 'seemed to me in bad taste', and disliked the 'dark, dingy melancholic olive green' in which the whole interior seemed to be coated.[69] The chapel also seems to have been somewhat

---

65 Wade, Walks in Oxford, i. 59 – 60.

66 J. D. Passavant, Kunstreise durch England und Belgien (Frankfurt am Main, 1833), 64 – 65.

67 Information from Dr Lucy Chiswell.

68 J. H. Parker, A Hand-Book for Visitors to Oxford (Oxford, 1847), 123 – 24.

69 Bodleian Library, Oxford, MS Eng. Misc. e. 1517 f. 26 (quoted in Colvin and Simmons, 58).

neglected: an observer in 1835 noted that some windows had been broken and replaced with glass of the wrong colour.[70]

However, by the 1840s, the age of Auguste Pugin had yielded to that of his son Augustus Pugin, the sworn enemy of classicism and Georgian architecture, and the passionate advocate of a true Gothic style. Even some Oxford colleges had detected a change in the air. In 1829, as the climax of a major restoration of the college, the president and fellows of Magdalen College decided to re-gothicise their chapel, commissioning Lewis Nockalls Cottingham, one of the most learned 'Goths' of the day. Cottingham was alarmingly ruthless. Just about all the wooden fittings and other fittings of the chapel were taken away: the medieval misericords were moved to the antechapel, but much else was sold off. Isaac Fuller's painting at the east end was removed, and, for the first time in at least two centuries, the remains of Magdalen's medieval reredos were revealed. Having scraped the chapel clean, Cottingham then reclothed it in proper Perpendicular dress, which included a recreation of the reredos. Some might find Cottingham's precision somewhat antiseptic, but his work was much more to contemporary taste, and his interior remains admired to this day.[71]

All Souls, in the meantime, rested content with its Georgian chapel. Admittedly, the costs of restoring it to a presumed medieval condition would have been high: the restoration of Magdalen's chapel cost that College over £11,000.[72] This figure might daunt even the keenest Goth among the All Souls fellowship – and, indeed, as will be seen, the great restoration of the chapel in the 1870s only proved possible thanks to some substantial benefactions. In any event, the College had devoted much of the 1820s and 1830s to a major restoration of its High Street and Catte Street façades.[73] Nevertheless, in the light of what had been rediscovered both at New College and at Magdalen it is perhaps curious that the fellows of All Souls of the mid-nineteenth century did not pause to think what might lie behind the Thornhill and the Mengs. Instead the reredos in the chapel of All Souls would remain hidden away for another quarter of a century.

---

70 Anon., *Advice to Proprietors*, 72.

71 See further Darwall-Smith, 'The Monks of Magdalen', 358 – 64 and Plate 17A (a drawing of Magdalen's medieval reredos after its rediscovery), D'Ancona *et al.*, 'Everyone of us is a Magdalen Man', 497 – 98, and Hall, this volume. As Hall shows, Cottingham's proposals for placing statues in the new reredos came to nothing at the time, thanks to contemporary protests. Anglicans were evidently still wary of putting graven (i.e. three-dimensional) images in their places of worship.

72 Darwall-Smith, 'Monks of Magdalen', 364.

73 Colvin and Simmons, 54 – 56.

PART 5
RESTORING

CHAPTER 10

REACTION OR RENEWAL? THE POLITICS OF ECCLESIOLOGY AND THE RESTORATION OF THE CHAPEL, c. 1869–1879

S.J.D. GREEN

In 1874, Montagu Burrows, the first Chichele Professor of Modern History in the University of Oxford, published what he conceived to be the first serious history of All Souls College.[1] In later life, the 'old commodore', as he was (sometimes) affectionately known by his colleagues, came to regard *The Worthies of All Souls* with a certain, quiet, satisfaction. What others sometimes dismissed as a minor contribution, even construed as part of a modest *oeuvre*, he celebrated as 'my first important book', the labour through which 'I learned what [historical] research [really] meant'.[2] For one so widely published, both before and after his elevation to the chair, this may seem a curious judgement. But it entailed neither false modesty nor obvious self-deception. This was because *Worthies* was a work motivated less by the demands of arcane scholarship than in the practical education of his ignorant colleagues: 'The Fellows of the College had not the least idea of its history, and could never explain how the institution had acquired its previous character.'[3]

---

1   S. M. Burrows (ed.), *Autobiography of Montagu Burrows* (London, 1908), 226: 'It led to the publication of the histories of all the other colleges at a later date'. Burrows was referring to the 'University of Oxford: College Histories' series, published by F. E. Robinson from 1899 onwards. It is difficult either to substantiate or to refute his claim to pioneering status in this respect.

2   M. Burrows, *Worthies of All Souls: Four Centuries of English History, Illustrated from the College Archives* (London, 1874); Burrows (ed.), *Autobiography*, 226; for a later, critical, account, see S. J. D. Green, 'Epitaph to the *Ancien Régime*: Montagu Burrows and the Worthies of All Souls', in S. J. D. Green and P. Horden (eds), *All Souls under the Ancien Régime: Politics, Learning and the Arts, c. 1660–1750* (Oxford, 2007), 372–93, esp. 379ff. Earlier books by Burrows included *Pass and Class* (Oxford, 1860) and *Constitutional Progress* (London, 1869). He also published a volume on *Parliament and the Church of England* (London, 1875) at much the same time.

3   Burrows (ed.), *Autobiography*, 226: 'The good old Warden was delighted with my plan, and promised hearty assistance'. The real significance of that support – and this remark – will become ever more clear in what follows.

Burrows believed that this deficiency threatened deeply deleterious consequences for the College. Worthies was intended to put it right – not merely in describing, but also by vindicating, the history of All Souls up to the age of the Selborne Commission.[4] In that way, he hoped to justify a particular view of its proper future development: one which would emphasise the achievements of the past as well as the challenges of the future.[5] He signalled these surreptitious purposes in the 'Preface' of Worthies by juxtaposing his historical narrative – 'the place of All Souls properly understood in relation to the political history of its times'– with a contemporary event – the (as yet) unfinished 'repair' of the College chapel, more particularly with the discovery and 'restoration' of the 'ancient reredos', at its eastern end.[6]

But let him tell his own tale. This began:

> The Chapel of the College had fallen in to a dilapidated condition.
> A thorough [and] necessary … repair brought the question to a point; should the work of the Sir Christopher Wren school be repaired … or should there be a thorough restoration [of] the Chapel left by Archbishop Chichele and his immediate successors? The discovery of the ruins of the Ancient Reredos … a discovery as unexpected as the sculpture of Nineveh, settled the question. Lord Bathurst … munificently undertook the renewal of this great work, and … under the judicious hands of Sir Gilbert Scott … the interior of the Chapel is now undergoing restoration to its original condition.[7]

It continued: 'The writer of these pages happened … in the autumn of 1871 to be on the roof-scaffolding at the very moment … when [some] workmen [innocently] scraping off the plaster from the eastern collar-beam' fortuitously exposed what was 'concealed behind Sir James Thornhill's fresco of the Apotheosis of Chichele [as] letter by letter, there began to appear on a faded gilt the famous expostulation – *Surgite mortui venite ad judicium*. [These were the words] of the founder.'[8]

Burrows concluded:

> Not the slightest tradition had survived that the modernized east end, with its fine fresco, its handsome marble entablature and its well-known

4 On which, see C. Harvie, 'From the Cleveland Commission to the Statutes of 1882', in M. Brock and M. Curthoys (eds), *The History of the University of Oxford, Vol. VII: Nineteenth-Century Oxford, Part 2* (Oxford, 2000), 67–95, esp. 79–80.
5 Burrows (ed.), *Autobiography*, 225–6. In his own words: 'it suggested the idea of an historical judgement'.
6 Ibid., 226.
7 Burrows, *Worthies*, 'Preface', vi. W. N. Bruce (ed.), *Sir A. Henry Layard: Autobiography and Letters*, 2 vols (London, 1903), ii, ch. 6; G. Waterfield, *Layard of Nineveh* (London, 1963), pt. 2; A. C. Brackman, *The Luck of Nineveh* (London, 1980), chs 17–22.
8 Burrows, *Worthies*, 'Preface', vi. On Thornhill see Johns, this volume.

picture of Noli me tangere concealed anything behind it save a bare wall. [Yet] on the removal of all this modern work ... perhaps the finest achievement of the fifteenth century stood revealed .... There was something suggestive ... in suddenly finding oneself standing face to face with an unsuspected past .... [I]t would not be too far from the truth ... to say that the scheme of this ... work dated from that moment. [For] the attempt to unravel the history of these transformations led to a search of the College archives, which revealed a past all but equally ... unsuspected by the present generation.[9]

Judged simply as a chronicle of what was going on in All Souls during the early 1870s, this account was almost entirely erroneous. It was simply not true that no one previously suspected the existence of a fifteenth-century reredos at the east end of the building. Henry Clutton's first report, undertaken as principal architectural adviser to the project from 1869, made it perfectly plain that he envisaged uncovering precisely such a feature on 'restoring ... the original fifteenth-century chapel'.[10] Moreover, the reredos was not accidently exposed by guileless labourers. The College's Chapel Restoration Committee had specifically recommended that this work be carried out. That was done, some time early in 1872.[11] Finally, the fellows then made it abundantly clear to that committee, by a time not later than April 1873, i.e., before the publication of Worthies, that they would not authorise any plan – not even one based upon the 'judicious ... designs' of Sir Gilbert Scott, to restore the chapel to its supposed original condition.[12] From that moment onwards, every proposal made to the College, whether for the alteration or decoration of the chapel, was painstakingly judged on its particular merits, by the whole College, and regardless of the source from which it came. Many projected plans, including some of Scott's, were rejected on that basis.[13] The sole exception was the reredos itself. In that case, Bathurst's 'munificence'

---

9 Burrows, Worthies, vii. Whether or not the reredos was actually constructed in the fifteenth century, or rather in the early sixteenth century, is a question that is considered by Wilson, this volume. No view is offered here. Those predisposed to prefer the claims to architectural pre-eminence of King's College Chapel, Cambridge, might wish to consult the remarks in A. Austen Leigh, King's College, University of Cambridge: College Histories (London, 1899), ch. 2, esp. 17–24; also C. Morris, King's College: A Short History (Cambridge University Press, 1989), 8ff.

10 H. Clutton, A Narrative and Correspondence Relating to the Restoration of All Souls College Chapel, Oxford (privately printed, 1872), 8.

11 ASC, College Meeting Minute Book [hereafter CMMB], 1858–1875 (LR.5.a.6, ms cccci(f)), 239; Report of the Chapel Restoration Committee, Easter 1872, item 3.

12 CMMB, 1858–1875, 267; Notices of Motion, Easter 1873; College Meeting, 15 April 1873.

13 CMMB, 1875–1888 (LR.5.a.7, ms.cccci(g)), College Meeting, 18 April 1876.

really did prove decisive. But even then, the eventual outcome was an inevitable compromise between 'restoration' and 'repair'.[14]

However, Burrows's otherwise fanciful conceit should probably not be judged by the standards of mere reportage. It was certainly not conceived in that vein. His narrative may have deployed many 'wearisome details'. But it did so to advance a subtle argument. His 'Preface', similarly, rehearsed a fictional drama to embellish a partisan cause. Burrows became an active member of the Chapel Restoration Committee in November 1871. This was barely a year after his election to a fellowship at All Souls.[15] Initially regarded by some of the traditionalists in College with suspicion, and that precisely because he was a professor, he first established his conservative credentials in All Souls by publicly associating himself with the goal of restoring a pure, fifteenth-century design to the chapel.[16] That beguiling scene, sketched at the outset of Worthies, permitted this controversial commitment to pass for avuncular instruction. No doubt, few then in College were entirely fooled. But Burrows spoke to an audience beyond its contemporary fellowship. This included quondams, families and friends. These were more likely to be persuaded. The point was to advance an otherwise uncertain goal. This seemed like a good way of doing so.[17]

The argument for restoration certainly needed to be made. For was a bitterly divisive project, arousing strong and contrary feelings both within and beyond the College.[18] Even during the years later characterised by Charles Grant Robertson as the era of its 'Constituent Assembly', a decade and a half after 1865 when the 'air in the College began to thicken with schemes to amend, amplify, or wholly reconstruct the Constitution of All Souls', each apparently related to the other only by its absolute inability to command the support of a stable majority in the College, the various plans for, and the haltering progress of, the repair and alteration of the chapel between 1869 and 1879 proved

14 CMMB, 1858–1875, 271; Report of the Chapel Restoration Committee, June 1873.

15 CMMB, 1858–1875, College Meeting, 1 November 1871. On the curious circumstances of Burrows's election to a fellowship at All Souls, fully *eight* years after his appointment as Chichele Professor, see Green, 'Epitaph', 378–9.

16 Burrows (ed.), *Autobiography*, 225. The Royal Commissioners of 1850–2 had originally proposed the suppression of 24 [sic] fellowships at All Souls to fund the endowment of four new professorships in the University; this the College had successfully opposed. Moreover, it went on resisting the creation of new chairs, attached to All Souls, for years (actually, decades) afterwards. See S. J. D. Green, 'The "Fremantle Affair" and the Destruction of the *Ancien Régime* in All Souls, 1857–1864', in Green and Horden, *All Souls under the Ancien Régime*, ch. 15, esp. 349–55.

17 Burrows (ed.), *Autobiography*, 226.

18 Colvin and Simmons, ch. 3, esp. 59–70, furnishes an outline narrative. It emphasizes the architectural, rather than the political history, of the matter.

especially corrosive of collective harmony. About few other aspects of communal life can the statutory obligations to brotherly love have been more conspicuously breached.[19]

To understand why it is necessary to delve into the curious world of mid-Victorian ecclesiology; more particularly, to consider the then fashionable but vexed question of church restoration.[20] But purely doctrinal and liturgical, and hence also ecclesiological, questions can only explain so much about this particular controversy. This is because All Souls chapel was alternatively 'restored' or 'repaired' – the distinguishing terminology was and is important – during the crucial years of what has been described as 'the nationalisation' of Oxford University.[21] In the quarter century after 1850, Oxford ceased to be an Anglican seminary. Its constituent colleges contemporaneously abandoned their erstwhile, geographic and dynastic, peculiarities.[22] The opening up of fellowships to merit and (eventually) marriage, similarly of undergraduate membership to non-conformists, papists and unbelievers, was matched by a massive expansion in numbers and a revolution in the curriculum.[23] All this is well known.[24] The particular effects of so much change wrought so quickly on the peculiar society of All Souls – a college with no students since the end of the seventeenth century – have been similarly well documented. There is no need to repeat that analysis here.[25]

It is, however, vital also to appreciate something easily neglected. This was that the implications of these reforms, both of the University and in its colleges, were never limited to purely secular purposes. To the

19 C. Grant Robertson, All Souls College (London, 1899), 202. This was the relevant volume in the 'University of Oxford: College Histories' series; see n. 1 above.

20 See W. Whyte, Unlocking the Church: The Lost Secrets of Victorian Sacred Space (Oxford, 2017), esp. chs. 1–4, for a recent introduction.

21 C. Harvie, 'A Nationalized University? Reform and Expansion, 1854–1871', in M. G. Brock and M. C. Curthoys (eds.), The History of the University of Oxford, Vol. VII: Nineteenth-Century Oxford, Part 1 (Oxford, 1997), 697–730.

22 See various chapters in Brock and Curthoys, Nineteenth-Century Oxford, Part 1, esp. W. R. Ward, 'From the Tractarians to the Executive Commission, 1845–1854', and M. C. Curthoys, 'The Examination System'; also A. J. Engel, From Clergyman to Don: The Rise of the Academic Profession in Nineteenth-Century Oxford (Oxford, 1985), esp. chs 1 and 2.

23 See Brock and Curthoys, Nineteenth-Century Oxford, Part 1, esp. chs 15–17, 'Subjects of Study'; and, of particular interest, P. R. H. Slee, Learning and a Liberal Education: The Study of Modern History in the Universities of Oxford, Cambridge and Manchester, 1800–1914 (Manchester, 1986), esp. chs 4 and 6; also F. H. Lawson, The Oxford Law School, 1850–1965 (Oxford, 1968), chs 1 and 2.

24 For a critical view of the effects, see S. Rothblatt, The Modern University and Its Discontents: The Fate of Newman's Legacies in Britain and America (Cambridge, 1997), ch. 4.

25 J. S. G. Simmons, 'All Souls', in Brock and Curthoys, Nineteenth-Century Oxford, Part 2, ch. 8, offers an outline. More detailed analysis is furnished in Green, 'The "Fremantle Affair"', and A. Wooldridge, 'Prizes, Fellowships and Open Competition in All Souls, c. 1850–1950', in S. J. D. Green and P. Horden (eds), All Souls and the Wider World: Statesmen, Scholars and Adventurers, c. 1850–1950 (Oxford, 2011), ch. 1.

contrary: reform raised fundamental questions about the proper place of organised religion in a modern academic community. In this respect, much publicised debates between 'traditionalists' and 'meritocrats' were matched by other, parallel, disputes between 'sacralists' and 'secularists' in Oxford. 'Sacralists' insisted that neither the opening up of college fellowships, nor the extension of University degrees to those outside the Church of England, still less the development of the curricula to include modern humanities and the sciences, had rendered – or should subsequently render – Oxford any less a place of religion. 'Secularists' argued, with varying degrees of emphasis, that they had and must do precisely that. The post-reform University was, in their eyes, primarily a place for the creation and dissemination of profane knowledge. For them, revealed truths now remained binding – if at all – on the private conscience alone.[26]

Abstract argument quickly assumed practical forms. Beyond the matter of non-denominational matriculation, beyond even the revocation of the Test Acts, lay grave, unresolved, questions concerning the proper distribution of resources between secular and sacred purposes: reduced to their most basic forms they often degenerated into conflicts about whether the library or the chapel might in future expect the lion's share of discretionary revenues.[27] Theoretical dispute was also made flesh. This was true with a vengeance at All Souls. The College's principal 'sacralist' was Francis Leighton. He was warden of the College from 1858 to 1881 and, simultaneously, ex officio rector of Lockinge, Wantage. He also served as Vice-Chancellor of the University between 1866 and 1870. He dedicated most of his adult life to the preservation of a religious dimension to England's academic life.[28] Its most important 'secularist' was Charles Henry Robarts, first elected to All Souls in 1864, later a controversial 'Remembrancer' to the Corporation of London, then a Judge of the Supreme Court of the Turks Islands and the man who presented Henry James to the Reform Club; eventually sub-warden and a redoubtable 'Codrington' Librarian. He would probably have been happy to let the College chapel fall down. Afforded the opportunity, he might also have turned All Souls into glorified shelf-space for the Bodleian.[29]

---

26 For a very thoughtful discussion of the effect, see C. Harvie, *The Lights of Liberalism: University Liberals and the Challenge of Democracy, 1860–86* (London, 1976), chs 2–4.

27 For the example of All Souls, see Colvin and Simmons, 71ff.

28 Our Oxford Correspondent, 'Obituary: Francis Kynett Leighton', *The Times*, 14 October 1881, 4.

29 Grant Robertson, *All Souls*, 199–200; Green, 'The "Fremantle Affair"', 370.

Leighton was both a 'traditionalist' and a 'sacralist'. He could hardly have been otherwise. Born in 1806, he was first elected a fellow of All Souls in 1829. After taking holy orders, he became curate of Ilford and then rector of Harpsden. As warden, he combined his Oxford roles with a canonry at Westminster. His obituary commemorated 'a good scholar of the old fashioned type [who] enjoyed a quotation from a classical author, and appreciated the scholarship of others'. This was conventional code for someone both learned and 'refined' but disinclined to original research.[30] That placed him within a perfectly respectable tradition. Such attitudes and attainments would become anomalous only when compared with those of (some) of his successors.[31]

By 1869, Leighton was also a battle-scarred 'traditionalist' and 'sacralist'. He had been elected warden at the very moment when William Henry Fremantle, Godfrey Lushington and Arthur Watson began their seven-year campaign to bring the College's electoral procedures in line with the University's Ordinances of 3 April 1857. These were particularly rigorous. Certainly, they were peculiarly demanding of All Souls. From that date onwards, the College was required to elect only from amongst those who had attained either a 'First Class' in one of the 'public examinations of the University', or to have 'obtained some prize or scholarship open to general competition amongst' its members. The examination it was enjoined to set for these candidates was also supposed to afford special emphasis to those subjects recognised in 'the [new] School of Jurisprudence and Modern History'. Finally, the College was expected to elect 'the candidate who after such examination, should appear to them of the greatest merit, and most fit to be a Fellow of the College as a place of religion and learning with special reference to the subjects recognised in the said school'.[32]

'The Fremantle Affair' plunged the College into internecine conflict about what that requirement really meant. To the young radicals, it entailed no less than meritocratic, academic, selection. For older hands, merit so defined also comprehended ancient learning, moral distinction and personal lineage. Their disagreement got bitter. The case went to court. The radicals won. Their will was legally imposed. Between 1864 and 1881 All Souls was compelled to appoint assistant examiners,

---

30 Our Oxford Correspondent, 'Obituary', 4.

31 Consider Warden Pember, now best remembered, perhaps, for his (apocryphal?) remark that 'anyone who has a First in Greats could get up science in a fortnight'; no less for Professor Lindemann's riposte, 'a pity that [you] never had a fortnight to spare'. See A. Fort, *Prof: The Life of Frederick Lindemann* (London, 2003), 74. F. W. Pember was warden of All Souls from 1914 to 1932. He published nothing of significance.

32 Green, 'The "Fremantle Affair"', esp. 349–55.

specifically charged with drawing up a strict order of merit amongst the candidates, these to be judged solely according to academic criteria. The College, conceived as the final examiner, was then required to elect accordingly. Only after 1876 was it permitted to make 'no election' if no candidate of sufficient merit offered himself for election.[33] That verdict, sensational and transformative in itself, unleashed a whirlwind of schemes for further, modernising, reform. Robarts's was only the most subversive. Max Müller seriously suggested merger with the Indian Institute as a way of producing suitably trained civil servants for the Subcontinent.[34] Leighton's own preferred scheme, probably conceived as the best means of putting an end to the vulnerability of peculiarity, was 'gradually ... to ... open ... the College to undergraduates'. It was defeated only by the narrowest of margins, in 1871.[35]

Not all 'meritocrats' were 'secularists' too. But Robarts was. In the spring of 1869, he introduced separate notices of motion to the Stated General Meeting concerning: the laicisation of the warden's office and the de-coupling of that position from the rectorship of Lockinge; a reduction in the number of College chaplains and the future appointment of the principal religious officer in College by the fellows themselves; minimisation in the number of chapel services 'to no more than one on any day other than Sunday', and putting an end to compulsory daily attendance at chapel by the Bible Clerks: finally, given 'that possession by the College of ecclesiastical patronage has a tendency to cause the fellowships (both) to be sought and ... to be filled up ... for reasons not the most worthy ... to appoint ... a committee to effect ... the sale of superfluous college livings with the least possible delay'.[36] It was in these circumstances – actually it was at the very next meeting of the College – that William Rolle Malcolm (elected 1864) and John William Nutt (elected 1858) proposed a counter-resolution: 'That a Committee be appointed to engage an architect to survey the Chapel and prepare plans for its restoration'.[37]

That this scheme was incompatible with Robarts's intentions needed no emphasis. Moreover, it came from on high. Malcolm and Nutt were only the nominal agents of the plan. The driving force behind this manoeuvre was Francis Leighton. His was the name at the head of the proposed committee. This putative body included himself, the

33 Ibid., 362–9.
34 Grant Robertson, All Souls, 203; Green, 'The "Fremantle Affair"', 370.
35 CMMB, 1858–1875, College Meeting, 19 December 1871.
36 Ibid., 153; Notices of Motion for Easter Meeting, 1869.
37 Ibid., 158; Notices of Motion for the Whitsuntide Meeting, 1869.

then sub-warden Charles Clifford (elected 1843), Charles Lee Wingfield (elected 1858), Walter George Phillimore (elected 1867) and Nutt. Even that action proved acceptable of a necessary compromise. Nutt originally proposed that 'a Committee be appointed to engage an Architect to survey the Chapel and prepare plans and estimates for its restoration'.[38] The College insisted on an amendment that deleted the word 'restoration' and omitted any mention of engaging an architect. Leighton went ahead and appointed an architect, all the same. His name was Henry Clutton.

This was an interesting choice. Clutton was a distinguished architect. He was a founder member of the Architecture Museum, a fellow of the Royal Institute of British Architects and a leading member of the Ecclesiological Society. He was also an acknowledged expert on fifteenth-century French building. His design for Lille Cathedral (presented with William Burgess in 1856) won first prize in an international competition. It was eventually rejected on the grounds of their inappropriate religion. This was ironic. Clutton was received into the Roman Catholic Church in 1857. Commissions from the rest of the Anglican establishment promptly ceased. But Clutton continued to thrive professionally. In 1867, he was appointed principal architect for the new Roman Catholic Cathedral in Westminster. That position continued for a further six years. He seems to have anticipated that his appointments in London and Oxford might run smoothly together during this period. This turned out to be a considerable mistake.[39]

But it was not a foolish thought. For Leighton had no less clearly signalled his determination to *restore* the College chapel. He also meant to achieve something concrete for Anglicanism in Oxford (he was, after all, its vice-chancellor) and Anglo-Catholic ecclesiology in All Souls. He knew from the first that this would be no easy task. Robarts was anything but a lone voice in the College at that time. Other secularists included Charles Wrottesley (elected 1847) and William Baillie Skene (elected 1864). Influential modernisers, such as William Reynell Anson (elected 1867), remained to be persuaded either way. Very probably, there was no obvious majority in favour of any particular course. In an active college of between 20 and 25 fellows, just a few votes, either way, might easily make all the difference.[40] So Leighton resolved to proceed

---

38   Ibid., College Meeting, 18 May 1869.
39   P. Hunting, 'Henry Clutton (1879 – 1893), architect', ODNB; Colvin and Simmons, 59 – 62; Hall, this volume.
40   The nominal size of the fellowship at that time was 40. But generally half that number actually attended College meetings.

subtly. He did so in three ways. First, he determined to work at all times through the Chapel Restoration Committee. The operative word here is 'through'. In fact, he often acted alone, albeit under its auspices – so frequently in the event that the College finally resolved that a quorum of three be obtained before the 'recommendations' of this body be properly construed as collective.[41] Secondly, he persuaded the Committee, and to a lesser extent the College, to acknowledge a working distinction between so-called 'repairs', that were to be paid for by *domus*, and 'restoration', which was to be funded, largely if not entirely, from 'private subscription', namely the contribution of quondam fellows, themselves much more likely to be both 'traditionalists' and 'sacralists'.[42] Thirdly, he hid whenever possible behind the recommendations – practical and aesthetic – of his architect.[43]

The purpose of such carefulness was not modesty. Rather, it was to permit Leighton the greatest possible freedom of action in relation to that advice. This sometimes entailed a rather loose interpretation of Clutton's counsel. The architect's initial report, privately conveyed to the Warden on 21 June 1869, outlined three quite distinct options: first, what he called 'work on the fabric', principally rebuilding of the walls and restoration of the masonry, repair to the roof and selected alterations to the antechapel; secondly, a profound but still partial restoration of the interior of the chapel, including the roof, the stalls and the stained glass; finally, 'the entire restoration of the original fifteenth-century chapel – roofs, stalls, screen plus, subsequent to the 'remov[al] of Thornhill's picture[,]... the skeleton of the once celebrated reredos [rising] from floor to ceiling'. Yet when the committee came to report to the College, Clutton's second and third proposals were curiously conflated rather than differentiated. Such deliberate obfuscation enabled Leighton to side with the majority in openly supporting the second (and less controversial) scheme whilst privately favouring the third (still quite unacceptable) proposal. More to the point, it prevented the third proposal from being ruled out *ab initio*.[44]

That meant collegiate battle was joined in a metaphysical fog. This is almost certainly what Leighton intended. If so, it was a wise strategy. For the odds against progress remained high. Even the second proposal

---

41 CMMB, 1858–1875, College Meeting, 21 May 1872.

42 Ibid., 170; Report of the Committee Appointed by the College at the Whitsuntide Meeting, 17 December 1869.

43 Clutton, *Narrative and Correspondence*, 6–7.

44 CMMB, 1858–1875, 177; Report of the Committee Appointed by the College at the Whitsuntide Meeting, 17 December 1869. Colvin and Simmons, 64.

initially proved unacceptable to the College, at least in the terms stated. Nutt's motion that the report be adopted was successfully opposed at the December Stated General Meeting.[45] It was replaced by a bromide that the Committee be empowered to pursue 'necessary repairs' to the Chapel and then 'to consult' with the acting bursar about the ways and means of raising the required resources to do so. This was a polite way of pointing out that the College had yet to recognise the legitimacy of 'independent private subscriptions' for such purposes. In many ways, it never did.[46] Just to add insult to injury, Robarts then successfully proposed 'adding' the name of an avowed sceptic, the Hon. Charles Wrottesley, to the Chapel Restoration Committee.[47] No one then knew that Wrottesley's indifference to all things religious extended even to attending the meetings of this crucial body.[48]

So Robarts had drawn first blood. But Leighton had discovered a way of moving forward. He had persuaded the College to acknowledge the principle of 'necessary repair'. He had also placed on record the view of the Chapel Committee that *some form* of restoration was desirable. Finally, he had acted in a way that enabled him to invoke the advice of the architect – above all, to deploy Clutton's reports and recommendations – as a way of translating his, that is, Leighton's, aspiration into their, that is, the College's, obligations. For instance, when the Committee sought to commence work on the antechapel in 1871, it reported that 'Mr. Clutton has shown that certain repairs ... to the Ante-Chapel are imperatively required'.[49] When, however, Clutton 'recommended' certain 'redecorations to the interior of the chapel' at much the same time, these were conveyed to the wider body as 'his views' of what might make the building 'worthy of the college'.[50] The purpose of all this verbiage was surreptitiously to grant the Committee a certain latitude of aesthetic interpretation. This ordinarily involved the partial substantiation of Clutton's judgements. Ordinarily, but not invariably: when he proposed to remove all of Christopher Wren's supposed additions to the chapel, the Committee pointedly recommended against him. In that way, the Committee sought (and sometimes succeeded) in promoting the image of itself as a moderate

---

45 CMMB, 1858–1875, 177; Notices of Motion for the December Meeting, 1869.

46 Ibid., College Meeting, 17 December 1869.

47 Ibid.

48 Ibid., College Meeting, 1 November 1871: 'Mr. Wrottesley resigned his place on the Chapel Restoration Committee'. He was 'replaced' by Professors Bernard and Burrows, also Mr Stopford and the Estates Bursar, after which the Committee became much more active.

49 Ibid., 194; Report of the Chapel Restoration Committee, 8 December 1870.

50 Ibid.

'third force', manfully serving the cause of ecclesiological sanity between one, over-enthusiastic, outsider and a few, otherwise unrepresentative, philistines within.[51]

This was how progress — both in the repair and restoration of the chapel — actually came about in All Souls between 1870 and 1872. The south wall was mended. Work was started on the antechapel, including the removal to the library of Blackstone's statue. Something similar happened to the sundial.[52] Confronted by a campaign for restoration through stealth, the secularists were compelled to propose alternative schemes or simply to stall, by invoking the rhetoric of financial prudence. In 1871, Robarts attempted to launch a parallel project for the 'restoration' of the library. To that end, he suddenly discovered that the library was in at least as bad a state as the chapel. This ploy came to nothing.[53] Later that year, Wrottesley (for once warming to his task) moved a motion 'that it is not desirable to proceed with the internal decorations to the chapel until the financial arrangements and general plan are clearly defined'.[54] This was, of course, precisely what Leighton wanted to avoid. His embarrassment was averted on this occasion by a counter-motion, successfully proposed by Messrs Wingfield and Garnier, 'that the Chapel Restoration Committee be not authorised to proceed with the proposed restorations of the roof until subscriptions have been promised to the amount of £1000'.[55]

The crunch came over the roof. Everyone agreed that the roof (or at least the ceiling) needed 'repairing'. Late in 1871, Clutton suggested (and the Committee recommended) that 'any ... worthwhile ... scheme for restoration' would also entail the removal of the 'canvass panelled ceiling' and the restoration of the 'original ... open timber roof'.[56] This plan was expensive. No estimate came in at less than £750.[57] In the event, it actually cost more than £1,000.[58] That action — specifically planned and paid for — also necessarily exposed the reredos. It was at this point that both sides fixed upon the fiction of its chance discovery. But their motives for this illusion were at variance. For Leighton, this really was the moment of truth. He laid out his case carefully:

---

51 Ibid.
52 Ibid., College Meeting, 30 May 1871; College Meeting, 22 August 1871. For an exhaustive account of its fate, see J. S. G. Simmons, *Wren's Dial Remov'd, or High-Victorian Hubris at All Souls* (Oxford, 2000), esp. 6–11.
53 CMMB, 1858–1875, College Meeting, 3 February 1871.
54 Ibid., 215; Notice of Motion for the Whitsuntide Meeting, 1871.
55 Ibid., College Meeting, 20 May 1871.
56 Ibid., 194; Report of the Chapel Restoration Committee, 8 December 1870.
57 Ibid., 208–9; Report of the Chapel Restoration Committee, Easter 1871.
58 Ibid., 239; Report of the Chapel Restoration Committee, Easter 1872.

Further investigations [subsequent to the uncovering of the roof] have resulted in bringing to light a most interesting portion of the chapel. All members of the College may not be aware of the existence of an original reredos ... on the Eastern wall of the Chapel, behind a fresco supposed to have been painted by Streeter, which in turn has been hidden behind Thornhill's fresco ... as well as the present marble altar and ... Mengs's ... Noli me tangere .... The reredos consists of very beautiful tabernacle work, richly coloured with blue, red and gold .... Only the extreme upper and lower parts have at present been uncovered [but] so far as it is possible to judge ... the whole work consisted of a representation of the crucifixion in a space over the altar, with one of the Last Judgement immediately under the roof: the middle portion, now covered up, probably represented the Resurrection .... The carving [is] singular and delicate [also] absolutely unique [sic] in character. Unfortunately, it has suffered much from the violence of misdirected zeal and bad taste, but there is no reason to fear that ... it could not be restored with the exercise of ordinary professional skill. [Certainly,] the marble alter-piece could be removed without difficulty [and] Thornhill's fresco could be taken off on linen and restored.

On that basis, he argued,

The Committee most earnestly recommend to the College that permission be granted ... to have the reredos uncovered and drawings made of it .... The College will then have ... an opportunity of deciding which restoration they prefer, whether of the original beautiful work of the founder, or of the present altar piece.

Even allowing for a momentary lapse of collective aesthetic judgement, he insisted that '[a]nother very urgent reason exists for uncovering the reredos, namely that the extreme eastern beam and wall post, on which part of the roof depends, are in a very decayed condition [and] being in part covered by the fresco, cannot be renewed without its renewal.' Therefore, 'In addition the committee would recommend[:]

1. The restoration of the floor of the chapel to its original level ... as the effect of raising the floor has been to cause the stalls to block up the lower part of the windows and then entirely spoil their proportions. N.B. This will involve the ... temporary ... removal of the present screen.

2. To clean and repair the stalls and repair their canopies. The Committee estimates the projected cost at somewhere in the region of £3,000. It proposes to raise this sum from a loan from the parliamentary Enclosure Committee, 'being manifestly a work of "restoration and improvement"', for which such monies were intended, and by way, if necessary, of further

private subscriptions, now bound to be increased [as] it becomes known that the College was [determined] on such a noble work of restoration and if really necessary, through the sale of Meng's picture … and the marble at the East End.

In conclusion, the Committee specifically recommended:

1. Completion of the work on the roof (i.e. uncovering, repairing and completion in plain oak)
2. The uncovering of the whole reredos
3. The levelling of the floor
4. Restoring of the stalls
5. Painting of the roof
6. Other necessary alterations.

The Committee also asked leave to sit again.[59]

Each of these recommendations was discussed, in turn, at a College meeting on 2 April 1872. There were fifteen fellows present. These included all the principal protagonists, save, unsurprisingly, Wrottesley. Recommendation 1 was passed. Recommendation 2 – that of uncovering the reredos – was lost. Francis Compton (elected 1846) instead proposed an amendment: 'that all accounts with Mr. Clutton be closed'. That was passed. Subject to this action, 'the committee was authorised to uncover the reredos, provided it be done in such a way as not to interfere with the free choice of a competent architect as a successor to Mr. Clutton'. Recommendations 3 and 4 were withdrawn. Recommendation 5 was lost, even after being subjected to a qualifying amendment. Recommendation 6 was also withdrawn. The Chapel Restoration Committee was reappointed only after the addition of John Andrew Doyle (elected 1869) and William Reynell Anson (elected 1867) to its ranks.[60]

In the immediate aftermath, the College disposed of Clutton's services.[61] Leighton delegated this task to his faithful lackey. John Nutt explained to the aggrieved architect that, in the view of the College, he had by that time completed those works actually commissioned, namely the repair of the roof, the adjoining masonry and at least some of the windows. No further tasks had explicitly been sought of him. Moreover,

No decision has been made with regard to any further works in the chapel [and] it was fair to say that there was a strong and general feeling against

---

59 Ibid.
60 Ibid., College Meeting, 2 April 1872.
61 Ibid., 245; Report of the Chapel Restoration Committee, Whitsuntide, 1872; Colvin and Simmons, 63.

placing such a work of restoration in the hands of an architect whose views are not found on the same theological basis as that of the members of the College.[62]

Clutton pointed out that the first statement, though technically true, contradicted clear assurances he had previously been given by the College, not least by Nutt himself. He observed that the second statement was misleading, presuming as it did the 'recent discovery' of something that had long been known. Finally, he noted the apparently transformative significance of a religious affiliation that had been known for longer still.[63] Nutt responded by assuring Clutton that: 'The College in general were not aware, at the time they first sought your professional services, that you were a member of the Communion to which you belong; it was not, indeed, till quite lately that all members of the Committee itself become acquainted with it'.[64] This was, of course, a preposterous claim.

But such disingenuousness served a purpose. Honours, if not honour, were preserved in College. The 'secularists' thereby removed Leighton's architectural trouble-shooter. They also neutralised his committee; or so they thought. In fact, 'their' committee recommended in its very next report that the College at least uncover the reredos.[65] Still, the vital question remained: what, then, should be done with it? The College met again on 21 May 1872 to determine this issue, once and for all. Compton proposed that it do nothing beyond what had agreed at the last meeting: that, in other words, it do nothing beyond the act of uncovering the reredos in a manner that allowed for the possibility of no further work being done on the monument. His motion was carried. Then, curiously, Anson proposed that the College at least raise money, for further, unspecified, repairs to the chapel. This motion was also carried. By one interpretation of this action, the College had agreed to do nothing and also to raise the money to do so. By another, it had even allowed itself the option of re-covering the reredos. Finally, Lord Bathurst, the senior fellow, first elected in 1811, peer of the realm, pillar of the Church and yet strangely uninvolved in this whole dispute up to that moment, rose from his chair to express 'his wish to restore the reredos at his own cost, or so materially to contribute as to enable the College to do so without inconvenience'.[66]

62 Clutton, *Narrative and Correspondence*, 15; the Rev. J. W. Nutt to Mr Clutton, 13 April 1872.
63 Ibid., 17–18; Clutton to Nutt, 23 April 1872; Colvin and Simmons, 63–4.
64 Clutton, *Narrative and Correspondence*, 22–3.
65 CMMB, 1858–1875, 245; Report of the Chapel Restoration Committee, Whitsuntide, 1872.
66 Ibid., CMMB, 1858–1875, College Meeting, 21 May 1872.

It is possible that this was a genuinely spontaneous gesture on Bathurst's part. He was rich, nothing if not an academic traditionalist, and he had for many years sponsored similar kinds of ecclesiastical restoration work in and around Cirencester, and other family seats.[67] But it is unlikely that he intervened unaided. The moment he sat down Mr Herbert proposed that:

> In consequence of Lord Bathurst's magnificent offer with regard to the reredos, the Chapel Committee be requested to apply as soon as possible to Mr. G. G. Scott to supply design for its restoration, and to obtain an estimate of its probable cost.

The warden seconded this motion. It was carried unanimously, with a vote of grateful thanks to Lord Bathurst. This proved a good day all round for the traditionalists. Anson's other motion – proposing that laymen be eligible for the office of warden – was lost almost immediately afterwards.[68] Bathurst was as good as his word. Over the next two years, he donated at least £2,000 towards the restoration of the reredos. That amounted to perhaps one-fifth of the total cost of the restoration of the chapel over the whole period from 1869 to 1879.[69] The Chapel Restoration Committee moved no less swiftly to secure 'the services' of George Gilbert Scott to advise on the 'restoration of the reredos'.[70] Then Montague Bernard succeeded in extending that remit to a general request that he – that is, Scott – 'furnish plans' for the 'restoration of the chapel', more broadly conceived.[71]

Scott was an excellent choice in the circumstances. Though a long-standing member of the Cambridge Camden Society, a frequent contributor to the *Ecclesiologist* and friend of A. W. N. Pugin, he was reared as an evangelical and remained a Broad Churchman for most of the rest of his life. He never became an apostle of the High Church School in architecture, following the examples of Carpenter and Butterfield.[72] But he boasted a distinguished ecclesiastical portfolio. This was rarely innovative, nor much influenced by Continental Gothic. Instead, he was content to accept the orthodoxy of 'English,

---

67 D. Vercy and A. Brooks, *The Buildings of England: Gloucestershire, I: The Cotswolds*, 3rd edn (London, 1999), 246ff.

68 CMMB, 1858–1875, College Meeting, 21 May 1872.

69 Grant Robertson, *All Souls*, 202; Colvin and Simmons, 65.

70 CMMB, 1858–1875, 254; Report of the Chapel Restoration Committee, 19 October 1872.

71 Ibid., College Meeting, 1 November 1872.

72 G. Stamp, 'Scott, Sir George Gilbert (1811–1878)', ODNB; *Sir George Gilbert Scott, Personal and Professional Recollections* (1879): *A Facsimile of the Original Edition with New Material and a Critical Introduction by Gavin Stamp* (Stamford, 1995), 112.

Geometrical, Decorated, Gothic', or what was often known as 'Middle Pointed'.[73] The results were there for everyone to see, and for most to admire, from the Martyr's Memorial and Exeter College Chapel in Oxford to the unexceptional – some said dull – new chapel at St John's College, Cambridge. Those suspicious of surreptitious Romanising tendencies had little to fear from this source. Those contemptuous of all revealed religion may have had scarcely more to worry about.[74]

Scott was also superhumanly productive, responsible for almost one thousand new building and restoration projects during his lifetime. Perhaps the most enduring was the Midland Grand Hotel, St Pancras.[75] Even the intervention of a stroke seems scarcely to have slowed him down. The All Souls challenge may even have invigorated him. According to *The Builder*, 'he [immediately] entered the work with that zeal and love of old examples that so eminently distinguished him'.[76] Moreover, his commitment secured the project national fame. He was famous, having been knighted in 1872 for his work on the Albert Memorial. Progress on the reredos was regularly reported not only in *The Builder* but also *The Architect* from the moment he took charge.[77]

Most importantly of all, Scott was Bathurst's man. The two had worked together as far back as 1852, when Bathurst had employed the architect to design the tower and spire that he added to Scott's church at Watermoor, Cirencester.[78] So too was Scott's sculptor, the controversial Emanuel Edward Geflowski. Born in Warsaw, and naturalised a British subject in 1864, Geflowski was declared bankrupt the same year. He may or may not have secured the commission to carve a statue of Sir William Fairburn in Manchester Town Hall, against a more famous competitor, subsequent to the surreptitious intervention of his father-in-law, a mercantile clerk with the Corporation.[79] But Bathurst trusted him. Geflowski carried out the carving for the interior of Watermoor and restored the reredos at Cirencester. He eventually produced 35 large statues and 84 smaller for the reredos at All Souls. Bathurst paid

---

73 Stamp, 'Scott'; Scott, *Personal and Professional Recollections*, 208.

74 Stamp, 'Scott'; Colvin and Simmons, 65–7.

75 Stamp, 'Introduction', in Scott, *Personal and Professional Recollections*, p. e [sic] (Stamp couples it with the Albert Memorial).

76 Anon., 'All Souls College Chapel, Reredos, Oxford', *The Builder*, 37, no. 1891 (3 May 1871), 489.

77 See, esp., Anon., *The Architect*, 10 (18 October 1873), 201. In fairness, Clutton's activities were also reported – albeit just once – in *The Builder*; see Anon., 'New Buildings and Improvements in Oxford: All Souls College', *The Builder*, 29, no. 1498 (21 October 1871), 830. However, Scott merited five entries in the same journal, during the period from 1874 to 1879.

78 Scott, *Personal and Professional Recollections*, 148; Vercy and Brooks, *Gloucestershire*, I, 256.

79 Colvin and Simmons, 67, 76.

for every one of these — including that of himself — to the tune of an additional £3,000–£4,000 before his death, in 1878.[80]

In this way, Bathurst became the 'third force' that the Chapel Restoration Committee had never been. The 'secularists' had successfully halted work in 1872 because they could prove that neither those loans secured from the Copyhold Commissioners nor the sums remaining in the private subscription list would cover the likely expenses involved in a complete restoration of the reredos. The bottomless pit of Bathurst's 'munificence' from that date onwards solved this problem. Moreover, it did so on Bathurst's terms. He never joined the Committee. However, he increasingly told it what to do. In Easter 1873, it reported progress on the reredos made 'at the instance of Lord Bathurst' and 'under the direction of Sir Gilbert Scott'.[81] Soon this was changed to 'the direction of Lord Bathurst' himself.[82] Bathurst got what he paid for. It was the Committee that first proposed, and the College that eventually voted for, his apotheosis in the final, altered version itself. In this way, they observed no more than the proprieties of the matter.[83]

They had good reason to do so. So too, in their different ways, did the principal protagonists. Leighton ceded direction of the project after 1872. However, by 1874, he had got much of what he wanted: the reredos, the roof, the stalls, the windows, even general alterations of the ante-chapel.[84] Moreover, Scott continued to make proposals, whether about the tiling of the floor, the paving of the east end, or the lighting of the interior, that were both agreeable to him and acceptable to the College. In February 1873 Skene bet Compton that no image would be erected behind the Communion Table in chapel. He lost.[85] But the 'secularists' were far from entirely defeated. Robarts and his confederates, having established the precedent that ecclesiological expenditure on this scale would no longer be borne from collegiate resources — the question of private donations remained unresolved

80 Ibid., 67–70.
81 CMMB, 1858–1875, 267; Report of the Chapel Restoration Committee, April 1873.
82 Ibid., 271; Report of the Chapel Restoration Committee, June 1873.
83 Ibid., 298; Report of the Chapel Restoration Committee, Whitsuntide 1874; College Meeting, 26 May 1874.
84 Hence, perhaps, the broader significance of Burrows's *Worthies*, published that same year.
85 CMMB, 1858–1875, College Meeting, 3 June 1873; College Meeting, 1 November 1873; College Meeting, 7 April 1874; College Meeting, 26 May 1874; C. Oman (ed.), *The Text of the Old Betting Book of All Souls College, 1815–1873* (Oxford, 1912), 173, entry no. 648, for 9 February 1873: 'Skene bets Compton half a crown that no image is put over the Communion Table in All Souls Chapel. Francis Compton, W. B. Skene (Paid for 2/6 for one image, 2nd June 1873, F.C.).' Oman added: 'The screen was in the process of being filled. Skene objected to the introduction of images, and remonstrated with the Warden on the subject.' I am grateful to Sir Keith Thomas for this reference.

– deployed the distinction between unfinanced proposals and gifted items to block other plans, and even to insist on a few 'preservations' of their own. At one meeting in 1876, the 'removal of the screen' was rejected, similarly the 'disposal of Mengs's picture'. At the same time, the Chapel Restoration Committee was 'instructed to see what can be done to preserve the broken fragments of ... Sir James Thornhill's fresco'. When the question of what precisely to do with those funds privately subscribed to 'erect the new screen' was indelicately raised, compromise was reached through an agreement to 'apply... those funds' to 'other matters connected with the repair ... and restoration of the chapel'.[86]

Repair, restoration and alteration work ceased in 1879. The Chapel Restoration Committee submitted its last report as a '*restoration*' committee that year.[87] This was perhaps just as well. Bathurst was already dead, his name having been inserted into the Prayer of Thanksgiving for the Benefactors of the College the previous December.[88] So too was Scott himself. He left £130,000 and the most successful architectural firm in the country.[89] Leighton passed away in 1881, exhausted by 'the labours of his various offices'.[90] Robarts proceeded to a suitably cantankerous and controversial career at the Bar and in the City of London. He died in 1904, never having quite fulfilled his early promise.[91] The real victor was Sir William Anson. His continual efforts to laicise the wardenship were eventually rewarded in 1873.[92] He inherited Bathurst's rooms in 1878.[93] He was the immediate successor to Warden Leighton in 1881.[94] No small part of this success may be traced to his ability to remain above this conflict, for most of its course. That achievement need not be ascribed to Machiavellian cunning. Anson remained both a churchman and a layman throughout. Leighton and Robarts distinguished all too determinedly between the two. They each paid a considerable price for so doing.

The divisions wrought in the College during the decade after 1869 were not quickly closed. It is possible to detect some of the bad blood they drew even in the (mildly disapproving) account of it, delivered

86 CMMB, 1875–1888, College Meeting, 18 April 1876; also, College Meeting, 1 November 1876.
87 Ibid., College Meeting, 15 April 1879.
88 Ibid., College Meeting, 18 December 1878.
89 Stamp, 'Introduction' in Scott, *Personal and Professional Recollections*, 9.
90 Our Oxford Correspondent, 'Obituary', *The Times*, 14 October 1881, 4.
91 He merits no mention in the ODNB, nor in its predecessor; more surprisingly still, perhaps, his name was omitted from *Who Was Who*, 1897–1915.
92 CMMB, 1875–1888, College Meeting, 8 February 1873.
93 Ibid., College Meeting, 23 April 1878.
94 Ibid., College Meeting, 3 November 1881.

twenty years later by an otherwise irenic Grant Robertson.[95] Was Burrows vindicated? Scarcely: Anson's All Souls proved altogether more agreeable to the 'secularists' than to the 'sacralists'.[96] When the time came, they chose to celebrate that fact in the appropriate place (see fig. 0.16).[97] The last major alterations to the chapel do not date back to 1879.[98] Anson's cenotaph was placed to the right of the reredos in 1915. It sits uniquely within the Sacrarium. Indeed, it occupies virtually the entire space to the north side of the communion rails. Below the stone canopy lies a recumbent figure of the late warden: hand on heart, three books (written by himself) at his feet. His image is larger than any of those on the reredos.[99] It was put there by a grateful College, shortly after his death, and paid for entirely out of corporate revenues.[100]

---

95 Grant Robertson, All Souls, 200–2.

96 H. H. Henson (ed.), A Memoir of the Right Honourable Sir William Anson: Baronet, Warden of All Souls College; Burgess for the University of Oxford (Oxford, 1920), esp. chs. 3, 8, 10; Simmons, 'All Souls', esp. 214ff; S. J. D. Green, 'All Souls College', in Wm R. Louis (ed.), Effervescent Adventures with Britannia: Personalities, Politics and Culture in Britain (London, 2017), 161–73.

97 CMMB, 1915–1925 (LR.5.a.10, ms. cccci(k)), Meeting of the Memorial Committee, 15 February 1915: 'That it is desirable that there should be a memorial to the late Warden in Chapel'.

98 A. H. M. Jones, 'All Souls College: Buildings', in H.E. Salter and Mary D. Cobell (eds.), VCH Oxfordshire, vol. III: The University of Oxford (Oxford, 1954), 183–93: 'By 1879, the work was finished and the chapel assumed its present appearance' (186). That so great a scholar as Jones should have made so simple an error is surely indicative of not so much of individual carelessness as of collective amnesia in this respect.

99 CMMB, 1915–1925, Meeting of the Memorial Committee, 15 February 1915: 'That a recumbent figure of the late Warden, resting on a cenotaph, placed ... by the North wall of the Eastern portion of the Chapel would ... be the most satisfactory and dignified form for such a monument'. The Committee came to this opinion in definite preference to several alternatives, viz. 'a standing full-length figure, a monument along the lines of that in the Ante-Chapel to Warden Hovenden, a portrait bust or bas-relief medallion, a figure incised in brass, and a memorial window in the College Hall'.

100 Ibid., College Meeting, 30 October 1915.

CHAPTER II

GEORGE GILBERT SCOTT
AND THE RESTORATION
OF THE REREDOS

MICHAEL
HALL

In April 1872 J. W. Nutt, secretary of the All Souls Chapel Restoration Committee, informed Henry Clutton (1819 – 1893), the architect in charge of the work, that his employment was to be terminated. He wrote that it had been brought to the College's attention that Clutton was Roman Catholic, and 'there is a strong and general feeling against placing such a work as the restoration of the newly discovered reredos in the hands of any architect whose views are not formed on the same theological basis as that of the members of the College'.[1] Clutton was both dismayed and nonplussed since there had been no intimation that the College was dissatisfied. As S. J. D. Green has shown in the preceding chapter, he had been commissioned to undertake the restoration of the chapel in May 1869, as a result of concerns about the structural stability of its south wall, and had produced his first report the following month. The work had been carried out successfully between April and December 1871, after which the project entered a more cosmetic phase when Clutton was instructed to remove the plaster ceiling that hid the medieval roof.[2]

An account of what happened next was given by the *Builder* magazine in 1879: 'During the restoration of the chapel roof a scaffold-pole was accidentally, and fortunately, thrust through the lath-and-plaster screen which covered the face of the wall and showed tabernacle-work behind'.[3] Once Mengs's altarpiece and Thornhill's mural had been taken down, there appeared 'to the view of astonished eyes the mutilated remains of a beautiful work of architectural and sculptural art'.[4] Astonished they may have been, but they cannot have been

---

1   H. Clutton, *A Narrative and Correspondence relating to the Restoration of All Souls College Chapel, Oxford* (privately printed, 1872), 16. For context see Green, this volume.

2   Until the present volume the fullest published account of the restoration of the chapel has been Colvin and Simmons, 61–70.

3   'All Souls College Chapel Reredos, Oxford', *The Builder* (3 May 1879), 489 (hereafter *The Builder* 1879).

4   Ibid.

completely surprised, as in his report of June 1869 Clutton had reminded the Fellows that it was likely that 'the skeleton of the once celebrated reredos, which rose from floor to ceiling' was concealed behind the eighteenth-century additions.[5] In March he sent the College 'an estimate of the probable cost for restoring such a work as the reredos, without filling the niches'.[6] Less than a month later he was dismissed.

Deeply wounded by the way he had been treated, Clutton published a pamphlet containing his correspondence with the Restoration Committee, in which he pointed out that All Souls had approached him with the offer of the job – 'it was not I who sought the college' – and that 'the charge upon which I am dismissed resolves itself into this, that I continue to hold the same religious opinions which I held when the college first employed me'.[7] In his reply, Nutt stated that 'the College in general were not aware, at the time they first sought your professional services, that you were a member of the Communion to which you belong; it was not, indeed, till quite lately that all the members of the Committee itself became acquainted with it'.[8]

These equivocating words seem to imply that some members of the College had indeed been aware of Clutton's religious affiliation from early on. Even allowing for the inward-looking nature of an academic community, it would have been strange if they had not, since Clutton was one of the best known Roman Catholic architects in England.[9] He had converted in 1857, after which his principal commissions were from Roman Catholic patrons. In 1860 he married Caroline Ryder, a niece of Henry Manning. As a result of Manning's appointment as Archbishop of Westminster in 1865, Clutton was asked to provide designs for a new cathedral, on which he laboured for the next decade, only for Manning to decide in 1873, largely for reasons of cost, not to go ahead. Painfully for Clutton, in 1882 the money for a new cathedral seemed to be available, only for the potential donor, Sir Tatton Sykes, to insist that an architect of his own choice, Heinrich Ferstel, be used instead.[10] Nothing came of that, and the project languished until the appointment in 1894 of J. H. Bentley, a former pupil of Clutton, to design a cathedral for a different site.

---

5   Clutton, *Narrative and Correspondence*, 7–8. Clutton's 1869 report does not survive.
6   Ibid., 13.
7   Ibid., 20.
8   Ibid., 23.
9   See P. Hunting, 'Henry Clutton (1879–1893), architect', ODNB; Green, this volume, 266.
10 See N. Wibiral and N. Pevsner, 'A Westminster Cathedral Episode', *Architectural History*, 20 (1977), 63–4 and 100–101.

Clutton's involvement in the Westminster Cathedral scheme was
not widely known outside Roman Catholic circles until he published
his designs in 1875, but All Souls had an opportunity at closer hand to
be informed about his religion. Following the withdrawal in 1859 of
the Jesuits from the Oxford Roman Catholic mission, permission was
given by Rome in 1866 for the establishment of a Congregation of the
Oratory in Oxford, and Clutton was commissioned to design a church
for it, which was to be Byzantine in style.[11] However, the project was
abandoned in 1867, and in 1871 the mission was returned to the Jesuits,
for whom J. A. Hansom designed the Gothic church of St Aloysius in
St Giles.

Although it seems unlikely, therefore, that the College was quite
so ignorant of Clutton's religion as Nutt claimed, it is not implausible
that it was considered a problem. Although Clutton had proposed
restoring the reredos without adding figures, the possibility of a full
restoration probably occurred to many involved as soon as the medieval
east wall was revealed.[12] That was a project unlike the restoration of
the chapel, as it would have involved the addition of sculptured figures
at the principal liturgical focus of the building. In 1872 that was an
issue of potential controversy. The fellows were presumably aware of
the histories of the restorations of the two other similar reredoses in
Oxford college chapels. In his restoration of that at Magdalen, begun in
1829, the architect L. N. Cottingham had removed the large mural by
Isaac Fuller to reveal three tiers of empty niches, which he proposed to
fill with sculptures of saints, but was prevented by objections from the
fellows, in particular Edward Ellerton, who regarded such imagery as an
offence to Protestant principles, and it was not until 1862 that opinion
within the College has shifted sufficiently for statues to be added;
they were carved by Thomas Earp to designs by Clayton and Bell (fig.
11.1).[13] At New College the remnants of the fourteenth-century reredos
were uncovered by James Wyatt during his restoration of the chapel
in 1789 – 94. Wyatt replaced the medieval stonework in plaster but no
figures were added, nor were they when George Gilbert Scott rebuilt the
reredos in stone in the restoration that began in 1877 and was completed
after Scott's death by his son John Oldrid Scott in 1881. The present

---

11   J. Bertram, *St Aloysius Parish, Oxford. The Third English Oratory: A Brief History and Guide*, 1793 – 2000
     (Oxford, 2000).

12   Green, this volume, reveals the complex divisions between the various parties within the College.

13   J. Myles, *L. N. Cottingham, 1787 – 1847: Architect of the Gothic Revival* (London, 1996), 83 – 4. See also R.
     White and R. Darwall-Smith, *The Architectural Drawings of Magdalen College, Oxford: A Catalogue* (Oxford,
     2001), 115 – 16; with Darwall-Smith, this volume, 255.

figures, designed by J. L. Pearson and carved by Nathaniel Hitch, were not installed until 1888–91 (figs 11.2, 4.22).[14]

The best known example of the sort of controversy that such schemes could provoke was the restoration of the high-altar reredos at Winchester Cathedral, begun in 1885 in the teeth of local opposition to the addition of sculptures of saints in the empty niches.[15] The most

14 See G. Jackson-Stops, 'The Architecture of the College', in J. Buxton and P. Williams (eds), *New College Oxford 1379–1979* (Oxford, 1979), 241–4, 250, 253–4.

15 G. Brandwood, '"Unlucky Experiments in Statues": Restoring the Winchester Great Screen', *Ecclesiology Today* (May 2003), 3–12.

contentious element was the Crucifixion scene in the central panel, designed by the architects Bodley and Garner in 1896. The news that Thomas Garner had recently converted to Roman Catholicism was exploited in criticisms of the project, as a result of which Garner dissolved his partnership with G. F. Bodley in the following year.[16]

In his account of the restoration of the chapel at All Souls, J. S. G. Simmons suggested that one reason why Clutton was dismissed was that his religion would have seemed problematic to Montagu Burrows, Chichele Professor of Modern History, who was 'an influential member of the Chapel Committee and a staunch anti-ritualist Church-of-England man'.[17] Burrows was indeed supposedly among the first members of the College to see the remains of the reredos, as he recorded in his book *Worthies of All Souls* (1874).[18]

Burrows' excitement was prompted by his sense that the discovery had reclaimed an important document in the College's history. In the preface to *Worthies of All Souls* he wrote that 'There was something suggestive, not to say weird-like in suddenly finding oneself standing face to face in this manner with an unsuspected past', and he explained that the uncovering of the reredos was one reason why he had embarked on the book, the first history of the College to be based on archival research.[19] Burrows' belief that the discovery of the reredos had more than an archaeological or aesthetic significance might well suggest, therefore, that he could have felt uncomfortable about employing a Roman Catholic architect, even if arguably there was something illogical about dismissing Clutton on the grounds of religion following the unveiling of a monument of the College's pre-Reformation past.

Simmons's description of Burrows' religious identity can be nuanced. Although in his autobiography, published in 1908, Burrows expresses opposition to Tractarianism and ritualism, his objections were principally to liturgical developments that went beyond the bounds of the Prayer Book. He was a Tory High Churchman who had been the chairman of the Oxford branch of the English Church Union, the principal lay Anglo-Catholic body and, although he resigned in 1866 on the grounds that it had strayed too far from 'the paths of moderation and practical reforms', he wrote that although this marked an official break 'from my Ritualist friends I still retained a certain amount of

16 M. Hall, *George Frederick Bodley and the Later Gothic Revival in Britain and America* (New Haven, 2014), 381.

17 Colvin and Simmons, 64.

18 M. Burrows, *Worthies of All Souls: Four Centuries of English History, Illustrated from the College Archives* (London, 1874), vi.

19 Ibid., p. vii. Burrows's motives in writing the book are explored by Green, this volume.

intimacy with them'.[20] In 1870 Burrows joined the committee that established Keble College, an unlikely appointment for anyone with deeply embedded anti-Tractarian views.[21] He was also the leading fund-raiser for St Philip and St James, Oxford, built in 1860–2. This was not an explicitly Tractarian project but had a High Church flavour thanks to the choice of G. E. Street as architect. In his autobiography Burrows explained that 'I had my wish on the two points in this work on which I was bent, – free seats, and Street as architect: I had observed his merits when he restored our dear old church at Hadley', referring to Street's restoration in 1848–9 of the church where Burrows's family worshipped, St Mary, Monken Hadley, Middlesex.[22]

That raises the question of why in May 1872, with Clutton out of the way, the College turned for the restoration of the reredos not to Street, who would have been well qualified for the task, but to George Gilbert Scott (1811–1878).[23] It may be explanation enough that Scott was the most eminent Gothic revival architect of the day: in August of that year he was knighted, principally in recognition of his design for the Albert Memorial in Kensington Gardens. Simmons takes Scott's appointment to be evidence of the College's hypocrisy in the reason it put forward for dismissing Clutton, since Scott 'was the man involved in a controversy which eventually went to the Privy Council in connection with so-called "superstitious" images put up under his direction in Exeter Cathedral'.[24] It is highly unlikely, however, that anyone in Oxford would have considered that incident as in any way compromising Scott's reputation as an architect who was theologically speaking neither High nor Low Church. By 1872 his career in Oxford stretched back thirty years to his design for a major monument to Protestant beliefs, the Martyrs' Memorial (1841–3). His numerous collegiate and university projects undertaken before he began work at All Souls included the chapel at Exeter College (1856–9) and the restoration of the University church, St Mary the Virgin, in 1856–7, and of Christ Church cathedral, in 1870–72.[25]

20 S. M. Burrows (ed.), *Autobiography of Montagu Burrows* (London, 1908), 220.

21 See A. H. Johnson, rev. Peter R. H. Slee, 'Montagu Burrows (1819–1905), Historian and University Administrator', ODNB.

22 Burrows (ed.), *Autobiography*, 222.

23 It is notable that Street received no significant commission from any Oxford college, despite his appointment as Oxford diocesan architect in 1850.

24 Colvin and Simmons, 65. Judgement was passed in the Privy Council case, Phillpotts v. Boyd, in 1875.

25 For a survey of Scott's work in Oxford, see G. Tyack, 'Scott in Oxford', in P. S. Barnwell, G. Tyack and W. Whyte (eds), *George Gilbert Scott 1811–1878: An Architect and his Influence* (Donington, 2014), 112–33.

There can in fact be little doubt that All Souls's dismissal of Clutton and appointment of Scott had nothing to do with the religious principles of either. As S. J. D. Green has explained in the previous chapter, the conflict within the fellowship between 'sacralists' and 'secularists', which shaped the College's approach to the restoration of the chapel – something that neither Clutton nor Scott is likely fully to have understood – was overtaken by an unexpected benefaction. It was no coincidence that the decision to offer the commission to Scott was taken at the same College meeting at which the senior fellow, William, 5th Earl Bathurst (1791–1878), offered to pay for the restoration of the reredos. He was a long-standing patron of Scott, whose professional relationship with the Bathurst family went back to 1847, when he was commissioned to design Holy Trinity, Watermoor, Cirencester, on land given by William's elder brother, Henry, 4th Lord Bathurst (1790–1866). It was also thanks to the Bathursts, who are seated at Cirencester Park, that Scott was entrusted with the restoration of St John the Baptist, Cirencester, in 1865–7.

If any objection was likely to be raised to the choice of Scott for the restoration of the reredos it would probably have been based not on his religious outlook but on his treatment of medieval architecture. Scott's reputation in his own lifetime – and long afterwards – for insensitive and even destructive restoration was focused in particular on the belief that he disliked late medieval architecture and would happily remove Perpendicular detail – in particular window tracery – in order to replace it with designs in his preferred style, early fourteenth-century Decorated Gothic – 'Middle Pointed' to use the Victorian term. This suspicion, which was reinforced by a growing admiration for Perpendicular architecture among younger architects – not least Scott's eldest son, George Gilbert Scott Jr (1839–1897)[26] – was sealed by the public attacks on Scott's abilities as a restorer by William Morris in the 1870s. In vain Scott justifiably protested that he had been a proponent of conservative restoration principles since early in his career, but Morris's scorn is still often echoed today despite the fact that recent research has emphasised that Scott's undisputed stature as a scholar of medieval architecture was in most instances matched by a thoughtful approach to

26 On the rise in the appreciation of Perpendicular, see G. Stamp, *An Architect of Promise: George Gilbert Scott Junior (1839–1897) and the Late Gothic Revival* (Donington, 2002), 38–50.

medieval fabric.[27] As his restoration of St John the Baptist, Cirencester, testifies, Scott usually treated Perpendicular architecture with respect. By the 1860s he was also prepared to work in the style where the context demanded it. At Gloucester Cathedral, for example, of which he was appointed architect in 1866, his new high altar reredos and screen, erected in 1872–3, was designed to be in keeping with the choir, one of the first major works in the Perpendicular style.

The appearance of the All Souls reredos before Scott got to work is recorded in a photograph that was presumably commissioned by the College in 1872 (see fig. 4.5). Since photographs taken at the outset of a restoration campaign in the nineteenth century are uncommon, it is possible that it was made at Scott's suggestion in order to forestall possible future criticism by demonstrating that although the medieval stonework was badly damaged it provided adequate evidence for the full-scale restoration that was planned. On 16 December Scott wrote to Lord Bathurst:

> Since I had the honour of meeting your Lordship at All Souls, – at which time I made a careful examination of the remains of the magnificent Reredos recently discovered by Mr Clutton, – I have had the most careful and minute sketches and measurements made of these remains, – a work which has taken a very considerable time, – From these sketches and measurements, I have had a large elevation made on which are laid down with accuracy all the features of the design, so far as they have at present been unravelled [...]
>
> The lamentable manner in which the tabernacle work has been hewn down, make it a work of some difficulty to trace out with certainty the whole of the details; but with patient perseverance the parts unfold themselves one after another, so that I do not doubt that the whole, or very nearly the whole, will be discovered with at least a near approach to certainty.[28]

The drawing – or more probably a copy of it – survives in Scott's papers at the Royal Institute of British Architects, London (fig. 11.3).[29] In

---

27 See Wilson's positive assessment of the restoration, this volume. One reason for the reluctance to give Scott his due, apart from the modern uncritical admiration of Morris, is that the major recent analyses of his restoration practice are unpublished: S. M. N. Branfoot, '"A Plea for the Restoration of our Ancient Churches": A Re-Appraisal of the Restoration and Conservation of Medieval Churches and Cathedrals by George Gilbert Scott', PhD thesis, University of Reading (2004), and C. Marx, 'The Restoration of Cathedrals and Major Churches in England during the Nineteenth Century and After', PhD thesis, University of Cambridge (2010). See, however, C. Marx, 'Scott and the Restoration of Major Churches', in Barnwell, Tyack and Whyte, George Gilbert Scott, 91–111.

28 Sir Gilbert Scott to Earl Bathurst, 16 December 1872, ASC archives, Anson Box 13.

29 RIBA Drawings Collection, London, PA1723/ScGGS[103](4).

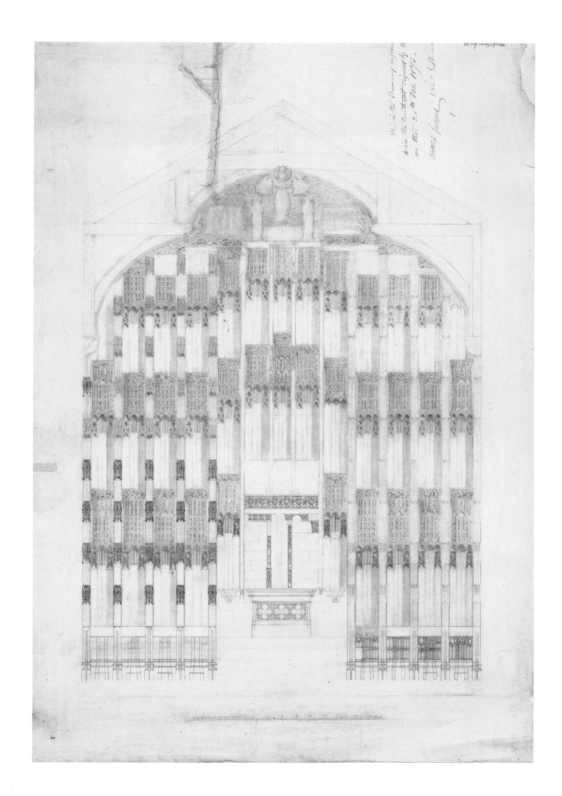

his letter to Bathurst, Scott explains that the recording of the remains of the reredos had been delayed as a result of 'one of my assistants having been laid up for three weeks with an attack of rheumatism arising from his work in the chapel'.[30] This assistant was John Medland (1840/1– 1913). Having been trained by his architect father, James, in Gloucester, he worked for Scott from 1862 until Scott's death in 1878, after which he went into independent practice in Gray's Inn, London.[31] Medland served as clerk of works for the reredos restoration, exercising day to day control over the intricate project following the guidelines laid down by Scott.

The greatest challenge was the addition of ornament to replace the carving that had been hacked away when the reredos was concealed (fig. 11.4). As The Builder put it in 1879: 'The whole of the projecting canopies had been axed off to a general surface, but the mason seems to have had a better feeling than his directors – perhaps with an eye to its restoration – and had left attached portions of pinnacles, canopies, tracery, groining and so on as a safe guide in working out the design correctly'.[32] According to a note published in The Builder in November 1876 describing the progress being made in the restoration of the chapel, 'the greater part of the work, and that of the reredos, has been carried out by Messrs Farmer & Brindley'.[33] Farmer and Brindley was a partnership based in Lambeth, south London, between the stonemason William Farmer (1823–1879) and an exceptionally talented architectural carver, William Brindley (1832–1919).[34] By the 1870s they were at the forefront of their profession, a status that they owed in considerable part to the patronage from the mid-1850s onwards of Scott, who regarded Brindley as a protégé. As Brindley's role in managing the firm grew he withdrew from carving himself and he seems to have given it up altogether as a result of Farmer's death, when he assumed complete control. This may explain why at All Souls, as recorded by The Builder in 1879, 'the practical restoration was carried out by Mr. Henry Terry, architectural sculptor, Lambeth-road'.[35] It seems likely that Terry (b. 1823) worked for Farmer and Brindley – he was Farmer's next-door neighbour in Lambeth – but the fact that The Builder did not in 1879

---

30 Letter cited in note 28.
31 Medland's part in the reredos restoration was referred to in The Builder's account of the work, which praised Scott's 'clever assistant, Mr. Medland'. See also his obituary in The Builder, 28 March 1913.
32 The Builder 1879.
33 The Builder, 4 November 1876, p.1078 (hereafter The Builder 1876).
34 See E. Hardy, 'Farmer and Brindley, Craftsmen Sculptors, 1850–1930', Victorian Society Annual (1993), 4–17.
35 The Builder 1879.

11.4 Detail of lowest tier of the reredos, showing ornament restored by Henry Terry and figures carved by Geflowski: left to right, Earl Bathurst, Catherine of France (wife of Henry V), Margaret of Anjou, and Archbishop Chichele

link his name with the firm's may imply that he worked at All Souls as an independent contractor, with Farmer and Brindley being responsible solely for the new carving needed for the chapel restoration, such as the credence designed by Scott for the north wall of the sanctuary.[36]

Terry's work was made more delicate by the wish to preserve the traces of medieval polychromy on the reredos. Scott does not mention this in his letter to Bathurst, but, according to *The Builder*, 'The whole had been highly decorated with gold, morone [maroon], vermilion,

---

36 See Colvin and Simmons, 71, where Scott's design for the credence is illustrated. The credence was removed in 1918 to make way for the monument to Sir William Anson, on which see Green, this volume, 277. Terry is recorded (as a 'stonemason') in the 1861 and 1871 censuses as living at 5 Meads Place, Lambeth; in 1861 Farmer was at No. 4. Although there is no other evidence that Terry worked independently, if he had been employed on the reredos by Farmer and Brindley it would have been exceptional for him to be named in the *Builder* report.

blue, green, &c., traces of which were found on the details in excellent preservation. Portions of the details, with the colour on them, have been cleverly inserted into the new work, giving the key for perfect restoration in colour if thought desirable.'[37] As part of his work on the chapel Scott employed the Oxford painter William J. Hill to execute new decoration on the ceiling,[38] and it is conceivable that Hill could have gone on to paint the reredos. The decision not to do so may have been for financial reasons or it could have been the result of the growing preference in the architectural profession for conservation over restoration – preserving the original polychromy undoubtedly makes it easier to distinguish the original work from the new – but it probably also reflected unease about coloured sculpture in a Protestant context. By the mid-nineteenth century it was widely accepted that medieval sculpture had almost invariably been painted,[39] but none of the other comparable reredoses restored in the nineteenth century was coloured, although it was known, for example, that when Wyatt uncovered that at New College he discovered that the backs of its niches were a 'deep ultramarine blue' and the carved work had been 'richly gilt'.[40]

The extent of the restoration of the reredos is graphically apparent in Scott's drawing made before work had begun, in which all the areas that were to be replaced by new carving were left blank. Presumably as a record of the number of niches that he was to fill, the drawing is signed and dated 20 October 1873 by the sculptor who had been chosen to carve the new figures, Emanuel Edward Gawłowski (1834 – 1898).[41] The choice of this Polish-born sculptor, known in England as Edward Geflowski, is a further example of the donor taking control of the project, as Scott reveals in his letter of 16 December 1872 to Bathurst: 'I have had several interviews with the sculptor nominated by your Lordship Mr Geflowski, who enters most enthusiastically into the work, and is making his arrangements for its commencement'.[42] Left to himself, Scott is much more likely to have offered the commission to Farmer

37 The Builder 1879.
38 The Builder 1876.
39 See, for example, J. T. Micklethwaite, Modern Parish Churches: Their Plan, Design, and Furniture (London, 1874), 328 – 9. Micklethwaite, who had been a pupil of Scott, recommended painting new sculpture in churches, emphasising that the colouring should not be naturalistic but 'strictly conventional'.
40 See Wilson, this volume, 126 n. 30, citing A. Chalmers, A History of the Colleges, Halls and Public Buildings attached to the University of Oxford... (Oxford, 1810), 135.
41 The fullest account in English of Geflowski's career is in 'Mapping the Practice and Profession of Sculpture in Britain and Ireland 1851 – 1951', https://sculpture.gla.ac.uk/view/person.php?id=msib5_1206733454 (accessed 20 August 2020). There are also Polish sources for his career: see Colvin and Simmons, 67, n. 43.
42 Letter cited n. 28.

and Brindley. Scott and Geflowski had worked together before, but only on projects for the Bathurst family. Geflowski was born in Warsaw. It is not known when he moved to England, but in 1857 he was baptised into the Church of England in Cirencester, suggesting that he might by then have been noticed by the Bathursts. In 1860 he was commissioned to carve the simple reredos for the chapel at the Royal Agricultural College, Cirencester, a building designed by S. W. Daukes; the Bathursts were among the College's principal benefactors.[43] Geflowski settled in Liverpool – where in 1864 he was naturalised as a British subject – and most of his principal works are in Lancashire. A continued trickle of commissions in and around Cirencester can almost certainly be ascribed to Bathurst patronage. In 1867–8 Geflowski carved a reredos for St John the Baptist, Cirencester, designed by George Gilbert Scott Jr as part of the restoration of the church by Scott's father, and in 1872 Geflowski supplied a reredos designed by Scott himself for St Laurence, Stroud. This was a collaboration with Geflowski's brother Maurice, who practised as a sculptor in Shrewsbury. The last known link between the Scott and Bathurst families and Geflowski is the reredos carved in 1880 by Edward for Scott's church at Watermoor (referred to above), designed by Scott but carried out after his death under the supervision of John Oldrid Scott.[44]

Following his conversations with Geflowski, Scott informed Bathurst that the sculptor 'has made an estimate at least of an approximate nature, by which he finds the value of the restoration of the architecture with the small figures about £2000 and that of the larger figures to be about £1600'.[45] Scott described the 'small figures' as forming part of one of 'the most remarkable features which have come to light' (see fig. 11.5). These were 'the little niches placed against the pillars which divide the main niches. The[re] are eighty-six in number, and contain statuettes whose attachments to the niches still remain visible'.[46] Geflowski's work was to consist therefore of two main elements: as well as the statues required for the principal niches, he was to carve new statuettes and restore the niches in which they stood. Presumably this last job was given to him rather than to Terry as the sculptures had to be precisely fitted to the niches, work best done in situ whereas the main sculptures could be carved in the studio.

---

43 D. Verey and A. Brooks, *The Buildings of England, Gloucestershire 1: The Cotswolds* (London, 1999), 260.

44 The patron was presumably Allen, 6th Earl Bathurst (1832–1892), who succeeded his uncle in 1878. Verey and Brooks, ibid., attribute the architectural carving in the church itself to Geflowski, but, as pointed out in 'Mapping the Practice and Profession of Sculpture', this carving must date from before 1851, when Geflowski was in his teens and not yet known to be in England.

45 Letter cited above, n. 28.

46 Ibid.

Discussion about the iconography of the new sculpture was initiated by Scott in an analysis of the original subject matter of the reredos, which he set out to Bathurst:

> The whole idea of the design was founded on the name of your college – it represents in the centre, below, the one sacrifice on which All Souls must rely and above the Judgement to which All Souls must submit; while the niches no doubt contained personages of varied positions and ranks representative of the same leading idea, these personages were by no means necessarily saints or sacred persons. This would rather befit a chapel dedicated to All Saints. That there were saints among them can be no doubt – as for example the four Doctors of the Church in whose names the chapel was dedicated. The major part, however, of the niches were no doubt filled by historical personages some of whom may however perchance have been saints.[47]

Scott explained that these 'historical personages' would have included Chichele and Henry VI as the College's co-founders and members of 'the reigning royal family', such as John of Gaunt and Humphrey of Gloucester, and benefactors of the College, including Bishop Goldwell. Scott concluded that 'nothing can be more interesting than to follow out

---

47   Letter cited above, n. 28.

the idea, at once historical and religious, – and recovering the thoughts and intentions of your Founder and those who followed up his work'. Scott was more than capable of drawing up such a scheme for himself but the reference to 'the thoughts and intentions of your Founder' recalls Burrows's *coup de foudre* on first seeing the reredos, and it seems likely that he and Scott had discussed its iconography. If so, there is a striking reciprocity between the reredos and Burrow's *Worthies of All Souls*: the uncovering of the reredos inspired the research that led to the book, which in turn shaped the subjects chosen for Geflowski to carve.

Scott's emphasis on the figures being as much if not more historical as religious was probably designed to deflect any Protestant objections. If that is the case, he had judged correctly, as the scheme closely follows that set out in his letter. As Christopher Wilson has explained above, Scott and Geflowski had some evidence for the original figures in the tympanum, a representation of the Last Judgement. The Crucifixion is placed above the altar, below a statue of John the Baptist flanked by the doctors of the Church. The historical figures include, as well as Chichele with Henry V and VI and their Queens, leading British figures in the Hundred Years War, such as Edward, Duke of York and John Talbot, Earl of Shrewsbury, together with an anonymous archer who must be intended to represent the bowmen at Agincourt (fig. 11.6).

For models, Geflowski turned to antiquarian sources – the College lent him an illustrated edition of Froissart's *Chronicles* and a copy of Samuel Rush Meyrick's *A Critical Enquiry into Ancient Armour* (1830)[48] – and it seems likely that, in the absence of any trace of the original figures, he also looked at the two principal sculptures remaining at All Souls from the fifteenth century, the statues of Chichele and Henry VI by John Massyngham, although close inspection cannot have been possible since they were then still in their original setting in niches in the gatehouse on the High Street. Now that the sculptures are displayed in the chapel it is possible to compare Massyngham's Henry

---

48 Colvin and Simmons, 70.

11.9 The figure of Earl Bathurst from the reredos, carved by Geflowski from a model by Count Gleichen

with Geflowski's (figs 11.7, 8); although he has given a Gothic sway to the figure, the king embodies an unmistakably nineteenth-century ideal of pious kingship. However, Geflowski was not expected by Scott or the College to produce pastiches of medieval sculpture, a point emphasised by the way he – presumably on the College's instructions – elided past and present by making some of his figures portraits of living personalities: John of Gaunt, for example, is the University's Chancellor, the 3rd Marquess of Salisbury, later to be Prime Minister. The left-hand figure on the lowest tier is a portrait of Bathurst, who is, however, depicted in his peer's robes and not as a person from history (fig. 11.9). According to *The Builder*, one of the figures was 'modelled by Count Gleichen'.[49] It seems plausible that Geflowski was asked to base his depiction of Bathurst on a portrait – perhaps a bust – by the London-based society sculptor Prince Victor Ferdinand of Hohenlohe-Langenburg (1833–1891). Known as Count Gleichen in England, he was the son of Queen Victoria's half-sister, Princess Feodora of Leiningen.

Inevitably Scott's treatment of the reredos was not admired by those who disliked on principle the idea of restoration. In a letter to the *Hampshire Chronicle* in 1887 protesting about the provision of new statues for the reredos at Winchester Cathedral – to which Geflowski contributed ten figures – the secretary of the Society of the Protection of Ancient Buildings, Thackeray Turner, compared what was being done to Scott's work at All Souls, where, he wrote, the reredos was 'now in reality a new screen'.[50] He would never have given Scott credit for accuracy in restoration but modern scholars have been more generous: the only point at which he seriously erred was the upper part of the Crucifixion group (fig. 4.10), but he can be forgiven for not having deduced the unusual design of the original, as Christopher Wilson explains above.

However, changing attitudes in the Church of England soon made the imagery chosen for the reredos seem old fashioned. In 1886 Pearson submitted a proposal to New College to install statues in its reredos on a scheme 'suggested by the Te Deum', depicting the Trinity, seraphim and cherubim, angels, apostles, prophets, martyrs, Christ, the Virgin Mary and saints. A young former member wrote to the College: 'May it prosper as it deserves, and not be a laughingstock alike to artists and churchmen (worthy of the name), like the All Souls reredos with its archers & men-at-arms of the period'. Expressing a hope that Pearson would not put the faces of contemporary celebrities or College fellows on to the bodies of saints, as at All Souls – 'portraits of the fellows in fancy dress!' – he offered to 'increase my subscription by HALF A CROWN if I received a satisfactory assurance on this'.[51] At Magdalen in the 1830s the idea of religious figures in a reredos had been thought unacceptable in a Church of England context; fifty years later, at New College, the thought that such figures might not be religious was equally objectionable, a mark of the drift upwards in Anglican churchmanship over half a century – a change that had left Scott's iconographical compromise at All Souls looking out of date.

49 *The Builder* 1876.

50 Quoted in Brandwood, '"Unlucky Experiments"', 12.

51 Letter from Sydney Cooper (who had matriculated in 1880), then a curate at Probus, Cornwall, to William Spooner, 24 September 1888, New College Archives, 3236, https://www.new.ox.ac.uk/sites/default/files/4NCN8%20%282013%29%20Chapel%20reredos.pdf (accessed 20 August 2020).

Scott had assumed that the restoration of the chapel at All Souls would remove all traces of its post-medieval history but that too by the 1870s was becoming an old-fashioned attitude. Almost everything he proposed doing when the commission was passed to him – a new 'altar table', new stained glass by Clayton and Bell, the restoration of the stalls and sedilia and the installation of a new floor in the sanctuary (of marble rather than the encaustic tiles that were originally envisaged) was carried out.[52] The main exception was the screen, on which Scott had written to the Fellows in 1873:

> The place of [the medieval] screen is now occupied by one of the early part of the last century, probably by Hawksmoor. It is a handsome structure, though of poor material (being mainly of deal) and of a character as far as possible from according with that of the Chapel; nevertheless I doubt whether it would be proper to remove it, unless some suitable place can be found for it in the college. The Library seems the most probable place and, as the character of the screen is scarcely ecclesiastical, there does not, as it appears to me, seem to be any objection to its removal there.
>
> I have designed a screen in a style suited to the Chapel; which design I submit for your consideration.[53]

The fact that the College did not replace the screen with one designed by Scott may simply be explained by lack of funds, as Simmons suggested.[54] Yet although Clutton had been instructed to prepare designs for a new Gothic screen,[55] there had always been an element in the College that was reluctant to contemplate the removal of the existing one: in response to Clutton's first report on the chapel in 1869, in which he had set out various possible approaches to the project, the Chapel Restoration Committee had expressed reluctance 'to remove the whole of the later additions and restore the fifteenth century Chapel as nearly as possible as it was originally built by the Founder. This would be very costly, and would probably not be acceptable to many persons who set a high value on the work of Sir C. Wren.'[56] That was, however, written before the uncovering of the reredos, which had it occurred

---

52 The proposals are set out in a letter from Scott to the Warden and Fellows, 7 April 1873. The choice of a marble floor rather than the tiles that Scott proposes in this letter may be a consequence of the decision to employ Farmer and Brindley, who specialised in importing foreign marbles.

53 Ibid. Scott's design for the screen is illustrated in Colvin and Simmons, 67.

54 Colvin and Simmons, 65.

55 Clutton, *Narrative and Correspondence*, 11. In the copy of the pamphlet in the College archives this reference to a design by Clutton for a new screen has been annotated in pencil, presumably by Nutt, 'by whom ordered?'

56 Report of the Chapel Restoration Committee, 8 Dec. 1870. For this Committee and its archive see Green, this volume, 260.

11.10 The reredos seen through the screen: illustration by H. W. Brewer for *The Graphic*, 3 June 1882

a decade earlier might well have created a momentum for a complete re-gothicisation of the chapel. But by the 1870s fashion was turning away from Gothic towards the eclectic classicism of the Queen Anne movement. At Oxford, in addition, Gothic was coming to be seen a symbol of all that was most disliked by those who wished to reform the university: 'Celibate fellowships, mediaeval buildings and the statutes of mediaeval founders'.[57] This hostility was evident in the repeated rejection of Gothic designs in the architectural competitions for the Examination Schools held in 1870–76 and the eventual victory of a Jacobean design by T. G. Jackson.[58] Debates about the restoration of medieval churches had also shifted in favour of the preservation of later fittings. In 1877 one of Scott's former pupils, J. J. Stevenson, a founder member of the Society for the Protection of Ancient Buildings, gave a lecture to the RIBA on the principles and practice of architectural restoration in which he provocatively argued that the willingness of architects such as Scott to do away with post-Reformation fittings implied a rejection of the Reformation itself. Among his targets was the work then being carried out to return Tom Quad to its appearance in the time of Cardinal Wolsey:

> I cannot sympathise with Mr. Bodley's alterations at Christ Church, Oxford. The classic balustrade may have been out of keeping with the perpendicular windows, but the general effect of the great court was dignified and interesting, and in its own way, complete .... The building told its own history, and typified admirably the spirit of compromise which had made the English Constitution and the English Church what they are.[59]

It seems unlikely that the fellows of All Souls were at that moment directly influenced by such debates in the architectural profession – although they would have been well aware of the arguments about the style of the Examination Schools – but the fact that visitors to the chapel first see the masterly restoration of the reredos by Scott, Terry and Geflowski through the frame of a baroque screen (fig. 11.10) embodies the broader understanding of the historical character of both the University and the Church of England that was beginning to emerge in the 1870s.

---

57 Goldwin Smith, 'Oxford University Reform', in *Oxford Essays* (London, 1858), 265–87, at 266, quoted in W. Whyte, *Oxford Jackson: Architecture, Education, Status, and Style 1835–1924* (Oxford, 2006), 89.

58 On the Examination Schools, see Whyte, 92–100.

59 J. J. Stevenson, 'Architectural Restoration: Its Principles and Practice', *Transactions of the Royal Institute of British Architects*, 27 (1876–7), 219–35, at 222. On Bodley at Christ Church, see Hall, *George Frederick Bodley*, 310–13.

INDEX

AD ILISSVM: 'By the banks of the Ilissus',
where Socrates bathed his feet
in Plato's *Phaedrus*, 230B, remarking:
καλή γε ἡ καταγώγη
(This is a beautiful place to settle)

Copyright © 2021

Texts copyright © the authors

ISBN 978-1-912168-18-7

British Library Cataloguing in Publication Data

A catalogue record for this book is available from the British Library

Produced by AD ILISSVM
an imprint of Paul Holberton Publishing
89 Borough High Street, London SE1 1NL
www.paulholberton.com

Designed by Laura Parker

Printing by Gomer Press, Llandysul

PHOTOGRAPHIC CREDITS

Oxford, All Souls College, the Warden and
    Fellows: all College-related images unless
    otherwise indicated
Oxford Archaeology: 1.1, 2, 3
Oxford, The Bodleian Library, University of
    Oxford: 0.13, 0.15, 4.5, 7.2, 9.2, 11.3
Oxford, Magdalen College, with the kind
    permission of the President and Fellows: 7.3, 4

Boston, Museum of Fine Arts: 4.33
Brussels, Musées Royaux d'Art et d'Histoire:
    4.49, 4.53
Budapest, Museum of Fine Arts: 8.5
Cambridge, Queens' College, the President and
    Fellows: 4.58
Chicago, Art Institute: 8.4
Dublin, National Gallery of Ireland: 7.9
Eton College, the Provost and Fellows: 2.25
London, Royal Institute of British Architects,
    British Architectural Library: 2.2, 2.27,
    4.26, 11.3
London, Tate Gallery: 8.6

London, The Trustees of the British Museum: 7.1
New York, Morgan Library and Museum: 4.28
Philadelphia Museum of Art, John G. Johnson
    Collection: 5.1
Winchester Cathedral, the Dean and Chapter: 6.1

Bridgeman Images, LIP1060811: 11.10
Creative Commons: 4.38, 4.62

Jill Channer: 4.11, 4.12
Robin Darwall-Smith: 9.4 – 9.6
Colin Dunn (Scriptura): cover, frontispiece,
    0.1 – 0.9, 8.7, 8.8
Jörn Günther Rare Books, Basel: 4.54
Benjamin Hahn: 4.57
Stuart Harrison: 4.23
Emily Howe: all images in ch. 2 and catalogue
    unless otherwise indicated
Christopher Wilson: all images in ch. 4 unless
    otherwise indicated